The Fall of Imperial Britain in South-East Asia

Nicholas Tarling

D1378061

KUALA LUMPUR
OXFORD UNIVERSITY PRESS
OXFORD SINGAPORE NEW YORK

Oxford University Press

Oxford New York Toronto
Delhi Bombay Calcutta Madras Karachi
Kuala Lumpur Singapore Hong Kong Tokyo
Nairobi Dar es Salaam Cape Town
Melbourne Auckland Madrid

and associated companies in
Berlin Ibadan

Oxford is a trade mark of Oxford University Press

Published in the United States
by Oxford University Press, New York

© Oxford University Press 1993
First published 1993
Second impression 1994

British Library Cataloguing in Publication Data
Data available

Library of Congress Cataloging-in-Publication Data
Tarling, Nicholas.
The fall of Imperial Britain in South-East Asia/Nicholas Tarling.
p.   cm.
Includes bibliographical references and index.
ISBN 0-19-588611-9:
1. Asia, Southeastern—History. 2. British—Asia, Southeastern—History.
3. Great Britain—Colonies—History. I. Title.
DS526.4. T37 1993
325'.3141' 0959—dc20
92—21081
CIP

Typeset by Typeset Gallery Sdn. Bhd., Malaysia
Printed by Kyodo Printing Co. (S) Pte. Ltd., Singapore
Published by Oxford University Press,
19–25, Jalan Kuchai Lama, 58200 Kuala Lumpur, Malaysia.

South-East Asia, 1939

0   100   200   300   400   500 miles

LUZON

THE PHILIPPINES

Manila

PACIFIC OCEAN

INDORO

SAMAR

PANAY

PALAWAN   Cebu

NEGROS

MINDANAO

Zamboanga   Davao

ndakan

Menado

HALMAHERA

MOLUCCAS

CELEBES

CERAM

BURU   Ambon   WEST NEW GUINEA

Makassar

BANDA SEA

UMBAWA

FLORES

(Portuguese)

SUMBA   TIMOR   *ARAFURA SEA*

INDIES

SOUTH-EAST ASIAN HISTORICAL MONOGRAPHS

The Fall of Imperial Britain in South-East Asia

For Barbara and Leonard Andaya

Contents

Introduction

THIS book has its origins in two lines of investigation which it seemed could be profitably brought together to the advantage of both.

One is into what might be called the decline and fall of the British empire. To this subject, of course, many other contributions have already been made, including John Gallagher's boldly titled *The Decline, Revival and Fall of the British Empire.*

It is necessary initially to decide what in this context is meant by empire. Britain's power in the world in the mid-nineteenth century did not rest on nor express itself merely in territorial possession. Above all, it rested, particularly because of its industrial primacy, on economic success. Its interests were world-wide. They were often more substantial in areas where it did not possess formal control than in areas where it did.

At the same time, there was, within a world-wide diversity of interests, a framework of political and territorial interests that were also diverse. One guideline was the provision of security for Britain itself. Another was the maintenance of strategic bases along the routes of a world-wide trade. A third, fitting less well into the pattern, was the empire of force and opinion built up in India during the period of rivalry with the French, but continuing to grow thereafter, taking on its own momentum, and requiring the adoption of continental policies.

The concerns of Britain may be placed within two circles of interests, economic and territorial, which would receive different emphasis at different times, in different areas, and in different circumstances.

These emphases helped to form British policy. It is suggested that in a general way the first circle of interests prompted policies that sought a minimum degree of control over other countries. The aim was a satisfactory economic relationship with them. Measures of control over them, if necessary at all, were only necessary to an extent that would ensure security and fair treatment for British economic enterprise. It is argued indeed that the British envisioned a future world of states rather than of empires. Existing states, it was hoped, would transform themselves. If need be, they would be prodded or guided into so doing.

Empire, in a restricted sense of the term, was thus an exceptional, even an undesirable, political configuration. Intervention, though often urged and sometimes undertaken, was regrettable or temporary. The assumption of responsibility was not necessarily to be welcomed: it might be better avoided or limited.

These are the policies of a power that enjoyed an unprecedented degree of primacy in the world. But that primacy could not last. It would be challenged by other states when they industrialized. It would be challenged when Europe ceased to be the focus of world power. But, despite these challenges, the emphasis remained the same. There was no attempt to build up a territorial empire in response to the undermining of economic primacy.

In the days of that primacy, it had been possible and seen as desirable to make adjustments and reach compromises with other powers. The same pragmatic approach was followed in the new context. Drawing together the fragments of territorial control into one great whole was not found possible: at most the units of empire were encouraged towards federal or regional relationships that might make them intrinsically stronger. Characteristically the empire was seen as an alliance of nations. Even the non-settler dominions were assimilated into this pattern.

It is argued that it was easier for Britain to handle its relative decline in this way, because it could be viewed for what in a sense it was: not a surrender but a creative act. Britain was following through a concept already formulated in the nineteenth century, that of a world of states the relationships among which were economic and diplomatic rather than territorial and imperial.

There was an undue degree of self-confidence in all this. Other attitudes were carried over from the days of primacy. There was a perhaps admirable assumption that Britain could still compete economically in such a world without the crutches of empire or protection. There was also a presumption about the mechanics of empire.

One of the most useful theories of 'empire' advanced by the historians Ronald Robinson and Jack Gallagher is that of 'collaboration'. Empires rely not merely on force, but on eliciting support. The exertion of British influence in the world—and indeed not merely its maintenance of imperial and colonial relationships—depended on the collaboration of élites in the states and territories concerned. The British recognized this. They looked to such élites to govern, to preserve stability in, and to transform the states with which they dealt, whether within or outside the bounds of empire itself. Intervention might be needed if they failed. But an élite would still be needed even so.

The framework for the exertion of British influence in the world was thus a dual one, made up of the limited application of external power, often through naval means, and of the eliciting of local support. The British were sometimes too confident that they could always find such an élite and that such an élite had enough mass support to carry out the appropriate policies.

They were particularly concerned at the threat of international Communism after 1917. It challenged the whole view of the development of a world of nations that they sought to advance. Perhaps characteristically, they emphasized its international threat, and gave less attention to its capacity to transform the relationship of élite and masses.

The other line of investigation in this book is concerned with the development of the British connections with the states of South-East Asia. Those who have written on the empire have normally approached it from the direction of the settler dominions, India, or Africa. While only parts of South-East Asia were formally part of the empire, all of it was in some sense within the circle of British interests. Examining the British connections with it may assist in understanding those interests more clearly. The very diversity of the formulas the British adopted makes it all the more a useful focus for studying Britain's empire and its decline. In so far as Britain may be seen, in Ingram's phrase, as a 'peripheral' power,[1] and the empire, in Headrick's, as a world-wide 'thalassocracy',[2] South-East Asia may be an especially appropriate field of study. It has characteristically been the scene of peripheral powers and 'thalassocracies'.

At the same time, the evolution of British policy in South-East Asia as a whole, and in respect of individual countries within it, can be seen with advantage in the larger context of British policy. The book does not present South-East Asia merely as a source of illustrations and examples for a wider historical discourse. It does not pretend to offer a narrative of British policy towards each country or territory in the area. But it does claim to offer the outlines of such a narrative, set in a regional context, and in a larger world context, too.

The book undertakes the ambitious task of pursuing two lines of approach and juxtaposing them. The aim is a better understanding both of the decline and fall of the British empire, and of the emergence of new South-East Asian polities in the twentieth century. The assumption is that both are a part of world history, best explained in that context. In some respects the book is more ambitious still. Studying the British empire brings out contrasts and similarities with other imperial powers also active in South-East Asia. It may also assist in appraising the historiographical use and meaning of words like 'imperialism'. The book offers, therefore, a survey of the conclusions historians have so far reached about British policy in South-East Asia. It tries to make these more meaningful in themselves, and more meaningful for those interested in the transformation of other parts of the old colonial world, by making them also part of larger histories still, including the history of the British empire and of the British view of world politics.

Along with the two lines of approach there are at least two risks. The one is that the role of Britain in the making of modern South-East Asia may be exaggerated. The other is that adopting the South-East Asian perspective on British power and planning may distort the picture of them. Juxtaposing the two, and placing them in a larger context, may, however, diminish the risks, rather than increase them. The attempt to secure a balance may have evaded the author. He is aware that the role of the Western element in South-East Asian history has long been a source of contention in South-East Asian historiography,[3] and that it is difficult to secure a balance between the indigenous and the exogenous.[4] But he will be pleased if his attempt is at least seen as valid enough to stir controversy. And he cannot help feeling that events since the mid-1980s may have given his work a relevance that he had not anticipated when he began it. The phase in world history dominated by two superpowers appears now to have ended, and, as in the nineteenth century, one power is now uniquely strong. How it shapes its policy in general, and in South-East Asia, will perhaps be better understood in the light of past history. So, it may be, will the attempts of the states and peoples in South-East Asia to respond to and to shape that policy.

The chapters in this book are designed to follow the two lines of approach and their juxtaposition through a chronological sequence. Each chapter covers a particular phase—the mid-nineteenth century; the late nineteenth and early twentieth centuries; the inter-war period; the Second World War; and decolonization—and they attempt to discuss the changing position of Britain's interests in the world, to outline the evolution of Britain's policy in respect of South-East Asian territories, and to point up the connections.

A work such as this draws not only on firsthand research but on the research of others. In particular this book owes a great deal to colleagues at the University of Auckland and to students in its Department of History who have over many years joined the author in studying topics which it covers. The interpretations it offers they would not entirely accept. They are not to be taken other than as a contribution to a continuing discussion. The author recognizes that he has undertaken an intellectually acrobatic task in ranging across a number of fields and in generalizing both about them and about their interconnections. He hopes that, if he slips, he does not fall.

1. E. Ingram, *The Beginning of the Great Game in Asia*, Oxford: Clarendon, 1979, p. 12.

2. Daniel K. Headrick, *The Tools of Empire, Technology and European Imperialism in the Nineteenth Century*, New York: Oxford University Press, 1981, p. 175.

3. The phrase is John Bastin's: *The Western Element in Modern Southeast Asian History*, Kuala Lumpur: Department of History, University of Malaya, 1960.

4. The words are used by H. L. Wesseling, 'Dutch Historiography on European Expansion since 1945', in P. C. Emmer and H. L. Wesseling (eds.), *Reappraisals in Overseas History*, Leiden: Leiden University Press, 1979, p. 122.

1

Concepts of Empire and Visions
of World Politics

In the nineteenth century, when Britain's power in the world was
least challenged, South-East Asia remained politically fragmented.
That makes the study of the region, interesting in itself, also an
important way of studying the operation of Britain's power in the
world at the time of its primacy. It illustrates the diverse means
by which that power was exerted and the diverse factors that
impinged on its operation. It illustrates, too, the limited and
contingent use of that power in respect of the establishment of
political and territorial control.

Primacy and Diversity

At the time of the Great Exhibition of 1851, Britain's dominion
was established in India, though soon to be challenged by the
Mutiny of 1857. It had played the lead in opening up China some
ten years before, though it was displaying much less interest in
opening up Japan, and the American Commodore Perry had not
yet welcomed Japan as 'the youngest Sister in the circle of commercial nations'.[1] In South-East Asia, its possessions included
coastal regions of Burma, Arakan, and Tenasserim, though not
Pegu or the mouths of the Irrawaddy. These possessions, like
India itself, were held by the East India Company, in turn
controlled by the Government in London through the Board of
Control. The same was true of Britain's only other major possessions in South-East Asia—Singapore, Penang, and Malacca—
the Straits Settlements, by contrast to the new acquisition of
Hong Kong, which was a colony administered directly by the
Colonial Office in London. So, too, however, was the most recent
acquisition in South-East Asia, the island of Labuan off Brunei,
secured in 1847.

If even the few territories the British possessed displayed a
characteristic political diversity, that was also a feature of their

relationships with other parts of South-East Asia. In Burma they had an uneasy relationship with the kingdom of the Alaungpaya dynasty, from which they had taken Arakan and Tenasserim. With Siam, ruled, too, by an independent monarchy, they had a more positive relationship, though it was currently under strain. In the case of Vietnam their efforts had not succeeded in establishing a commercial or political relationship with the independent kingdom of the Nguyen dynasty that was increasingly at odds with other Western powers.

In maritime South-East Asia the British sought to avoid official intervention in the Malay Peninsula, and they sought to limit it in northern Borneo. The Indonesian Archipelago they had largely left to the Dutch, though they were not convinced that the latter were meeting their side of the bargain set out in the treaty of 1824 by allowing proper access to British trade, either in Java, their main possession, or in the outer islands. Their relations with the other minor European power in the region, the Spaniards, who had been established in the Philippines since the sixteenth century, were not dissimilar. They did not challenge it politically, but sought to enjoy commercial opportunity in the territories it held.

It is an argument of this book that a study of South-East Asia helps to explain the nature and objectives of what is loosely called British imperialism. It was an area where Britain's primacy was felt but its power deployed in a variety of ways that did not foreclose opportunities for others or involve territorial control. That is not, of course, to say that British policy alone determined what happened. The role of other states, European and Asian, was essential and the action and reaction of masses and élites important in determining the modes in which British power itself was exerted. But it is to say that British policy was an essential part of South-East Asian politics, usually taken account of by others, sometimes ignored at their peril.

It is the further task of this book to trace these relationships through phases in which the British no longer enjoyed primacy. These are in fact its special focus. The story of the establishment of British interests has already been told more fully elsewhere not, of course, only by the author. This book aims initially to place that story, briefly told here, in the context of an interpretation of British imperialism, a way of looking at the exertion of British power in the world that the story indeed seems to validate.

The rest of the book is concerned with the continued interconnection of Britain and South-East Asia. Still on the premise that a study of British imperialism and of South-East Asia are mutually enlightening, it seeks to illuminate both by placing them in the context of Asian and world politics. The attempts of the British to react to the challenges they faced within and outside South-East Asia offer an opportunity for commentary on the nature of their imperialism and of their view of the world. What is striking is the persistence of certain assumptions and aspirations. They were to prompt the framing of policies and plans designed to effect South-East Asia's decolonization.

This chapter seeks to outline features of the British relationship with other parts of the world by relating them to common concepts in the history of imperialism. The main focus is on the period of primacy. But the chapter also points to the changes and continuities in subsequent periods. The second chapter forms the South-East Asian counterpart of the first. It summarizes policies the British had adopted there and outlines their relationship with the region at mid-century. The subsequent chapters bring the two approaches together.

Definitions

In writing of empires, it is impossible to avoid thinking, however presumptuously, of classic phrases and patterns: rise and fall; decline and fall; and decline, revival, and fall. But there are risks other than that of presumption, some of which may be diminished by preliminary attempts at definition.

The above phrases imply periodization. There is a risk in most modes of periodization, and there is a risk in the one presented in this book, too. The obvious risk is one of over-simplification. There is also a suggestion of purpose—God's or man's—that may be overemphatic. Perhaps, too, there is a sense in which a phrase like decline and fall, if only because of the Gibbonian precedent, suggests a particular form of empire, territorial in extent, administrative in purpose, its decline and fall measured in these terms.

To apply such concepts, even implicitly, to the British empire, is at once to raise issues that need resolution if confusion is to be avoided. Which British empire is referred to? Even if, as in this book, the focus is on the 'second' and 'third' empires and on the nineteenth and early twentieth centuries, the question of periodization is only partly resolved. It cannot be further tackled without considering the nature of the 'empire'. Are territorial dominion, India, the colonies, protectorates, and dependencies, or only the colonies of settlement that became dominions, or all these and more referred to? Or is it not Britain's empire that is referred to after all, but Britain's power in the world by whatever means it was exerted, taking 'empire' as symbol or shorthand for that? Much confusion has resulted from avoiding these questions.

Discussing it in the last way may indeed be helpful. Britain's power in the world during the period of its second and third empires did not rest merely on territorial dominion. 'The imperial metropolis of a far-flung polity' became, as the great Australian historian Sir Keith Hancock put it, 'the commercial metropolis of a farther-flung economy'.[2] Its power may be described as falling into two circles of interest. One was sketched out by the enveloping ambit of its world-wide commerce. The other was drawn by the ambit of its political and territorial control. The two were not coterminous. Though it might be supported by the second, the first was larger and more important to the British, particularly as their industrialization, preceding that of other powers, got under way. 'The sun never sets upon the interests of this country.'[3] So Lord Palmerston, a long-serving Foreign Secretary, significantly modified the phrase used by Philip II, according both to tradition and to the German playwright Schiller, to describe Spain's world-wide empire.[4]

Drawing such a distinction helps to define the problem of periodization. The chronicler of the advance of Britain's power will find that the chronicling of its territorial empire proceeds at a different pace, as well as covering, even at its greatest extent, a smaller portion of the world. The two are related, not in a simple way, but in a range of ways. There are, perhaps, two chronicles to be written in conjunction and to be read together. The decline and fall of the empire has often been taken to be the explanation for the decline of British power. The relationship is different. Though one has sometimes stood as a symbol for the other, the relationship of the two chronicles is in fact more complex.

The distinction may help to deal with other problems in the history of British imperialism, and to appraise explanations of and generalizations about its nature. The concept of 'collaboration' is clearly a useful one.[5] No empire has been without its indigenous or local collaborators, though the word has not always had quite the pejorative nature it acquired in the Second World War. But the concept is almost too useful. Exertions of governmental power other than imperial are unlikely to be successful without collaborators. Indeed, it may be that it is only when collaboration is either not forthcoming, or collaborators are ineffectual that formal territorial or political control is required. The decision would partly depend on the policy and judgement of those exerting power, but the British certainly tended to take this view. As a result their relationship with a territory might change, slipping perhaps from the first to the second circle of their interests. All the same there would be a kind of continuum between the pre-imperial and imperial phases. The second phase might in fact not occur and the first would thus be a misnomer.

There might also be some continuum into a late imperial or post-imperial phase. The collaboration concept has again proved useful in considering decolonization in general and in explaining British policy in particular: if collaborators have seen an interest in working with the imperial power, they or their successors might see an interest, personal or otherwise, in continuing to do so when the relationship has been put on a new footing, even though other options would now also be given to them. Optimism about such a prospect could be the more easily generated in the British since the main thrust of their policy throughout was after all economic and financial. It was in a sense a matter of creating conditions in which the territory concerned could find its way back into the first circle of British interests. It would then—once more, or for the first time—be part of a system of at least theoretically sovereign states whose internal governance and interstate diplomacy guaranteed that measure of stability and security that commercial interests required.

The concept may also help with tackling another issue: the application of the term 'imperialism' to the activities of the British or other powers. The word originated in one political arena and was transplanted to another; it remained a political word, and its use as an historiographical term is at the very least an ambiguous one. There has been a tendency, particularly in the post-imperial phase, and in academic as well as non-academic discourse, to apply it to any form of control, even to any form of external influence. 'An imperial policy', writes A. P. Thornton, 'is one that enables a metropolis to create and maintain an external system of effective control. The control may be exerted by political, economic, strategic, cultural, religious, or ideological means, or by a combination of some or all of these.'[6] Imperialism the Indonesian nationalist Sukarno saw as 'a concept, an idea, a lust, a programme, a system, a policy of subjugating or controlling the country of another people or the economy of another nation . . .'.[7] Such generalized definitions risk making the word meaningless, even if still emotively useful in politics. The element of control is certainly a necessary part of its definition. But it is surely more helpful to consider 'imperialism' in reference to political or territorial control, and to regard it as the aspiration or policy relative to the establishment of such control.

The definition helps to bring another issue into focus. 'Imperialism' has been used in particular to describe the 'age' that includes the last two decades of the nineteenth century and the first of the twentieth. But it is necessary to consider whether it is the history of the great powers or that of their activities overseas that is being described. In this period, Africa was partitioned and China threatened: the world was further divided up. But in applying the description a trend may be overemphasized. It may have been a matter of aspiration rather than actuality. The transmission of purpose into policy has to be demonstrated. Were the aspirations of imperialists more related to their ambitions at home than abroad? Were they trying to change the nature of their own societies more than others? Were the changes that came about the result of those aspirations or were they the result of other trends within or outside Europe? Were they the culmination of earlier aspirations that merely differed in their attitude to territorial control?

Yet another issue comes into view. The American historian Martin Wiener has offered an explanation of British 'decline' that relates to an emphasis in the attitude of the British ruling-class, in its educational system, and in the orientation it fostered, on the aristocratic rather than the entrepreneurial, and the generalist rather than the specialist. Such would certainly at first sight accord ill with the suggestion that the first circle of their interests was the primary focus of the British. But, as Wiener himself says, finance was more respectable than trade,[8] and finance clearly related Britain's interests to the world at large. Imperial rule, it is true, was seen by some as out-relief for the aristocracy, and again, as more respectable than trade: Frederick Lugard, Wiener points out, turned down a business job to sit for the Indian Civil Service examination.[9] But there may be a broader consideration, partly diminishing, or shifting, the distinction between Britain and other societies that Wiener seeks to draw. The answer may again be that interests overseas were seen through the prism of British society at home. At a time of change, the British, like other Europeans, sought also to retain traditional values. It was as if the capacity to innovate had to be combined with the capacity to preserve. Perhaps the former was in some sense conditional on the latter: without some confidence about the past, it was hard to advance into the future. The creative cultures of late nineteenth-century and early-twentieth century Europe seem after all to be associated with a fructifying tension between old and new. Wilhelmine Germany has been presented as distinctively 'modern' just because of it.[10]

The Interests of the British

The historian C. A. Bayly has stressed the emphatic way Britain's leaders sought to reassert its power in the world after the loss of the American colonies. Historians since Vincent Harlow may have been tempted to overemphasize that the objects of overseas policy in the late eighteenth or early nineteenth century were now commercial rather than territorial.[11] But the very success Britain enjoyed, together with its triumph in Europe and its early industrialization, brought out the emphasis that Harlow may have predated. It tended, it might be said, to adopt the model, not of Sir Robert Walpole, but of the French Physiocrats.[12]

The main chronicle of the period since the late eighteenth century is thus not one of imperialism: it is rather that of the exertion of British power to the extent required not by imperial purpose but by the prescription of Britain's economic interests. That is at once broader and more limited: broader in the sense that those interests concerned the commerce of the world at large, and more limited in the sense that they did not necessarily require the establishment of territorial control. What they prescribed was the minimum conditions under which economic activity might be satisfactorily carried on. These included a measure of security and stability among and within the political entities of the world and their avoidance of monopoly and protectionism. There was no disposition to intervene to create a new world order. If these conditions were satisfied, commerce would help to civilize the world, and a stable world of more or less sovereign trading states would emerge. Empire, in the sense of territorial control, was necessary only if the goal could not be realized by other means. Even then the goal remained the same: empire was a transitional arrangement. *The Economist* in 1858 favoured a British take-over of Sarawak. But it saw the argument against useless imperial expenditure and the multiplication of imperial responsibilities. 'There is a moral frugality which is at the root of all pecuniary frugality; and no nation which is lavish of pledges and promises which it may be unable to redeem, can have any grasp at all of the first principle of a true State economy. . . .'[13]

These were presumptions primarily associated with the first circle of British interests. In general these prevailed. Alliance prevailed over federation; free trade over protection. But interests from the second circle affected the exertion of British power. In some respects they were after all connected. Even interests in the first circle required the exertion of political power internationally. Above all the homeland had to be secure. Trade routes and strategic *points d'appui* had also to be protected. World-wide security was necessary as well as internal stability: the latter might help to produce the former and so, it was presumed, would the civilizing effects of trade. But it was likely that even in the long term some political action would be needed, and in the transition it was certainly essential. The expansion of economic activity, it was soon realized, would not at once produce order. It might initially enhance instability within or among political entities, threatening trade or security.

Less directly connected with interests in the first circle were others in the second circle. In particular these were associated with India. British rule there, which had begun to expand in the eighteenth century even as the first empire in America was being lost, depended on dominion and control, direct and indirect, and it gave rise to a complex of interests, values, and attitudes that were often at odds with those directly associated with the commercial and industrial interests of Britain itself. Yet India could also serve those interests. It could help to preserve security and stability in Asia, providing men and resources. It could make up deficiencies, temporary or lasting, in Britain's commercial resources, providing at one time goods for trading to China, and at another markets for goods which had lost their markets elsewhere.

If India provided resources and opportunities it also posed problems in foreign policy and demanded initiatives not always in keeping with Britain's normal interests. Sometimes Britain had two foreign policies: that made in London, and that in Calcutta, Delhi, or Simla; that of a 'peripheral' power, and that of a 'continental' power. India was a source of strength so long as the English were strong, as the early twentieth-century Conservative leader Bonar Law put it: the moment they were no longer believed to be strong, it was a source of weakness.[14] Maintaining the position of the British required the sustaining of prestige within India and the insulation of the sub-continent from foreign political contacts. 'India is like a fortress ... with mountains for her walls,' Lord Curzon, Viceroy 1898–1905, was to put it.

... beyond these walls ... extends a glacis of varying breadth and dimension. We do not want to occupy it, but we also cannot afford to see it occupied by our foe. We are quite content to let it remain in the hands of our allies and friends, but if rivals and unfriendly influences creep up to it ... we are compelled to intervene.[15]

These objectives did not necessarily coincide with those of an industrial and commercial state in Europe. From the first, the growth of Indian empire had been of concern at home. No less than the empire of the Habsburgs, Queen Victoria's was, as Max Beloff has suggested, a dual monarchy.[16]

Britain's own security posed special problems, too, and at times they might themselves demand initiatives at odds with the dictates of commercial and industrial priorities. There was no value in empire if the metropolis was lost; no power was useful on the periphery if none were available at the centre. To a remarkable extent, indeed, interests in Europe and interests overseas coincided at least while Europe dominated the world. A navy helped to ensure Britain's own security in Europe as well as to protect its trade and colonies overseas. The division among the powers of the European continent helped to prevent a challenge in Europe by an aggregation of armies as well as a challenge overseas by an aggregation of navies. But the two sets of interests were not identical. To ensure that Europe was not dominated by one international power, it was useful to sustain minor powers, and one means of so doing was to permit them to retain colonial empires, the relationships with which might require some compromise with the dictates of a merely economic policy. To sustain a concert in Europe, it might be desirable, moreover, not to obstruct the creation of empires overseas by more significant powers, such as France or even Germany, though they might conflict with the commercial and even the strategic objectives of Britain's policy elsewhere in the world.

Even at the height of Britain's power, there was a recognition of the need to compromise. A live-and-let-live attitude of this kind was after all compatible with a world-wide cumulation of power such as Britain achieved in the nineteenth century, though it was not the attitude of previous European world-empires. In a sense it also prepared the British for a policy of adjustment when their primacy was challenged. There was room, as there always had been, for others who could fit into an emerging world of sovereign states trading with one another. There remained difficulties. Was the adjustment acceptable to the British? Was it acceptable to their rivals? Did they wish for more than adjustment? Or a different world order? Or a greater say in the timetable of change?

The Relationships with Other States

Britain, it may further be suggested, conceived of its relationships with the rest of the world in terms of a framework. It was not a fixed framework. It was in a state of movement, of adjustment, at different times and places, and the patterns within the framework were diverse. But the British vision was of a world of sovereign states, and the framework was intended to approximate, ever more closely over time, to that objective. Britain's interests would be met in such a world: it would provide security, stability, and economic opportunity. It would, however, do this only if other states were satisfied with their role in this venture. Liberal as the British might be, that could not be presumed.

Here let me say, with regard to the action of our country over the centuries, that in all the struggles in which we have been engaged we have survived and emerged victorious not only because of the prowess of great commanders or because of famous battles gained by land and sea, but also because the true interests of Britain have coincided with those of so many other states and nations, and that we have been able to march in a good Company along the high road of progress and freedom for all.[17]

Churchill's rhetoric, occasioned by the Italian invasion of Albania in 1939, no doubt exaggerated. But his view in some sense echoed that of Kurt Riezler, assistant to the German Chancellor, Bethmann-Hollweg, twenty-five years before. Britain was, in his terms, a Rome, not an Athens. It was 'the protector of everything free and progressive'.[18] Both Riezler before the First World War and Churchill before the Second had Europe in mind. But the concept applied with increasing explicitness to the rest of the world, too.

Suggesting the validity of this approach perhaps runs the risk of adopting a Whig interpretation of the history of Britain's relationship with the rest of the world since the early nineteenth century. It is necessary to be careful not to read back into the past what was said of it by statesmen of the twentieth century without an examination of that past. Other superordinate powers have adopted the pose of protectors and advocates of lesser powers. But there was a consistency in Britain's approach throughout times of change, and it was supported by its interpretations of its interest as well as by ideology.

While its power in the world was unrivalled, Britain tended to use its power in ways that largely accorded with the desire to see such a framework of relationships emerge. In Europe it sought a concert of powers; outside it sought to bring about new forms of collaboration rather than to take over direct control. Often such policies were pursued with insufficient understanding or were in any case vain. But the emphasis continued to be on the external application of power, mainly by naval means; on devolution rather than integration in respect of settler colonies; and on self-development for independent entities and even for dependencies. It was a recognition of the limits of Britain's power; but it was also a decision about the priorities in the use of that power and the proper purpose of it. There had after all always been a sense in which the British recognized that their primacy owed something to the lack of rivals and that they should therefore even when enjoying the primacy conduct their policy in a conciliatory manner. It was characteristic that, if they fought major wars, they sought the support of coalitions; it was also characteristic that, in victory, they sought to avoid the elimination of the defeated.

There were times of crisis. The emergence of rivals—from Europe and from outside—required adjustments: some in Britain and, in a different way, among the rivals, believed that more was needed than adjustments. Such rivalry indeed made adjustments more difficult to achieve: the frontiers of colonies became more difficult to adjust, like those of the European states of which they had in a sense become part. The British themselves, when challenged, or when apprehensive, were not always as flexible as their principles suggested they should be. But on the whole they sustained striking optimism about their approach and even about their own future.

Collaborators

The concept of a framework can both draw upon and amplify the debate on 'collaboration'. Empire, it has been argued, can rarely, if ever, be sustained by mere force: it rests also upon co-opting the support of indigenous élites, whose role in society is, however, changed as a result. Aware how few French officials there were in Indo-China, Paul Beau, the Governor-General, was clear that they 'neither can nor should act directly on the population itself; they must have, as their intermediary, a corps of Vietnamese officials, who are devoted and loyal to our political régime and satisfied with the respect we show them and the initiative we give them'.[19] But the concept of collaboration, it has also been argued, should be seen in the context not merely of empire, but the exertion of power. In some sense it is a matter of degree or of process. If the interests of the British were adequately served without the assumption of control, it may have been as a result of collaboration by the ruling groups or indigenous leaders, in the sense at least of their perception of a common interest. Their failure to continue the collaboration, or their inability to do so, may help to lead to their displacement, to be followed, it might be, by the assumption of imperial control. That provides in the event a new, but more constricting, approach for collaboration. The imperial phase may be no more than a phase. If collaboration is adequate without it, the control can be diminished or relinquished.

That perception the British attained in the nineteenth century in respect of what are seen as settler territories like Canada, Australia, and New Zealand. The Radical John Bright put it rather crudely with respect to the first that it would be 'cheaper for us and less demoralising for them that they should become an independent state, and maintain their own fortresses, fight their own cause, and build up their own future without relying upon us'.[20] In respect of India and other territories, it was at first only a dimly perceived and unprogrammed prospect, but the idea was there. 'We should look upon India, not as a temporary possession, but as one which is to be maintained permanently', Sir Thomas Munro, a great Indian civil servant, had written,

until the natives shall in some future age have abandoned most of their superstitions and prejudices, and become sufficiently enlightened to frame a regular government for themselves, and to conduct and preserve it. Whenever such a time shall arrive, it will probably be best for both countries that the British control over India should be gradually withdrawn.[21]

'The mere extent of empire is not necessarily an advantage,' Lord Macaulay, MP and historian, proclaimed.

To many governments it has been cumbersome; to some it has been fatal. . . . To the great trading nation, to the great manufacturing nation, no progress which any portion of the human race can make in knowledge, in taste for the conveniences of life, or in the wealth by which those conveniences are produced, can be a matter of indifference. . . . It would be, on the most selfish view of the case, far better for us that the people of India were well governed and independent of us, than ill governed and subject to us—that they were ruled by their own kings, but wearing our broad cloth, and working with our cutlery, than that they were performing their salams to English collectors and English Magistrates, but were too ignorant to value, or too poor to buy, English manufactures. . . .[22]

The same kind of attitude guided British policy in China. There was no wish to take it over—India was a warning, not an example—but its large population suggested the prospect of a large trade. There had been a clash in 1840–2, but the British had accepted the compromise the Ching dynasty had offered, and looked to it, and the expansion of commerce, gradually to modernize China and the Chinese. 'We do not wish to revolutionise the country,' Frederick Bruce wrote, 'for I am convinced that we are more likely to get on with a Manchu than with a purely Chinese dynasty.'[23] China should remain independent but collaborative, and transform itself. That was the object of 'Palmerstonian blows'.[24]

Such views were also later to make it possible to consider dealing with the emergence of nationalism in dependent territories in a positive, even an optimistic way, to assimilate the treatment of the 'Roman' portions of the empire to the treatment of the 'Greek'.[25] There might be differences of timing over withdrawal. There might be paradoxes in the advance towards independence: Will Rogers, the American humorist, made the sharpest comment on the concept in imagining a conversation between President Hoover and Patrick Hurley on the Philippines. ' "I say how can you tell when a Nation is ready for Independence?" He says, "I don't know. I never saw a Nation that was." '[26] Was independence something people could be prepared for without having the responsibility for sustaining? But within an adjusted international framework, and with sufficient internal stability, it should be possible again to stress the first circle of British interests, and to rely on the commercial opportunities Britain had long put ahead of others.

Such a programme implied a number of presumptions. One

was that the priorities in Britain's policy should remain the same when its power was relatively in decline as when it enjoyed primacy. The fact that the 'first circle' of interests had always enjoyed priority virtually ruled out change. Stressing territorial control, pulling the territorial links closer, were rarely seen as realistic options or even positive ones. Britain's influence in the world must still depend on its economic strength and its diplomatic resource. That meant in turn, however, that it might not dispose of the power to determine or programme the development of the framework. Increasingly it would have to enlist the support of other major powers, for which a price would probably have to be paid, even if it might be thought, under Churchillian persuasion, that their larger interests were identical.

There were other presumptions that related particularly to the search for collaborators within the framework. Some compromises with other states had already been made. In South-East Asia, for example, it had been decided that the Dutch should retain their empire in the Indies, and in a sense therefore the Dutch were the collaborators of the British. But that meant that the British were in their hands, so far as the search for collaborators among the ruled was concerned. The British could have relatively little influence on the way other colonial powers handled the problems of colonial rule, even though that might affect the development of the framework as a whole.

Moreover, the search for collaboration was not necessarily a simple task. Initially, perhaps, it might be forthcoming. But it was difficult to make a change without risking an upset, and difficult to avoid an upset without risking a change. Economic and social development did not stand still, and outside powers might do well to seek new collaborators. But it was not easy to jettison the old and to win the new. The Spaniards in the nineteenth-century Philippines, for example, were unwilling to drop their ties with the old élite and the friars, and risk collaboration with the *ilustrados*. But, as a result, the *ilustrados* turned from a moderate political stance to a more revolutionary one. A stronger power might have been bolder. But changing collaborators was essentially a difficult task for any colonial state. The same was true of other states, too: the decline and overthrow of the Manchus in China posed the British with problems of revolution they had sought to avoid.

There was yet another problem with the concept. It was concerned with the leadership of a society, and the value of an understanding with the local élite rested on its ability to mobilize popular support or at least neutralize popular opposition. In fact it contained an in-built contradiction. If they were too closely tied to an imperial power, the élites might lose their local influence; but if they were insufficiently influential, they would be useless. No doubt all colonial powers have realized this: the Dutch in Netherlands India, and the Japanese in occupied China. The French despatched the mutinous Vietnamese Emperor Duy Tan into exile in 1916. 'Is it absolutely necessary', the Governor-General asked in telegram and querulous anger, 'to begin again disappointing experience crowning of a king who if active and intelligent can easily become dangerous and if incompetent gives us no strength?'[27] Possibly, given their own political culture, the British were particularly inclined to assume that an élite was influential, and looked for one that seemed—like Indian zemindars or Malay rajas—to be recognizably landowners and/or gentlemen. Other élite elements they often found less trustworthy, particularly if Western educated, and there was always tension between the recognition of the importance of conciliating the élites and the belief that imperial rulers would be recognized and accepted by the masses as fairer and less oppressive, a belief that, however, was sometimes no more than an assumption. 'It is a mistake to suppose that these people were anxiously awaiting annexation,' George White found during the third Burma war.[28]

After the 1917 revolution, international Communism was to see British empire and British influence as its major opponents in the colonies and underdeveloped countries. The British in turn were particularly apprehensive of Communism, and the foregoing discussion helps to explain why. No doubt, there was at times a tendency to overemphasize its threat, perhaps partly explained by the anxiety to win the support of other powers for the international framework to which Britain's interests were tied. Indeed, one aspect of the threat of Communism was that it presented itself, more than any other challenge, as an alternative to the British world-view, a wholly different and ideologically based framework for the future. The other part of its threat—made more threatening by its connection—was that it also aimed to capture the allegiance of emerging élites and to offer them a prescription for winning the support of the masses. It was not surprising that Communism sometimes led the British to intervention or manipulation that extended well beyond their norms.

In general, of course, there were bound to be differences of approach among British policy-makers and their decisions would be affected by a range of contingencies. Not only, for example, were there differences of interest between London and Delhi: there were, more widely, differences between those in the metropolis and those on the spot, and the relationships between them changed over time. Interpreting British policy along the lines suggested can and must allow for such differences. It must also of course allow for the context in which policy was made. The working-out of a policy is at least a two-way affair, and that was particularly so where the policy rested so largely on influencing and winning over others.

Concluding Remarks

The object of this chapter has been to offer some hypotheses about the relationship of Britain with the rest of the world since the early nineteenth century. They are in themselves not new, but they may be drawn together in a new way. An emphasis on their persistence seems both justified and helpful.

The essential hypothesis is that Britain's relationship with the rest of the world rested on economic connection rather than territorial control. Territorial control was limited in extent and, where it was not limited in extent, limited in duration. Britain had come to enjoy an unusual primacy in the world. But the expression of that primacy was not an aspiration to universal empire. That was unnecessary, if not impolitic, even immoral. Other powers had a legitimate place in the world. The world was, or should become, a world of states. The approach to world politics was diplomatic not imperialistic. 'Sufficient unto the day', a biblical phrase once invoked by Robert Meade, Assistant Under-Secretary at the Colonial Office,[29] was perhaps a maxim for nineteenth-century policy. It might even be acceptable to generalize a definition offered by the Foreign Secretary in respect of the Eastern Question in 1877, that British policy was 'to float lazily down-stream occasionally putting out a diplomatic boathook to avoid collisions'.[30]

The hypothesis is expressed through a number of metaphors, though none as appropriately marine as Lord Salisbury's. First, there is the notion that Britain's interests fell into two 'circles', one economic, one territorial, the former global in extent, the latter more limited. It is also argued that policies were based on a recognition of these interests and that their primary direction was and remained the preservation and development of Britain's economic relationships with the rest of the world. The aim was to provide the minimum conditions for its prosperity, a measure of world-wide stability and security.

Second, there is the notion of a framework through which Britain's world-wide interests were pursued. That naturally rested on a minimum application of force and the maximum acquisition of collaboration. Its ideal was a nation-state which accepted a role in a world of nation-states that provided security and access for commerce and handled interstate relations by diplomacy and adjustment. 1851 was a symbol, 'this peace festival', as Queen Victoria put it, 'uniting the industry and art of all nations of the earth . . .'. The opening was 'indeed moving, and a day to live for ever. God bless my dear Albert, and my dear Country, which has shown itself so great today.'[31] The framework was not a rigid one but necessarily one in a permanent condition of partial transition.

The chapter has suggested that there are some striking consistencies in British policy. That runs the risk of Whiggism, and the advance of territorial dominion in India, or the 'new imperialism' of the late nineteenth century, will at least challenge such an interpretation. But such consistencies surely help to explain the decolonization of the twentieth century and the positive attitude that in general the British managed to develop towards it.

Though by then Britain no longer enjoyed the primacy of the mid-nineteenth century, nor the industrial pre-eminence which, along with the lack of rivals, was so powerful a support for it, the attitudes it had adopted it substantially retained and developed. There was a worse alternative. Perhaps indeed Britain exaggerated the threat of an alternative world-system, that of the Communists.

One line of investigation in this book is thus summarized, that concerned with the exertion of Britain's power in the world. The other line of investigation is concerned with South-East Asia in particular. Each should cast light on the other. What the British did in South-East Asia is better explained in the context of their policies and attitudes world-wide. At the same time, South-East Asia offers a means of testing the validity of the hypotheses advanced on those policies and attitudes. It may be possible as a result to reach a better understanding of the making of modern South-East Asia and of the role of the British in it.

1. Quoted in Marius B. Jansen, Introduction, *The Cambridge History of Japan*, Cambridge: Cambridge University Press, 1989, Vol. V, p. 17.

2. W. K. Hancock, 'Agenda for the Study of British Imperial Economy 1850–1950', *Journal of Economic History*, XIII, 3 (1953): 257.

3. Quoted in R. Hyam, *Britain's Imperial Century 1815–1914*, London: Batsford, 1976, p. 48.

4. F. Schiller, *Don Carlos*, Act I, Scene 6.

5. Put forward by R. Robinson, 'Non-European Foundations of European Imperialism: Sketch for a Theory of Collaboration', in Roger Owen and Bob Sutcliffe (eds.), *Studies in the Theory of Imperialism*, London: Longman, 1972, pp. 118–40.

6. A. P. Thornton, *Imperialism in the Twentieth Century*, London: Macmillan, 1978, p. 3.

7. Robert K. Paget (ed.), *Indonesia Accuses!*, Kuala Lumpur: Oxford University Press, 1975, p. 137.

8. M. J. Wiener, *English Culture and the Decline of the Industrial Spirit 1850–1980*, Cambridge: Cambridge University Press, 1981, p. 128.

9. Ibid., p. 136.

10. M. Eksteins, 'When Death was Young', in R. J. Bullen, H. Pogge van Strandmann, and A. D. Polonsky (eds.), *Ideas into Politics*, London and Sydney: Barnes and Noble, 1984, pp. 25–35.

11. C. A. Bayly, *Imperial Meridian*, London: Longman, 1989; V. T. Harlow, *The Founding of the Second British Empire*, London: Longmans, 1952, Vol. I.

12. The contrast is drawn in James C. Thomson, Jr. et al., *Sentimental Imperialists*, New York: Harper and Row, 1981, pp. 11–12.

13. *The Economist*, 4 December 1858.

14. Quoted in Thornton, *Imperialism in the Twentieth Century*, p. 88.

15. Quoted by Hugh Tinker in reviewing D. P. Singhal, *The Annexation of Upper Burma*, Singapore: Eastern Universities Press, 1960, for *JSEAH*, I, 2 (September 1960): 106.

16. Max Beloff, *Imperial Sunset*, London: Methuen, 1969, Vol. I, p. 37.

17. W. S. Churchill, 13 April 1939, Speeches, p. 6104.

18. Wayne C. Thompson, *In the Eye of the Storm: Kurt Riezler and the Crisis of Modern Germany*, Iowa City: University of Iowa Press, 1980, pp. 19, 105.

19. Quoted in P. F. Baugher, 'The Contradictions of Colonialism: The French Experience in Indochina, 1860–1940', Ph.D. thesis, University of Wisconsin, Madison, 1980, p. 307.

20. Quoted in N. Mansergh, *The Commonwealth Experience*, 2nd edn., Toronto and Buffalo: University of Toronto Press, 1982, Vol. I, p. 67.

21. Quoted in G. Bennett (ed.), *The Concept of Empire: Burke to Attlee 1774–1947*, 2nd edn., London: Black, 1962, p. 70.

22. Ibid., pp. 72–3.

23. Quoted in Masataka Banno, *China and the West 1858–1861: The Origins of the Tsungli Yamen*, Cambridge: Harvard University Press, 1964, p. 237.

24. The phrase is from Ronald Robinson and John Gallagher, *Africa and the Victorians*, London, Macmillan, 1961, p. 32.

25. The adjectives this time are Sir Charles Adderley's. W. D. McIntyre, *The Commonwealth of Nations: Origins and Impact, 1869–1971*, Minneapolis: University of Minnesota Press, 1977, p. 24.

26. Quoted in Lewis E. Gleeck, 'President Hoover and the Philippines', II, *Bulletin of the American Historical Collection*, Manila, IX, 4(37) (Oct–Dec 1981): 39.

27. B. M. Lockhart, 'Monarchy in Siam and Vietnam, 1924–1946', Ph.D. thesis, Cornell University, 1990, p. 20.

28. Quoted in Muhammad Shamsheer Ali, 'The Beginnings of British Rule in Upper Burma: A Study of British Policy and Burmese Reaction 1885–1890', Ph.D. thesis, London University, 1976, p. 41.

29. Minute, 1 August, on Leys to Derby, 30 May 1883, 39, C.O. 144/57 [12509].

30. Quoted in K. Bourne, *The Foreign Policy of Victorian England*, Oxford: Clarendon, 1970, p. 132.

31. Quoted in C. Hibbert (ed.), *Queen Victoria in Her Letters and Journals*, Harmondsworth: Penguin, 1985, p. 84.

2
South-East Asia in the Period of British Primacy

THIS chapter takes up the second line of investigation pursued in this book, the application of British power in South-East Asia. That, of course, is a subject that has been studied by a number of authors, particularly in respect of the nineteenth century. But it has been rather less often studied in the context of the application of British power more generally. Moreover, historians of South-East Asia have studied the period of decline less often than the period of primacy, and it may be that the juxtaposition of the general and the regional will be especially instructive in that respect. It may throw some new light on decolonization and independence though they have, of course, themselves been the subject of many studies.

At the same time, the study of South-East Asia has rarely been the focus of historians of British foreign policy or those of British imperialism. India, Africa, and the dominions have virtually monopolized the latter. But, though not much studied by writers on the British empire or on the exertion of British power overseas, South-East Asia affords them a range of opportunities. It was diverse in itself; British power was exerted in it in diverse modes. It was ruled by native monarchies, Buddhist, Islamic, Confucian, and custom-based, and by older European colonial powers, Spain and the Netherlands. The French had ambitions in South-East Asia; the British had interests. These related not only to trade, in particular the trade, actual and prospective, with China, but also to India, where the British had founded a realm with its own strategic imperatives, and to Australasia, where they established colonies of settlement. The interaction of British and local purpose differed from area to area and from time to time.

At the height of Britain's power, its interests in South-East Asia were sustained by a range of devices and modes of collaboration. Essentially that reflected not only the diversity of interactions with British interests, but also the diversity of those interests; some placed within the first circle, and some within the second.

The Dutch and the Archipelago

The Dutch had been established in the Indonesian islands since the earliest days of their venture into Asia in the late sixteenth century. In the following century, the leading commercial power in Europe, they had become the leading European power in Asia. But they had not built a territorial empire. Their purpose had been to secure a prosperous commerce and that object they had ruthlessly pursued, particularly in the recession of the latter part of the century. In the eighteenth century, they were increasingly overtaken by the British as the main European traders within Asia as a whole. Their growing concentration on the Archipelago, and on Java in particular, was a sign that they had not risen more generally to the challenge of the new period of expansion. They sought to retain the monopolies they had established of the fine spices of Maluku and to extract coffee from parts of Java they came to dominate. But they had established no unified territorial control over the Archipelago, nor even over Java itself. Their realm was a complex of treaties and contracts with native rulers, largely of a commercial character, and entrepôts and *points d'appui*, like Batavia, Malacca, and Makassar.

Before its wars with France Britain had challenged the claims of the Dutch to monopoly, as in the Anglo-Dutch treaty of 1784: 'They are afraid', as Henry Dundas put it, 'that the communication we may have with the Natives would lay the foundation for their total shaking off of the miserable dependence in which they are held. . . .' [1] In fact the British hesitated to overthrow the Dutch empire before the French overran the Dutch republic. During the time of the French wars they took over the Dutch possessions: Malacca in 1795, Maluku in 1795–6, and Java itself in 1811. Lieutenant-Governor of Java during the occupation, Stamford Raffles wanted Britain to remain in the Archipelago, and secure 'a general right of superintendence over, and interference with, all the Malay states'.[2] The British connection with the islands of the Malay Archipelago, he argued more moderately,

stands on a very different footing from that with the people of India. However inviting and extensive their resources, it is considered that they can be best drawn forth by the native energies of the people themselves, uninfluenced by foreign rule, and unfettered by foreign regulations, and that it is by the reciprocal advantages of commerce, and commerce alone, that we may best promote our own interests and their advancement. A few stations are occupied for the security and protection of our trade, and the independence of all the surrounding states is not only acknowledged, but maintained and supported by us. . . .[3]

These plans were rejected. The possessions of the Dutch in the Archipelago were returned in the convention of 1814. On their return they sought to renew their treaties and contracts, and this alarmed local British merchants and, more significantly, made British authorities apprehensive about complete Dutch control of the Straits of Malacca. But Britain did not take up the policies Raffles had advocated, even in that more moderate form in which he had sought to place them in the context of Britain's commercial interests. An effectively independent and friendly Dutch state was important to the British in Europe, both as part of the balance of power, and part of the defensive outwork of Britain itself: a Dutch empire overseas was the price to be paid. It could be paid more readily if other British interests were met: the economic interests of the first circle and the strategic interests of the second. Lord Castlereagh, the British Foreign Secretary, had written in 1819 that 'a good understanding is to both states more important to their general interests than any question of local policy . . .'. Such a conviction would make it easier to reach a settlement, 'the Basis of which, on the part of the British Government, will be to endeavour to provide adequately for the commercial Rights and Interests of British Subjects, without being incidentally drawn into a practical struggle for Military and Political dominion in the eastern seas, with the Government of the Netherlands . . .'.[4] The outcome was the treaty of 1824, which redefined the position of the two states in the Malay world.

Singapore, occupied by Raffles in 1819, was retained, and certain conditions were imposed on the Dutch, particularly in the commercial sphere. Britain's needs in South-East Asia were limited and had to be related to its needs elsewhere: security for the dominion in India and the trade to China, command of the Straits of Malacca, a fair share of the trade of the islands, and, later, protection of communications with Australia and New Zealand. But the Dutch had lost Malacca, which had been the defence outwork of Java: they had to rely on the new treaty instead. More generally they had to accept that their tenure in the Archipelago itself was in a sense conditional.

For the Dutch the essential relationship in the nineteenth century was, therefore, with the major imperial power in South-East Asia as in the world, Great Britain. It involved the recognition that the

one was a risky business, and an insecure power might try to avoid so problematic a transition. In the case of the Anglo-Dutch relationship, yet further difficulties were involved. Two powers in an established pattern of collaboration might wish to react differently to a challenge from outside. The British could contemplate coming to terms with a new power at the expense of their old partner. Whether or not they actually did so, the latter might in any case fear that they would and, either as a result or on recognition of a changing distribution of power in the world, itself consider coming to terms with the new power. But in the inter-colonial collaborations, there was, as it were, a third party. The colonial government relied not only on international acceptance, but on co-opted local support. The connection between a minor colonial power, like the Netherlands, and its subjects was of concern not only, of course, to itself, but to its patron. It might pursue policies at odds with its patron's wider interests: its treatment of Islam was a case in point. How the Dutch treated their Muslim subjects or opponents might affect the position of Britain, which, as ruler of India, came to have more Muslims under its rule than any other power. Yet the amount of everyday control Britain could exert over the Dutch was limited. If collaborators are always difficult to control, trying to determine the way they might collaborate with a third party is still more difficult.

The Netherlands was an independent state within the ambit of international relations: its sovereignty could not be easily openly abused, any more than it could be exercised with complete freedom. Furthermore, to state the obvious because its implications are less so, it was European, rather than native. The Europeans had had a long history of intra-European disputation which had extended overseas: indeed it was a major impulse behind their overseas ventures. But, as colonial powers, they had something in common. A 'second-circle' interest in sustaining the prestige of European rule encouraged the British to see the Europeans as hanging (or being hanged) together. Again, however, that did not mean that the British could support the Dutch come what might. But it might be hard to dissociate Britain from the implications of their policies.

In the period up to the 1870s, these issues were not prominent. What that period saw was the working-out of the relationship consolidated by the treaty of 1824 and of its implications for the Indonesian peoples. The two powers were indeed 'exclusive Lords of the East' in another sense besides their relationship with other

Europeans. Besides fending them off—indeed, in so doing—they were, of course, affecting the relationship of the Indonesians with the outside world. The independence Indonesian states enjoyed diminished, whatever the wording of the treaties they had made.[10] Any independence the Indonesian states in contractual relationship with the Dutch possessed was reduced by their incapacity to act on the international scene; any attempt they made to do so would be opposed by the Dutch and would embarrass the British, who could only anticipate or recommend their coming to terms with the Dutch. The British could not seek a direct relationship, of collaboration or otherwise, with native rulers or élites in the area consigned to the Dutch: the primary relationship had to be with the Dutch.

The Dutch would be anxious to foreclose British intervention if there were any risk of it. Generally, however, they had no need to fear it. They had been nervous about British interest in northern Australia in the 1820s, and that had induced them to dispatch Captain D. H. Kolff to reaffirm the allegiance of the chiefs in the islands off West Irian, to set up a fort at Triton Bay, and to assume possession of the coast between Humboldt Bay and the Cape of Good Hope.[11] The Borneo venture of the British also prompted them to strengthen their claims in the island and to set up a Government of Borneo in 1846, while the involvement of foreign traders in Bali, together with news of the shift in British views in 1838, prompted intervention there. Only, however, in Sumatra, where Aceh remained independent and the plans of the Dutch to expand had to be deferred, and in northern Borneo, where they were pre-empted, was there any real opposition from Britain. Generally they had no need to fear it.

The attitude of the British made it possible to adopt *onthouding*: not abandoning Dutch claims, but refraining from active intervention. Itself not challenging the Dutch, Britain had a relationship with them that helped to keep out others. They could extend their control as and when and to the extent that it seemed profitable, sheltered by their patron's position in the world and its attitude towards other powers, and more or less secure in the knowledge that the Indonesian peoples were thereby insulated from the outside world and unable to play a role on the world scene by conducting truly international relationships. For much of the time the Dutch in many areas did so little that the true position may not have been apparent to Indonesian rulers and peoples.

Certainly Dutch policy towards the Muslims was in general a

cautious one, born of a consciousness of latent opposition, enlivened by periods of antagonism, and opened up and deepened by occasional war. The British were conscious of their need to avoid a clash between European and Muslim, but rarely needed to enforce this view on the Dutch. The concern of the British was more evident in regard to the empire of the Spaniards, which indeed rested on bases rather different from that of the Dutch, though also dependent on the British.

Filipinas

The British relationship with the Spaniards in the Philippines in some ways paralleled that with the Dutch in Indonesia. A fragment of South-East Asia was held by what had now become a minor European power. That fragment was less important to the British than the Indonesian region, but it was not unimportant. So far as the second circle of interests was concerned, it had no connection with the defence of India, but it was adjacent to the route to China. It was also, like other parts of the world, within the enveloping commercial interests of the British, partly for its own sake, partly because of its relationship with China. Spain itself was also of less critical significance to Britain than was the Netherlands, and it was, of course, not of direct significance to the defence of the British isles themselves. But its continued independence was important as part of the overall security of Europe and the maintenance there of a balance of power in which no one continental power dominated. If the Spaniards (like the Dutch) lost their empire to the British when they lost their independence in Europe to others, that only illustrated the relationship the two elements, empire and independence, possessed for the British. The loss of almost all the Spanish American colonies in the 1820s was permanent: the new world had thus, in George Canning's terms, to redress the balance of the old. But the loss of the Philippines was not, and its role in the balance was different.

The Spanish empire in the Philippines certainly differed from the Dutch empire in the Indonesian Archipelago. Both dated back to the late sixteenth century. But, though, like other Europeans, the Spaniards had been anxious to share in the trade of Asia, in the event their capital at Manila had become an entrepôt for exchange between China and their possessions in Mexico and Peru, and commercially they had developed few other interests even in the islands they named after the future Philip II. Their position in

Luzon and the Visayas came to rest on the missions of the various Catholic orders the monarch patronized, and on a collaborative relationship with the local élite. The Spaniards claimed to control Mindanao and Sulu as well, but there their position remained far weaker. They faced established Muslim sultanates, which their disposition to Christianize only provoked. Spanish power was insufficient to bring them under control by forceful means. The relationship remained one of mingled peace and war, occasional expeditions by the Spaniards mixed with a diplomatic approach, and answered, more often than not, by piratical attacks on Luzon and the Visayas which they could not prevent, but which at least consolidated the loyalty of the Christianized *indios* there.

Attacking an ally of France in the Seven Years War, the British seized Manila in 1762, but they returned it when peace was made. In the interim there was a revolt in Ilokos, headed by Diego Silang, to which the British gave some support. They had also made contact with the Muslims in the south, and concluded a number of agreements with the Sultan of Sulu. An emissary of the British East India Company from Madras, Alexander Dalrymple, envisaged making Balambangan a capital for 'oriental Polynesia', and establishing a state called Felicia in northern Borneo.[12] But after the return of Manila in 1764, the British Government was unwilling clearly to back any British venture in the area, and, though the East India Company finally occupied the island of Balambangan in 1773, its corrupt and disobedient servants were soon after driven out by the Sulus and it abandoned the settlement.

The British remained cautious about again upsetting Spanish rule in the Philippines, though the Spaniards were apprehensive that they might. That encouraged them on the one hand to open up the islands to British commerce, though without the formal treaty stipulations to which the Dutch had to submit in 1824. Manila was formally opened in 1834, though in effect earlier; other ports followed in 1855. It also encouraged them, on the other hand, to press ahead with asserting their political predominance in the Philippines over against the British or any other power; that was generally acceptable to the British who wanted no other power there, and had no urge to secure territorial control, only economic opportunity. If the French should establish themselves in Basilan, an island off Mindanao, Consul J. W. Farren wrote in 1845, then Britain should consider 'the expediency of selecting from the archipelago of Islands which separate our possessions and interests in the Pacific and China Seas, some position calculated to connect and to support them'. Britain needed no more colonies 'for objects of aggrandizement or Empire . . . but the extent and ramifications of her maritime and commercial system render such supports to them necessary, besides that there are geographical positions which it is obviously important to command . . .'.[13] But French failure made such a venture superfluous.

Spanish predominance itself rested for the most part on a version of the colonial collaboration that specially applied to the Philippines, based not only on the presence of the religious orders and the Christianization of the people, but also on the collaboration of a 'mestizized' élite. It remained weak in two areas, in the Luzon Cordillera, and in the southern islands. The attempts to affirm it in the nineteenth century were incomplete in both areas, but they were more effective in Luzon than in Sulu and Mindanao. There the Spaniards faced Islamic-inspired opposition. The methods they adopted, frustrated and frustrating violence, were at once provoked by the British and provoked them.

Like its relationships with the Dutch, Britain's relationships with the Spaniards were damaged in the 1840s, and their actions prompted renewed Spanish attempts to establish control. Picturing himself as reviving the policy of Raffles, and making use of British dissatisfaction with the Dutch implementation of the treaty of 1824, the English adventurer James Brooke had established himself in Sarawak, then part of Brunei. 'The entire coast will fall under our influence. . . .' The British should push their interests 'along the coast to Sulu, and from Sulu towards New Guinea'.[14] It was the activity of the Dutch in eastern Borneo and the Sulu Archipelago that prompted him, now Her Majesty's Commissioner and Consul-General, to make a treaty with the Sultan in 1849, designed, Dalrymple-style, to preserve his country's independence. But that, of course, provoked diplomatic opposition from Spain, against which Brooke argued. The aggression of Spain was prompted by the British 'attempt to preserve the freedom of trade through the native states', which, he argued, could and should be 'supported and improved'. He urged 'the independence of Sulu—the ratification of the treaty—the increase of trade from that place and the determined and systematic suppression of Piracy . . .'. He added his opinion 'that we should never compromise our position and our power in native estimation; and I believe our recession would have that effect—in these countries, as in India, not to advance is to retrograde'.[15]

Brooke's advocacy was in vain: the British Government did not ratify his Sulu treaty.

Spain, however, failed to occupy the sultanate. Its attempted blockade of Sulu in the early 1870s was to test British readiness to associate with another colonial power. 'A shameful story,' Robert Meade declared at the Colonial Office. 'It seems a pity that Spain should be allowed to behave in this way; the war is being carried on in a part of the world which is not open to whatever influence public opinion might possess.'[16]

When I consider what has been the course of events in this unhappy group of Islands and the spectacle afforded to orientals of a Christian Power murdering, pillaging and burning with no adequate excuse—and that Power so weak that the slightest intimation from us that proceedings must cease, would no doubt be attended to—I think a more vigorous course might well be adopted. . . .

A colleague added: 'It is not a matter for pride or pleasure to contemplate our position and the acts we tolerate in the far East.'[17]

Britain's challenge to Spain was, however, limited, in particular because of its concern for its interests in Europe, and ultimately the challenge was to be dropped. The relationship became less tripartite: the Sulus were left to struggle alone behind an internationally recognized Philippine frontier. The clash between colonial power and indigenous people was, more sharply than in Netherlands India, one between Christian and Muslim, and the British had perhaps been especially concerned because of the implications for their position in the Muslim world, in particular in India.

The Malay Peninsula and Borneo

Sulu was left to Spain. In the Malay Peninsula and in northern Borneo, the British relationship became over time dyadic, too, but in a different way. In the former during the late eighteenth and nineteenth centuries the British had a number of interests. Their economic concern with the Peninsula itself was for most of the time limited. Even with the opening up of tin mines, more particularly from mid-century onwards, Britain's interests in the Peninsula fell far short of the significance they were to attain from the early twentieth century onwards with the development of rubber and the rise of the automobile industry. Economically the British were interested in the area rather on account of the entrepôt opportunities its geographical position afforded it. They established themselves in three Straits Settlements: Penang (1786), Malacca (1795, 1825), and Singapore (1819). Their trading interests did not merely, or even primarily, look inwards: they looked outwards, to the trade of India, China, and the islands consigned to a greater or lesser degree to the Dutch.

Overlaying concerns that fell into the first circle of British interests were those of a strategic nature. They, of course, also related to the geographical position of the Peninsula. It lay across the routes between the two greatest centres of the world's population, in both of which Britain had interests; empire in the one and trade in the other. Penang, furthermore, was, at least in the days before steam, an important defensive position for the Bay of Bengal, and thus for insulating the empire on the sub-continent from foreign invasion. Singapore was not only a trade entrepôt: it was on the route to China from India and from Europe. As such it had strategic significance, even before the major changes in Britain's position gave it special naval importance after the First World War. In turn the strategic importance of these settlements gave the peninsular hinterland an importance that extended beyond its direct economic significance. The establishment of a rival power on the Peninsula would undermine the security of the Settlements and of the interests beyond the Straits that they protected. The Dutch and the Spaniards were acceptable in the Indonesian and Philippine islands under certain commercial guarantees, and indeed their collaboration helped to preclude the intervention there of other more threatening powers. Even the Dutch were, however, excluded from the Peninsula under the treaty of 1824.

Under the treaty, Borneo was, it seems, to be left to the Dutch, like the rest of the Archipelago. The establishment of a British political regime in northern Borneo was not anticipated, and it came about as a result of an exceptional confluence of interests and personal initiatives. The economic interests of the British there were limited. A trade in antimony developed at Sarawak, then part of the sultanate of Brunei, soon after Raffles' establishment of the Singapore entrepôt in 1819. More significant was the impact of the development of steam navigation. That made the supply of coal of economic and also strategic importance, and Borneo possessed a certain amount of coal, for instance in the region of the Brunei capital and offshore on Labuan. Later the strategic significance of the area was increased as a result of the re-establishment of French interests on the opposite shore of the South China Sea in Vietnam and Cambodia: that made it more important to keep the southern shore of the route to China free from a major European power. The possession of the area by the Dutch might have foreclosed the intervention of others in Borneo as elsewhere in the Archipelago. But a British political intervention had made that impossible.

At the time the Spaniards had first established themselves in the Philippines, they had attacked Brunei as well as Sulu, but they had not succeeded in overthrowing it. On the periphery of the Archipelago, it had, like Aceh, also stood outside the contractual system developed by the Dutch. By the early nineteenth century, it no longer had the aspirations or the actual power of the previous centuries, but it was still a large realm. It was not the truncated, though wealthy, Brunei of today. From the superb position of its present capital, it ruled, with greater or lesser degrees of effectiveness, all the present territory of Sarawak and much of that of Sabah.

Even though, or perhaps in part because, Britain probably intended under the treaty of 1824 to leave the political fate of all of Borneo to them, the Dutch did not establish themselves there. They thus left the way open to James Brooke and his Rafflesian aspiration for a British policy that would in fact reverse that of the 1824 treaty. The Dutch had destroyed the independence of native states in the Archipelago and degraded their commerce. They could be revived. Politically reformed, furthermore, they could participate effectively in the development of British commercial interests. Intervention was, however, needed. He would set an example in Sarawak, which he hoped Brunei as a whole could be induced to follow. He advocated a collaboration between Europeans and Asians.

The experiment of developing a country through the residence of a few Europeans, and by the assistance of its native rulers has never been fairly tried; and it appears to me, in some respects, more desirable than the actual possession by a foreign nation.... Above all it insures the independence of the native princes, and may advance the inhabitants further in the scale of civilization, by means of this very independence, than can be done when the government is a foreign one, and their natural freedom sacrificed....[18]

For this venture he had a surprisingly substantial, though still limited, degree of British support. This he secured on a number of grounds. Perhaps it was important that he conceived of it and presented it as a collaborative venture. He argued that it would serve Britain's economic interests, and the point was made more effective than might have been anticipated by the contemporaneous Anglo-Dutch dispute over the interpretation of the treaty of 1824 that suggested that the Dutch were anxious to limit the opportunities for British commerce in the rest of the Archipelago. He pointed, too, to the impediment piracy placed in the way of legitimate commerce, and extended the commitment to destroy it, included in the treaty of 1824, by offering a wide application of the term. He also drew attention to the coal that Borneo might be expected to afford. These arguments were presented to the authorities. But he also sought to drive them home by a public campaign that would arouse philanthropic as well as commercial interests. 'The press—the press—agitate, agitate, ding dong, knock it into their ears. . . .'[19]

The Government in London was induced to afford him some support, but it remained limited. The British did not abandon their general acceptance of the Dutch in the Archipelago, nor did they take over Sarawak as a colony. They did, however, acquire Labuan, despite the opposition of Gladstone, then Colonial Secretary:

I confess that . . . I am struck by the enormous field as yet unoccupied but distinctly belonging to us which we have to fill; by the singular complication which distance gives to our affairs in that quarter; by the weight of our responsibilities there already incurred, and by the extent of the opportunities open to us for every kind of material and some kinds of social development. . . .[20]

The Government also made a treaty with the sultanate of Brunei in 1847, binding it to exclude other powers, and they appointed Brooke Commissioner and Consul-General, with a wide brief that encouraged him to take up, too, the cause of the Sulus against the Spaniards. The policy, never firmly institutionally based, was the more easily dropped when public opinion turned against Brooke. But he remained in Sarawak, increasingly asserting its independence, and, though the Sulu treaty was not ratified and the commissionership ceased, neither the treaty with Brunei nor the colony of Labuan were abandoned. The British Government tried, however, to delimit its policy towards Brunei. At the Foreign Office the Under-Secretary Lord Wodehouse (later Lord Kimberley) wrote:

We have nothing to do with the domestic troubles of Brunei, or the other dominions of the Sultan. . . . Mr St John [the Consul-General] evidently contemplates exercising the sort of power which is possessed by a

British Resident at a native Indian Court. . . . I apprehend we should hardly wish to make Borneo another India. . . .[21]

With both Brooke and the Sultan the British acquired in northern Borneo collaborators who were difficult to handle but could not be jettisoned, obligations unwanted but unavoidable. 'I believe the policy of Mr Canning's treaty was much the wisest: viz to leave to the Dutch the Eastern Archipelago,' Wodehouse wrote in 1860.

I know that this Treaty does not strictly apply to the North West Coast of Borneo, but the general intention of Mr Canning was clearly that we should not acquire territory in the Archipelago south of Singapore. . . . It seems to me in many respects very advantageous to us that the Dutch should possess this Archipelago. If it was not in the hands of the Dutch, it would fall under the sway of some other maritime power, possibly the French, unless we took it ourselves. . . .[22]

But it was impossible to return to 1824. Brooke had still some hold on public opinion, which made his enterprise difficult to desert; and his vaunted independence led him to negotiate with other powers. The sultanate could hardly be abandoned to the Dutch. Its most likely fate seemed to be absorption by an expanding Brooke Raj. But the anomaly and unreliability of Brooke rule made that an impossible option for the British, too. The fear of intervention by other foreign powers in the remnant of Brunei was to lead the British to adopt a new policy, though one that still stopped short of acquisition.

The ideas of Brooke had been derived in some sense from those of Raffles. They reflected not only his wish to establish an empire in the Archipelago to rival that of the Dutch, but also his notion of reviving and reforming the remaining Malay states. These ideas were also to influence the nature of British intervention in the Peninsula when it ultimately came about. There was another source, too, perhaps not wholly distinct. Raffles, of course, was an official of the East India Company, and Brooke had been in its army. Ideas associated with intervention, responsibility, and reform were derived in some degree from practice and precept on the subcontinent. There was a more direct influence still. The initial centre for the Straits Settlements was Penang, and for a while it was a Presidency equivalent to Calcutta, Bombay, and Madras. That encouraged officials there such as W. A. Clubley to develop notions of larger responsibility than those befitting a merely commercial post. They wished to intervene in the Peninsula as their colleagues did among the Indian states. In their eyes Raffles was an intruder, but his aims competed rather than contrasted.

[S]upposing that commerce alone first brought an English settlement to this island, it must be recollected that the same duties which on a larger scale have fallen to the other Presidencies in India have in a more contracted sphere now devolved on us ... other Duties than those which would strictly fall within the sphere of a mere Commercial Residency. ... We have become a preponderating Power on this side of India and we ought to hold in our hands the scales of justice, to protect the weaker power against the usurpations of the stronger, to mediate between them all on every occasion when our interference can be effectual, and even at times to exhibit a tone of superiority to check the extravagant pretensions of the different states. ... [23]

No such intervention was approved by the superior authorities. Attempts to intervene in fact prompted a reaffirmation of the non-intervention policy in a despatch from the Governor-General of 1827. The fact that, with the loss of its monopoly of the trade with China, the Company also lost its main interest in the Settlements only encouraged a non-interventionist policy after 1833. Nevertheless the Governors intervened in a number of more or less informal ways. They worked against piracy, and conducted operations so as to involve Malay rulers. They worked with the ruler of Johore, in the event so closely that they provoked jealousy on the part of the ruler of Trengganu. They thus established a pattern of collaboration with peninsular princes that helped both to limit the scope of the formal intervention that was to be sanctioned in the early 1870s and to define its shape.

Before that time, however, the local government could secure no sanction from their superiors for a more formal programme of intervention. It was not for want of asking. Governor Orfeur Cavenagh, for example, argued in 1861 for engagements

recognizing our paramount authority, and thus enabling us, without any undue grasping after power, to imperceptibly extend our influence over the surrounding chiefs and to exercise over their activities that legitimate control which our position so justly demands, a control that whilst enlarging the circle of operations of our own trade, and thus improving its prospects by opening up new fields hitherto but imperfectly explored, could only tend to the benefit of the rulers and people over whom it might be extended. [24]

Two years later, he urged the adoption of

some specific line of policy with regard to the native states on the Malay Peninsula, and were the Governor of the Straits empowered when occasion might require to assure them that the British Government will not allow the general peace to be disturbed, there would be little difficulty in maintaining perfect tranquillity by inducing the chiefs to refer all disputes to our arbitration and to acknowledge our paramount authority.[25]

The Government was, however, not prepared for a change of policy: 'we have hitherto waited to hear of disturbances and threatened aggressions before using any influence to stop them; a letter of advice or an authoritative injunction has then ordinarily been found sufficient to restrain an aggression and prevent disturbances.'[26] The Colonial Office, taking over supervision of the Straits Settlements from the India Office soon after this, took over its policy, too. Only in the early 1870s was a new policy adopted. But it was limited in scope—it related to Perak, Selangor, and Sungei Ujong, all on the west coast—and in concept—it took the form of appointing Residents who were to advise the rulers.

The line of policy Cavenagh advocated, the Indian Government had pointed out, would involve 'interfering in the domestic as well as the external affairs of the native states, and might possibly be looked on with jealousy by the Government of Siam'.[27] The restraint of the British in the Peninsula indeed derived from another source, too: they had competing interests. The relationship with at least some of the Malay states was tripartite, like the relationship with some of the Indonesian states. The third point in the triangle was not, however, as in that case, a European power, but an Asian one, the kingdom of Siam. The Thai kingdom in times of prosperity and success extended its power into the Peninsula and following the installation of the Chakri dynasty in Bangkok it looked south again. It was indeed the Thais' assumption of Kedah's vassalage that encouraged the Sultan to welcome the East India Company to Penang. It was their prompting his invasion of Perak, and their subsequent invasion of Kedah itself, that alarmed the officials in Penang and led them to argue for British intervention. Their arguments and their activities, however, elicited caution and restraint from their superiors. Henry Burney was sent to Bangkok and made commercial and political treaties in 1826. But the terms of the latter were disappointing to the Penang officials. The northern states seemed to be more or less lost to Thai supremacy and their attempts to redeem Perak from that fate only led to the 1827 despatch. 'Our only national object of policy hereafter in relation to the Siamese should be to endeavour to allay their jealousy of our ultimate views . . . and to derive from our connexion with them every attainable degree of commercial advantage. . . .'[28]

While leaving Patani to the Thais, however, the Burney treaty did enable the British to restrain the exertion of Thai supremacy in Kelantan and Trengganu. The subversion of Thai authority in Kedah in the 1830s enabled Governor S. G. Bonham—assuming what Rama III called 'the middleman's role'[29]—to promote a compromise which again in a sense represented the tripartite sharing of political power in these states. It was a relationship more to the advantage of the Malay rulers than the relationship in which the Indonesian states were involved. Generally the latter had lost their contact with the British and any power but the superordinate Dutch. Other than Patani, the Malay states retained their British contact in one form or another.

There were occasions on which the relationship with the British seemed disadvantageous, for instance the British bombardment of Trengganu in 1862. The special relationship with Johore that the Straits authorities had developed had promoted an imbalance on the Peninsula and risked destabilizing it rather than promoting peace and security. Among the princes that were opposed to the Johore ruler's ambitions—which his association with the British seemed to encourage him to advance, particularly by intervention in neighbouring Pahang—were not only other Johore–Lingga princes but also the ruler of Trengganu. It was in part the latter's counter-intervention in Pahang that led Governor Cavenagh to authorize bombardment; it was also his apparent readiness to re-affirm the suzerainty of the Thais in order to counteract the influence of the Anglo-Johore combination. In fact the bombardment did not secure its objectives. The anti-Johore faction prevailed in Pahang, while the bombardment produced a protest from Siam, led the British Government to reaffirm its recognition of Thai claims over the northern states, and even prompted Cavenagh's successor, Sir Harry Ord, the first Colonial Office-appointed Governor, to attribute the good order established in Kedah, Kelantan, and Trengganu to the influence of the Thais. The long-term effects, however, were less damaging than the immediate outcome suggested they might be. The new ruler of Pahang proved anxious to sustain an independence of both Trengganu and Johore, while Trengganu saw an advantage in maintaining a friendly relationship with the British so as to avoid submergence beneath Siamese supremacy. The tripartite relationship could be preserved.

The reason for the initial distrust of the Anglo-Johore combination had been its apparent exclusivity. The other princes sought to avoid the extension of Johore's power through its association with the British, but they sought their own relationship with the British, whether they were under Thai supremacy, like the northern states, or not, like Pahang. The extent of British influence with the states was not yet an issue. It was only when the effects of the Resident system began to be felt in the west coast states and noticed in the others that another attitude towards the British developed and collaboration was put under strain.

Clearly the policy of the British towards the peninsular states was deeply influenced by the relationship between Siam and the British and between Siam and the states. For most of the nineteenth century, the economic interests of the British in the Peninsula were limited. The political and strategic importance of the area was greater than its direct economic value and it was probably the political and strategic arguments that were to be decisive in the partial formalizing of intervention. No other power could be allowed to establish itself along this part of the route to China. The Dutch had been excluded: another power could be still more damaging. The relations of the British with the Peninsula were thus largely determined by factors extraneous to it. The same was true of their attitude towards the Siamese relationship with the Peninsula. It was marked, in general, by moderation and caution, at times undercut, but never undermined, by the actions of the local authorities.

Siam

The policy of the British towards Siam was in turn determined by their interests and by the attitudes of the Thais. Britain's interests were again in a sense external to Siam. Economically Siam was of no special importance, though it was to become a major supplier of rice to the colonial and pseudo-colonial territories in the latter half of the century. Its importance to the British again depended upon its geographical and political position in relation to British interests elsewhere. In the earlier part of the period the relationship with China was of special significance. After the China war of the 1840s the relationship with the British became more significant, together with the relationship with the other European powers that increasingly penetrated the region after the change in the European relationship with China that the war had precipitated.

Siam had a place in the so-called tributary system, which the Manchu rulers of China had sought to sustain and which was substantially undermined in the 1840s. Like other states within this system, the Thai preserved effective independence by recognizing ineffective suzerainty. The early rulers of the Chakri dynasty legitimized their position by accepting a tributary relationship, while they also sought to enforce such a system on their own neighbours in the Peninsula and elsewhere. The emergence of European states with different views, differing interests, and different power, and in particular the emergence of the British, presented a challenge to the dynasty's perception, and to its capacity to adapt, and to enforce its adaptation over its subjects.

Initially the British were, however, exceedingly cautious. Their relations with the Chinese empire were in the hands of the Company and until 1833, it retained its monopoly of the trade in tea, increasingly paid for by the sale of Indian opium. The ground rules were still determined by the Manchu authorities and trade was confined as a result to Canton and conducted through a peculiar commercial regime. A challenge to that regime might undermine a profitable trade. A challenge to Manchu claims elsewhere might also destroy the relationship. The British authorities deprecated any obligation to the Sultan of Kedah in respect of the cession of Penang, avoided intervention on his behalf, and disapproved of the adventurousness of the Penang authorities. Their reasons lay not only in their recognition that the Peninsula was in itself of limited importance; it lay also in their recognition that, while Siam had claims there, it also accepted a tributary relationship with China. That could not be disturbed without risking the British relationship with China and the really important economic interests attached to that.

The relationship with Siam was also affected by the attitude of the Thais, however. The Chakri rulers displayed a flexibility that in some degree may be attributed to a Thai tradition of diplomatic self-preservation. It may also in part be attributed to the crisis the Thai kingdom had faced in the second half of the eighteenth century. The centuries-old struggle between Thais and Burmans had come to a climax with the destruction of Ayuthia in 1767. Seeking to restore their kingdom, the Thais adopted positive and innovative policies.[30] Though its power on the periphery was uncertain, the kingdom of the Thais had a strong core, and the Chakri capital at Bangkok uniquely commanded the contacts with the outside world. That gave the rulers an unusual confidence in dealing with other powers and an unusual capacity to carry through any obligations they undertook or decisions they made. Though still accepting a tributary relationship with China, Rama III was prepared to make treaties with the Company in 1826. As a result of this approach, and that of Burney and his superiors, the treaties had considerable advantages for Siam. The greatest advantage was that they were made at all. Thai diplomacy was able to take account of new factors in South-East Asia. It had taken a first step towards preserving its existence in a changing world. In a sense it had become one of Britain's collaborators, though yet still one of China's vassals.

This course stood Siam in good stead when relations with China changed in the 1840s. The British defeat of China, the treaty of Nanking, the opening of treaty ports, and the acquisition of Hong Kong were dramatic changes the impact of which was felt among all the tributaries of the Manchus, the Siamese as well as the Vietnamese and the Japanese. The Thai reaction, like the Japanese, was positive; it was also prompter. True, no real change took place in the remainder of Rama III's lifetime. The British at Hong Kong argued that a new approach to the tributaries following the change in the relationship with the suzerain would be well received, but at first the forecast seemed mistaken. A mission sent by the home government, which now conducted relations with China, was also vain: though Raja Brooke was hardly an ideal choice to undertake it. He argued for force, using arguments that related to India as he had over Sulu.

The hope of preserving peace by an expedient Policy—by concession, submission, by indifference, or by any other course, than by rights firmly maintained by power justly exerted, is both a delusion and a cruelty; and after years of embarrassment and the sacrifice of a favourable prestige leads to a sanguinary war.

An adherence to this principle has raised our Indian Empire, and established the reign of Opinion which maintains it; and the departure from this principle has caused the present deplorable condition of our relations with Siam, and the consequent and embarrassing circumstances which no longer permit of Palliation or inactivity. . . . I can only arrive at the conclusion that there is no other course open to Her Majesty's Government, except, to demand . . . either a more equitable Treaty in accordance with the observance of civilized nations, or a total withdrawal of British subjects and their property from Siam.

Should these just demands firmly urged be refused, a force should be present immediately to enforce them by a rapid destruction of the defences of the river, which would place us in possession of the capital and by restoring us to our proper position of command, retrieve the past and ensure peace for the future, with all its advantages of a growing and most important commerce.[31]

Palmerston did not follow this advice. The new king, Rama IV, responded positively to the next British mission, that of Bowring in 1855, and readily accepted many of the changes that China had been forced to accept, and more. It was an 'unequal' treaty, but it had advantages for Siam. Aside from promoting its economic transformation, it enabled Siam to enter the 'family of nations'. The very fact that it made a deal with the predominant power in the world helped to limit the threat other powers could present. The Kralahom told Bowring that the Siamese 'had trusted that he would be the pioneer of the new relations to be opened between them and the West, as they could then count upon such arrangements being concluded as would both be satisfactory to Siam, and sufficient to meet the demands that might hereafter be made by other of the Western Powers'.[32] Treaties with other powers followed the British model, but went no further. By making them, the Siamese avoided total dependence on the British. But their most important gain was British interest in their future.

The presence of a British envoy in their capital—something the Chinese had declined—stood them in good stead, even against other protagonists of British power, like Cavenagh. Siam could not be treated merely as a colonial antagonist. Its protests were more telling in London as a result of Robert Schomburgk's presence in Bangkok. But there was always a vein of moderation in British policy anyway. That, for example, had no doubt explained the non-acceptance of Brooke's fiery recommendations. The British attitude helped Rama IV to shift away from the latter-day obstinacy of his predecessor, to build upon the precedent of the Burney treaty that predecessor had made at the outset of his reign, and to renew collaboration with the major world power of the day. Following up Bowring's mission, Harry Parkes delivered a letter from Queen Victoria, which gave Mongkut

genuine satisfaction. . . . To be as he believed the first Sovereign in Asia to receive a letter from Her Britannic Majesty, to be styled by Her not only 'an affectionate friend' but 'sister' also, and thus to be admitted unreservedly into the brotherhood of European royalty, and have his position as a King thus clearly recognised by the Sovereign—as it may probably appear to him—of the most powerful European State, was indeed an honor and a satisfaction which at once touched his heart and flattered his ambition.[33]

British policy towards Siam thus came primarily into the hands of the Foreign Office, since it became one of the family of nations. That limited the challenges the Straits Governors could present—the obligations of this collaboration were not all on one side—and helped to consolidate acceptance of Thai supremacy in the northern Malay states. But the Company, ruling India and the Straits Settlements up to 1858, made a moderating input, too. Even after the change of relations with China, it had been doubtful about the advantage of a new mission to Siam: it might make matters worse, even provoke the need to retaliate. One reason for this caution was that it meanwhile acquired parts of Burma. It had no wish for collision with a state on the periphery of British territories there or in the neighbouring of the Straits Settlements for which it was still responsible. That this concern was shared elsewhere in the British Government was demonstrated when Brooke's recommendations were not followed. In the post-Bowring years this approach was reinforced by the advent of other powers in South-East Asia, in particular the French. Increasingly Siam seemed to be a buffer state between the territories they came to acquire in Indo-China and those the British possessed in Burma and controlled in the Peninsula. The British gained a further political interest in preserving the independence and integrity of Siam; the Chakri kings at once a further antagonist and a further diplomatic resource. In some sense, the preservation of Siam's independence was dependent on the loss of independence on the part of its neighbours. But the major factors lay elsewhere, in the nature of Siamese policy and of British interests.

Burma

Burma had been far less successful, both because of its different policy and of the different nature of British interests. Its policy was certainly less flexible than Siam's. Both the Thais and the Burmans had a tradition of assertiveness over neighbours and bordering minorities. But in the case of the latter it seemed to condition their outlook on foreign relations in general more fully than in the case of the former. The assertiveness of the dynasty founded by Alaungpaya was marked. That was at once related to the history of the kingdom and to its Buddhist character. The kingdom had long tried to sustain the dominance of the Burmans, and in particular Alaungpaya had to destroy the claim of the Mons to renewed independence. At the same time the king had the universalistic claims of a *cakkavartin*. Alaungpaya built a great pagoda designed to mark the end of the strife. But there were other challenges for Alaungpaya's heirs. Not only did Hsinbiyushin invade Ayuthia, he sought to control Arakan. His successors extended their realms to the frontiers of Bengal. But, again by contrast to the Thais, the Burmans there faced a territory that was under British dominion.

The British empire in India had begun to grow at the same time as the Alaungpaya dynasty established itself in Burma and asserted itself over the Mons, the Arakanese, and, though only temporarily, over the Thais themselves. But it was no ordinary empire. Connected with the major world naval power, it was even so a dominion especially dependent upon military prowess and political prestige. That made it peculiarly susceptible, even before the Mutiny of 1857, to challenge from within and suspicious of challenge from without and particularly anxious to avoid the coincidence of the two. It gave the British not only a peculiar advantage but a peculiar problem, and their policy in India hardly coincided with their policy overall. It aimed indeed at stability and at security. But its policy in India was necessarily continental in character: it was an Indian policy, not the policy of an insular commercial state.

Even if no European power were involved, the British in India, unlike the British in Europe, were unlikely to recognize the full sovereignty of their neighbours. A continental power seeks security on its frontiers by requiring a degree of subordination, something less than the equality that European nations at least theoretically enjoyed one with another. Even if the Burman kings had been less pretentious, their full independence would have been difficult to accept. Their kingdom, especially as they asserted themselves over the Arakanese, ran alongside the dominion of the British. There were border disputes, in themselves no abnormal feature of inter-state relations, but, in the context of the different attitudes of the two main parties involved, the more difficult to resolve. There were also commercial disputes. But again the problems of British traders at Burman ports could not readily be resolved. They were complicated by the political pretensions of both sides. Britain did not act on behalf of its traders in the ports of the kingdom in the same manner as it did in respect of those in Siam. The fact was that Burma was not merely in the first circle of British interests, but, because of India, in the second as well, and perhaps more importantly so.

In any case, for much of the time another European power was involved, or the British thought or feared that it was involved. The French had initially competed with the British on the continent of India: their rivalry may have precipitated the establishment of British territorial control. Failing in the contest in India, they sought other means of undermining Britain's triumph in Asia. Naturally they looked to Burma, for from the further side of the Bay of Bengal the security of the shores of the Indian subcontinent might be undermined, especially as before the acquisition of Ceylon, the British had no naval bases that could afford shelter in the northerly monsoon. French contacts with Alaungpaya prompted the initial British venture at Negrais. That ended in humiliation and disaster for the British in 1759. In succeeding years, Anglo-Burman clashes were avoided. But the development of the respective attitudes of the two parties in the meantime boded ill for the future.

The renewal of war with the French in the 1790s again made the British in India worry about Burma. At the same time their frontiers had become contiguous. The missions of Michael Symes and Hiram Cox averted conflict. But it was significant that the solution Governor-General Wellesley's adviser, William Francklin, advocated was the extension to Burma of the 'subsidiary alliance' system that was being developed in India itself. The aim was not so much to counter a French threat as to ensure that Burma assumed a less pretentious stance vis-à-vis the British: its position on the confines of India was to be less than fully independent. Its independence could as it were be sustained only if it were qualified. The British did not wish to take Burma over, but they wished it to accept its subordinate status. No real attempt was made on Symes's second mission of 1802 to carry out this policy. It would surely have failed in any case. Busy elsewhere, and recognizing that the French were unable to establish their influence in Burma either, the British contented themselves with Captain John Canning's diplomatic missions. And he found the king quite unrealistic. 'It seems that he will treat with no power on earth as an equal, but he graciously receives under his protection China, Ceylon, Burma, and the British Empire in India. He will grant a boon but will not make a treaty. . . .'[34]

The first major conflict between Britain or British India and Burma came well after the French wars had concluded. The advance of the Burmans beyond Arakan and their threat to Bengal played its part. But the core problem—making other problems insoluble—was the inability to reconcile diplomatic traditions and political stances. The British and their Indian troops were victorious, though only after a laborious struggle. Governor-General Amherst's aim had not been to acquire a Burman empire—even the rulers of India had no such objective—but to force Burma's recognition of British superiority by a prompt and dramatic military success: 'to produce such an impression of the power and resources of the British Empire in India as will deter the Court of Ava from any attempt again to disturb the friendly relations which may be re-established by the result of the present contest'.[35] That had evaded him, and he had to find another means of so doing. The British attempted to put the relationship with Burma on a new footing not by annexing the whole kingdom nor by entering into a subsidiary alliance. They annexed part of the kingdom, though not the mouth of the Irrawaddy. The object was to mark their superiority over Burma, and they hoped the Burmans would adjust their views accordingly. They also made treaties with Burma, but hesitated over placing a Resident—he was, significantly, not an ambassador or an envoy—at the Burman capital.

The position was finally filled with success and distinction by Henry Burney, who had made the Bangkok treaties of 1826. Even he, however, could not persuade the Burman kings to accept the situation. Bagyidaw he found 'full of the most ungovernable pride and arrogance, ... most unwilling to admit the British Government as equal to his in pride and strength. More than any other man in his empire he feels and broods over the disasters of the late war, and of all his subjects that war has left the least impression of our superiority upon his mind.'[36] The Amherst policy had failed. On coming to the throne in 1837, Tharrawaddy declared that the treaty of Yandabo, made by his predecessor, no longer applied. He said that

the Burmese officers had been frightened into signing the treaty of Yandabo, and that it contained everything for the English and nothing for the Burmese, that some of its articles were too hard, that the late Government had never shown him the whole of it, which he had only lately seen, and that at all events the English had not conquered him or made the treaty with him, and that he was determined to have nothing to say to it.[37]

There was little chance of the kind of progressive development that the Chakri kings managed. The Burmans could not accept the position the British victory was designed to assign them.

The origins of the second Anglo-Burman war of 1852–4 are controversial: they were at the time the subject of Radical criticism at home, illustrated in a pamphlet 'How Wars Are Got up in India' by Richard Cobden, for whom commerce was 'the grand panacea'.[38] Its title at once hints at bases for action in the second circle differing from those in the first. The kind of incident that led to the war was less likely to have provoked war elsewhere in the world. But the reason it provoked war in South-East Asia did not, as Cobden suggested, lie in fact that India paid the bill; nor did it lie in the aggressiveness or irresponsibility of the Governor-General, Lord Dalhousie; nor did it really lie in the assertiveness of his deputies, as Oliver Pollak has argued,[39] or the aggressiveness of agents like the 'combustible Commodore', George Lambert. The prime factor was Burma's propinquity to India. 'The Government of India could never, consistently with its own safety, permit itself to stand for a single day in an attitude of inferiority towards a native power, and least of all towards the Court of Ava,' Dalhousie minuted.[40]

The simple question is whether, before all Asia, England will submit to Ava, desert its subjects, and be driven out of the Irrawaddy; or whether, protecting its subjects, it will enforce its treaty rights by arms, and if no less alternative will do, take possession of the Irrawaddy itself. God knows I lament the alternative, but I did not create it. I have laboured to avert it, and as it has been forced upon us, I say that if we shrink from it our power in India will be shaken by our short-sighted and cowardly policy worse than ever it has been shaken by our enemies.[41]

Once the incident had developed, the stand-off in Anglo-Burman relations that had been brought about by the first Afghan war had to be terminated. It was terminated by a second war, more effectively conducted by Dalhousie than the first had been by Amherst. The annexation of Pegu followed, but this time no treaty was made. The Governor-General argued persuasively against the attempt to do so. The Burmans would resent it, and infringements would compel further punishment. He was relying on annexation alone to mark Britain's superiority and Burman defeat. 'I believe that the Court of Ava would silently acquiesce in a loss, though it would not openly assent to a cession. A conviction of its own interests would dissuade it from disputing our possession, while its extravagant pride would not allow it to give us possession by a formal act of its own. . . .' If, despite all the risks, the Burmans did challenge the British, 'still I earnestly contend that an onward territorial movement should be avoided to the last. So injurious do I consider the extension of our sovereignty over Burma would be, that I would exhaust every honorable expedient before I would advise recourse to that measure. . . .' A substantial military force would be required, great expense, and there would be no corresponding revenue.[42] 'To stop at Prome, taking Pegu, and without a treaty, was better than going on to Ava, taking it, and still without a treaty.'[43]

Though its new king, Mindon Min, hoped to regain the Pegu territory, the remnant kingdom cultivated good relations with British India, partly with that object in mind. He behaved like an ally in the Crimean war and in the 1857 Mutiny. He even proceeded to make commercial treaties, facilitating British access to the Burman lands and through them, it was hoped, to China. But there were limits beyond which, in the British Indian view, a king of Burma could not go: he was a collaborator who could not pass certain limits that others could. In his later years, Mindon began to overstep them. Relations with other powers were, as the Thais saw, a reassurance against total dependence on the British. But, for the Burmans more than the Thais, they were risky. Too obvious a demonstration of independence would alarm the British, and perhaps prompt a further and final conflict. If Mindon's judgement waned in his later years, his successor had less. Furthermore the Burman court became divided and its factions were fatally to use the issue of foreign relations as a focus for their conflict. This was the more dangerous because of the reappearance of the French upon the scene, following the establishment of their control in Vietnam and Cambodia. Their interest was no longer in the Bay of Bengal, nor in undermining British dominion in India. But the British became apprehensive that their interest in upper Burma could destroy its submissiveness and indirectly at least undermine their security.

The Andaman and Nicobar Islands

Geographically part of South-East Asia, the Andaman and Nicobar islands shared little of its history. But they were affected by the conquests of the British in India and Burma. The search for sheltered bases on the east side of the Bay of Bengal led not only to the establishment of Penang, but also to settlements on the Great Andaman island, finally abandoned as unhealthy in 1796. The Danish settlement on the Nicobars, established in 1756, was removed by the British in 1809, following their acquisition during the French wars of the Danish factories in India. Post-war the Danes established a settlement on Kamorta in 1831, but they withdrew in 1838. The Nicobars increasingly became the scene of disputes between islanders and traders from Sumatra and Burma, but the Indian Government, despite references to alleged French intentions, did not intervene: it had 'no apprehension of the designs of other European nations and no desire to establish relations . . . with the chiefs and tribes of the Nicobar Islands'.[44] The Andamans, of even less commercial value, were also the scene of violence. They lay in the track of vessels crossing the Bay and in the track of mainland traders to the Nicobars. Slave-raiding by Burmese and Siamese–Malay vessels did not mitigate the savage treatment islanders meted out to crews who stopped for water or were wrecked; all this in islands 'situated as it were in the centre of the peculiar sea of the Indian Empire'.[45] By 1855 the Indian Government was considering a return to the Andamans. The Governor-General, Lord Canning, was opposed: '. . . we must consider our means and the further and more weighty liabilities which we may bring upon ourselves before we undertake even a duty. The possession of an island, unless it be so situated and armed as to be a bulwark or an advanced guard, becomes in war a positive weakness. . . .' 'Whatever was the case before, the conquest of Pegu has made the Bay of Bengal a British Sea,' his colleague J. P. Grant argued by contrast. No foreign power could be allowed to establish itself there and Britain should anticipate such a prospect.[46] What turned the balance was the Indian Mutiny. A vastly increased number of Indian convicts had to be disposed of. Port Blair was established as a convict station. Danish claims to the Nicobars were taken over in 1869, and convicts sent to Kamorta in 1871.

Vietnam

The French had interested themselves in Vietnam in the second half of the eighteenth century, at the same time as they had interested themselves in Burma. In Burma, they had hoped to undermine British success in India; in Vietnam they hoped to undermine the link between India and China. The notion lay behind the designs of Choiseul and Vergennes. The latter lamented in 1775:

It seems that there remains only Cochin China which has escaped the vigilance of the English: but can one flatter oneself that they will delay in casting their glance there? If they decide on that place before us, we will be excluded for ever and we will have lost an important foothold on that part of Asia which would make us masters by intercepting in time of war the English trade with China, by protecting our own in the whole of India, and by keeping the English in a continued state of anxiety.[47] But again French plans were impeded both by their own weakness and by the attitude of the Asian state concerned. Independent Vietnam had had a long history of southward expansion, but that had made it difficult to hold the state together. By the early eighteenth century it had absorbed most of Champa and much of Cambodia, and it had secured the Mekong Delta. But since the late sixteenth century the kingdom had been divided *de facto*, though *de jure* under one ruler: the north was ruled by the Trinh family, and the south by the Nguyen. It was the latter who were the French target. But their rule, and that of Trinh, was overthrown by the uprising led by the Tay-son brothers. In this great crisis, the Nguyen sought French help. A treaty was made at Versailles in 1787. No help was, however, officially offered, though a limited amount of unofficial assistance had a limited role in bringing about the Nguyen triumph and the reunification of the Vietnamese state under its leadership. The British were apprehensive that the grateful Nguyen rulers would welcome French influence. But they did not. Their policy was one of isolation, which they hoped would at once avoid the subversion of the Confucian doctrines on which they built their hopes of sustaining political unity and deflect the attentions of the rival Europeans. Attempts at isolationism were, however, unsuccessful, though less because of the limited British commercial interest in Vietnam than because of the persistent endeavours of Catholic missionaries to sustain and expand the long-standing Christian communities there.

Isolation was, however, sufficient to prevent any commercial treaties being made with the British, though they were sought particularly after the defeat of China in 1840–2: even the Bowring precedent was of no avail. 'It is obvious that the policy of the Cochin Chinese will continue to be that of repudiating the advances of foreigners, so long as foreigners can be kept in positions too remote to cause any anxiety. . . .'[48] No collaborative relationship was established. The British felt little interest in the fate of Vietnam, therefore, when a new regime in France, that of Napoleon III, took up the cause of the Catholics and displayed a new interest in the political fortunes of the area. 'We hear that the French are about to send five thousand men to Cochin China,' wrote Bowring. 'They have long had a fancy for locating themselves there. It will tend to the extension of Trade and there is perhaps no locality where less mischief will be done as regards our interests. . . .'[49]

With ships in China since its opening, the French had no base, like Hong Kong, though they sought one: Danang, allegedly promised them by the Nguyen, was a possibility. In fact their expedition, though augmented by Spanish and Tagalog troops, failing to secure the submission of Emperor Tu-duc, moved south, and took Saigon in 1859. This formed the nucleus of the French colony of Cochin-China. There they found collaborators, and from there, successfully challenging the Thais, the French extended their protection over the intervening remnant of the ancient Khmer state. So long as the French left Siam and Laos untouched, the British resolved not to object. Perhaps indeed, as the *Hong Kong Register* put it, the French would be able to open up Vietnam to European commerce where the British themselves had failed.

We may doubt the success of any commercial settlement at Tourane, but if it is to form a link in the chain of European intercourse with the East, if it is to aid in spreading western civilisation and a more liberal policy in this quarter of the globe, it is not France alone that will profit by the step, and we of all others, should be the first to wish the expedition God speed, even though the motives in which it first originated were those of opposition to our own power. . . .[50]

Vietnam lay within the first circle of interests. But the fate of Laos and Siam could affect those in the second circle.

Concluding Remarks

The nature of the British connection with the South-East Asian region at mid-century illustrates the nature of Britain's priorities. India was an exception to the rule. The general aim was not to take on additional territorial responsibilities, except in so far as they were essential to provide strategic support for Britain's naval and commercial interests. India required additional guarantees. But even its security did not require the conquest of Burma; it was the latter's subordination, not its governance, that the British sought. India was in a sense a warning. The British said over Borneo, as they were to say over China, that they did not want 'another India'. Their wish to avoid territorial responsibility was sustained by their need for good relations with the minor European powers in maritime South-East Asia. But their unwillingness to intervene existed all the same. The aim was security and stability, not dominion. Other states, Asian as well as European, would, it was hoped, survive, modernize themselves, and remain part of the emerging framework of states that formed the British vision of world politics.

If a survey of South-East Asia at mid-century supports the kind of interpretation this book offers of the use of British power in the world, that interpretation may also help in understanding the development of South-East Asian history. That was, of course, substantially determined by South-East Asians themselves, who had to face the major challenges of the nineteenth century, the impact of industrialization, the advance of European power. But the way they met these challenges was much affected by the role of the British in mediating, seconding, limiting, and shaping them. Where other European powers were left in control, or expected to prevail, the local élites could make no direct contact with the British. Elsewhere they could, though their opportunities differed, and so did the use they made of them.

This, of course, provided a starting point for the challenges of the next phase. The same applies to the British. The next phase challenged them, too, and they answered by adaptation rather than by revolution. The overall outcome was to bring South-East Asia under the hegemony of the Western powers. Even then, however, the British programme stopped short of imperialism.

1. Quoted in H. Furber, *Henry Dundas, First Viscount Melville, 1742–1811*, London: Oxford University Press, 1931, p. 103.

2. Sophia Raffles, *Memoir of the Life and Public Services of Sir Thomas Stamford Raffles*, London: John Murray, 1830, pp. 59 ff.

3. Raffles' Minute on the Malay College, quoted in H. Egerton, *Sir Stamford Raffles*, London: Unwin, 1900, p. 229.

4. Castlereagh to Clancarty, 13 August 1819, F.O. 37/107, Public Record Office, London.

5. Quoted in N. Tarling, *Anglo-Dutch Rivalry in the Malay World, 1780–1824*, St Lucia and Cambridge: Cambridge University Press, 1962, p. 155.

6. Sjahrir, *Our Struggle*, trans. B. Anderson, Ithaca: Cornell University, 1968, pp. 24–5.

7. Elizabeth E. Graves, 'The Ever Victorious Buffalo: How the Minangkabau of Indonesia Solved Their "Colonial Question" ', Ph.D. thesis, University of Wisconsin, 1971, p. 144.

8. Backhouse to Wood, 9 January 1838, Board's Collections 77129, India Office Library, London.

9. Quoted in Tarling, *Anglo-Dutch Rivalry in the Malay World*, p. 155.

10. See G. J. Resink, *Indonesia's History between the Myths*, The Hague: van Hoeve, 1968, pp. 137 ff.

11. D. H. Kolff, trans. G. W. Earl, *Voyages of the Dutch Brig of War Dourga, through the Southern and Little-known Parts of the Moluccan Archipelago*, London: Madden, 1840.

12. N. Tarling, *Sulu and Sabah*, Kuala Lumpur: Oxford University Press, 1978, pp. 23–4.

13. Farren to Aberdeen, 13 March 1845, private, F.O. 72/684, Public Record Office, London.

14. Quoted in N. Tarling, *British Policy in the Malay Peninsula and Archipelago 1824–1871*, Kuala Lumpur: Oxford University Press, 1969, p. 193.

15. Brooke to Addington, 26 January 1852, F.O. 71/1, Public Record Office, London.

16. Minute, 12 December 1873, C.O. 133/41 [11857], Public Record Office, London.

17. Minutes, 12 August 1874, C.O. 144/43 [9188A], Public Record Office, London.

18. Quoted in N. Tarling, *The Burthen, the Risk, and the Glory*, Kuala Lumpur: Oxford University Press, 1982, p. 50.

19. Brooke to Templer, 22 August 1842, in J. C. Templer (ed.), *The Private Letters of Sir James Brooke*, London: Bentley, 1853, Vol. I, pp. 210–13.

20. Memorandum, 18 January 1846, C.O. 144/1, Public Record Office, London.

21. Minute, 4 November 1855, F.O. 12/22, Public Record Office, London.

22. Memorandum, 18 June 1860, F.O. 12/28, Public Record Office, London.

23. Minute by Clubley, 16 September 1823, G/34/91, India Office Library, London.

24. Cavenagh to Secretary, 16 December 1861, 213, Collection 6 to No. 94 of 1862, Collections to Political Dispatches 63, India Office Library, London.

25. Cavenagh to Offg. Secretary, 25 August 1863, 156/1073, Collection 2 to No. 33 of 1864, Collections to Political Dispatches 72, India Office Library, London.

26. Minute by Prinsep, 4 May 1864, attached to No. 33 of 1864, and wrongly dated 1863, Political Dispatches to India 7, India Office Library, London.

27. Viceroy to Wood, 8 February 1864, 156/1073, Collection 2 to No. 23, of 1864, Collections to Political Dispatches 72, India Office Library, London.

28. Amherst to Governor-in-Council, 23 July 1827, G/34/142, India Office Library, London.

29. Quoted in Kobkua Suwannathat-Pian, *Thai–Malay Relations*, Singapore: Oxford University Press, 1988, p. 89.

30. Hong Lysa, *Thailand in the Nineteenth Century*, Singapore: Institute of Southeast Asian Studies, 1984, pp. 38 ff.

31. Brooke to Palmerston, 5 October 1850, F.O. 69/1, Public Record Office, London.

32. Quoted in N. Tarling, *Imperial Britain in South-East Asia*, Kuala Lumpur: Oxford University Press, 1975, p. 180.

33. Parkes to Clarendon, 22 May 1856, F.O. 69/5, Public Record Office, London.

34. Quoted in D. G. E. Hall, *Europe and Burma*, London: Oxford University Press, 1945, p. 96.

35. Quoted in G. P. Ramachandra, 'Anglo-Burmese Relations, 1795–1826', Ph.D. thesis, University of Hull, p. 391.

36. Quoted in W. S. Desai, *History of the British Residency in Burma 1826–1840*, Rangoon: University of Rangoon Press, 1939, p. 196.

37. Ibid., p. 295.

38. Quoted in M. J. Wiener, *English Culture and the Decline of the Industrial Spirit 1850–1980*, Cambridge: Cambridge University Press, 1981, p. 28.

39. Cf. O. Pollak, *Empires in Collision: Anglo-Burmese Relations in the Mid-nineteenth Century*, Westport: Greenwood, 1979, p. 68.

40. Quoted in D. G. E. Hall, *The Dalhousie–Phayre Correspondence*, London: Oxford University Press, 1932, p. xiii.

41. Ibid., p. xxi.

42. Minute, 3 November 1852, Papers Relating to Hostilities with Burma, Presented to Both Houses by Command, 4 June 1852, pp. 82–94.

43. Quoted in Aparna Mukherjee, *British Colonial Policy in Burma: An Aspect of Colonialism in South East Asia, 1840–1885*, Delhi: Abhinau, 1988, p. 156.

44. Prinsep to Crisp, 7 December 1836, Board's Collections 72400, India Office Library, London.

45. Rogers to Littler, 9 April 1850, Board's Collections 131280, India Office Library, London.

46. Minutes, 15 and 19 March 1856, Board's Collections 171873, India Office Library, London.

47. Quoted in A. Lamb, *The Mandarin Road to Old Hué*, London: Chatto and Windus, 1970, p. 64.

48. Bowring to Clarendon, 8 October 1855, F.O. 17/233, Public Record Office, London.

49. John Bowring to Edgar Bowring, 12 July 1858, Eng. MSS 1228/220, John Rylands Library, Manchester.

50. *Hong Kong Register*, 31 August 1858.

3

The 'New Imperialism' and South-East Asia

MAJOR changes mark South-East Asia in the last quarter of the nineteenth century. The 1880s witnessed the third Anglo-Burman war and the absorption of the remnant of the Burman kingdom, after guerrilla resistance, into the British Indian empire. That decade also saw the extension of the Resident system in the Malay Peninsula from the west coast states, where it had been established in 1873–4, into Pahang, and the following decade saw the creation of the Federated Malay States (FMS). The 1880s, too, saw the extension of formal British protection over the three states by then established in northern Borneo, Sarawak, North Borneo, and the remnant sultanate of Brunei, though no equivalent of the FMS evolved there in the next decade or subsequently.

The changes in South-East Asia outside the territorial ambit of British influence were also major. In Netherlands India the phase was marked by persistent attempts to extend and deepen the Dutch hold on the outer islands, thus developing an empire extending from Sabang to Merauke. There were new deals with the British over Sumatra and Borneo; there was also conflict with Indonesians, particularly in Aceh.

The French built an empire on the Indo-Chinese Peninsula from their beginnings in Cochin-China and Cambodia. They acquired a protectorate over central Vietnam and more or less direct control in the north. They moved into Laos too, incorporating a large part of it in what they called French Indo-China. Even in this phase of European expansion, however, Siam retained its independence, though shorn now of claims in Laos, as earlier of claims in Cambodia, and ceding to the British early in the new century its claims over the northern Malay states.

The Spaniards, reaching a frontier agreement with the British in Borneo shortly before the Dutch, dropped their claims there, but strengthened their control in Mindanao. They also endeavoured to assert their control in Sulu, but had still not succeeded when the

Americans intervened and displaced them. The Americans also displaced the Republic the Filipino nationalists had established in the north.

South-East Asia and the Trends in British Policy

These developments in South-East Asia illustrate trends in Britain's policy more generally, as it reacted to changes in its position in the world. The trends indicate a continuity of approach, and a tendency to shift tactics rather than strategy. The image the British had of world development did not disappear from their view, though its detail and its timing might be altered.

The previous chapter outlined the integration of South-East Asia into the system of policy operated by Great Britain at the height of its power in the world. Its priorities were commercial and strategic rather than territorial. Its relations with other states and polities fell into a number of patterns, all relating, though in various ways, to the concept of a world of independent states, stable and open to trade. Such a world did not yet exist, but the policies followed were to be consonant with and contribute to its emergence. Inside the states and polities Britain looked to find collaborators who shared its views. Within such a system, adjustments would be needed, and it allowed for them both in respect of the framework as a whole and its component parts. Perhaps Britain presumed too often that those adjustments were easy to make. But given its great power in the world, that was not usually an unreasonable presumption. There was room to make deals, to offer trade-offs to rivals, to redraw frontiers, and to displace rulers. But it was all the same a moderate use of world power. The British retained a consciousness of limits beyond which it was not sensible to go. China would not be another India, as *The Times* put it.[1] There were limits to the amount of control Britain should seek within an overall framework that facilitated the prime objective, the pursuit of its economic interests.

The adoption of this attitude during the nineteenth century helped to determine Britain's response to the changes in the last two decades. This response proved at the time easy to misinterpret and has so proved since, too. The main change was the re-emergence of European rivals, closely followed by a much more novel and ultimately more far-reaching change, the emergence of new centres of power outside Europe. These changes challenged Britain's primacy in the world and therefore challenged the system of policy it had pursued during the period of that primacy. The British did not, as it is sometimes argued, react by a vigorous imperialism. Their assumptions of territorial control were selective. They made compromises with rivals where they could. They adjusted. Their system of policy allowed for that, and in some sense they may be seen as merely continuing it. In another sense, the change was more fundamental. What had been a liberal way of deploying world power became a feasible way of responding to its relative decline. The appearance of confidence was part of this response. It was indeed true that the framework looked for the emergence of a world of states. That was in the interest of others, and they might be encouraged to go along with British initiatives, British leadership, and British timetables. History might still seem to be on Britain's side. But there was, it may be, an element of deception in this. The changes were perhaps more fundamental than the British admitted to themselves, or wished others to admit. Some recognized Britain's decline and over-emphasized it; others tended to assert its greatness at the end of the long Victorian age.

The Spread of Industrialization

The changes within South-East Asia from the later 1870s clearly relate to larger changes that affected Britain, the other colonial powers, and the South-East Asian states themselves. The most important of those changes were connected with the spread of industrialization outside Britain to other countries in Europe and beyond. In Europe the most striking transformation was that of Germany, though the 1880s and 1890s also witnessed the beginning of industrialization in Russia. Outside Europe the most striking transformation was that of the United States after the Civil War, which combined the rapidity of the Germans with the resources of the Russians. Less striking in scale, but striking also in novelty, was the industrialization of Japan that followed the Meiji restoration of 1868. The most obvious result of these changes was to produce rivals for the British in commerce and in politics. The changes they had initiated now confronted them with challenges.

The other changes were still more extensive. Railways and steamers transformed communications within states and among them. The Suez Canal was opened in 1869, and Panama in 1914. The telegraph reached Singapore in 1871. The automobile, the bicycle, and the oil-bunkered ship were to follow. By these means not only was trade revolutionized: states could be more integrated, and administrations more demanding and more effective. Books, ideas, and people travelled more. More education was needed, even in colonial dependencies. New aspirations were to develop there as a result, and old ones to be given new forms. The nature of collaboration, even its continuance, came into question, within territories under Britain's control and within those under Britain's patronage.

These changes weakened the underpinnings of Britain's primacy and thus its capacity to determine and programme the evolution of the world state-system. Its power had so far been applied less in pursuit of some larger imperial purpose than in the pursuit of world-wide economic opportunities and necessary strategic objectives. Its application had been influenced by a perception of the world as divided among states, as Europe was. Their nature might differ, but they could be dealt with on a relationship of full or modified equality, if their rulers could provide stability and freedom of trade or, if not, could be moved towards that objective by intervention or, if need be, by control, in association with local élites. The concept had its liberal aspects: it did not aim to monopolize world power, and it left room for others. But there was a presumption that Britain, the leading power in Europe when Europe led the world, would be there to regulate it. It was thus challenged when Europe ceased to be the sole centre of world power, and when Britain's position as the leading European power was challenged. How did Britain respond?

Imperialism

It was the 'age of imperialism'. But the extent to which that modified Britain's overall policy is limited. At home in Britain imperialism did not rule. It was a political concept, struggling with rival concepts in an increasingly democratic political system, often picked up by those concerned over social change at home as much as or more than over shifts in the distribution of power abroad. 'Popular imperialism, or jingoism, was one thing; popular support for the whole panoply of "new imperialist" policies was quite another.'[2] A renewal of international rivalry and economic competition was certainly an argument that could be used for restructuring British society at home. But it is far from clear that this 'imperialism' in turn affected policy abroad, either in principle or even in practice. The British in general chose to retain the policy adopted in the mid-century period. On the one hand, its pursuit then made it difficult to reverse now. On the other hand, its nature then made it easier to adapt now. Britain could proceed from concession to compromise. It would have to make sharper decisions about priorities; its trade-offs might become more conflicting. But adaptation was the easiest type of response, and perhaps the only one. This the British pursued, at times with pessimism, at times, more often perhaps, with optimism, at times with both, and always with flexibility.

In some areas fuller territorial control was established. That seemed to some, and to some still seems, a manifestation of imperialism. But it may rather be seen as a response to the rivalry of other powers, and the pressure exerted by economic and political change on the stability of the indigenous states. The response was a selective rather than a general one. There was also a tendency to foster larger units of government, like the federation in Australia or the federation among the Malay states. But that was no precursor of centralization, nor even of imperial federation. It was really an alternative, much more in keeping with traditional views, and it remained one of the modes of imperial thinking. Territories should be strengthened so that they could take on more responsibility for their own stability and development, and even for contributing to international security. Yet a third tendency was the disposition to transfer the programme for self-government from the colonies of settlement to other imperial territories, in particular India. If this was imperialism, it was imperialism of a refined kind. Designed to enlist the support of new collaborators, it also set India more clearly than before into a place in an emerging world state-system. In that Britain would have economic opportunity; it would also retain a leadership role, but one that would increasingly be exercised by diplomacy rather than dominance.

Accusations over 'imperialism' were part of a political struggle at home. Abroad they were often the work of envious or disappointed rivals. And it was true that not everyone could be appeased in a policy of adaptation. Priorities were established in respect of certain territories: some were essential strategically, some merely desirable economically; and some were more worth securing than others. There were other priorities. If it was a matter for compromise, with which power was it better to compromise, and why? The mid-nineteenth century system allowed for trade-offs. Now they had to become more numerous: they might become contradictory; and they could not help arousing antagonism. Adapting the mid-nineteenth century system was perhaps the only course. But, if there had been alternatives, it might be argued that adaptation was at once too idealistic and not idealistic enough. Britain seemed to assume that other nations would accept the patterns as it laid them out. But it also realized that such an assumption was often unfounded. That was the source of the combination of optimism and pessimism to be found among its policy-makers. They were resourceful, but were they, or could they be, resourceful enough?

The Philippine revolution offers evidence of the problem. The new limits on Britain's power explained why it did not itself intervene. What policy should it then follow? The continuance of Spanish rule was ruled out. Britain had no confidence that an independent Philippine Republic could survive or, if it did, provide stability. If another power were to take over, it preferred the United States to Germany, which seemed to see itself as the other contender.[3] And this choice points to a problem that Britain could not solve.

Clearly it sought to allow scope for other powers, and if possible to enlist their assent to the international system it favoured: 'If Germany is to become a colonising power, all I say is "God speed her!" She becomes our ally and partner in execution of the great purposes of Providence for the advantage of mankind.'[4] In this case the establishment of US rule in the Philippines was in some sense to enlist US support for the nineteenth-century pattern in the rest of South-East Asia. Why not choose to enlist German support? No doubt the claims and the presence of the United States made it difficult to do that. Elsewhere concessions had been made to Germany; and both Germany and the United States were, unlike Britain, protectionist. There were perhaps two main issues. First, there was the old concern to avoid the establishment of a major European power along the route to China. But perhaps more important there was increasing concern at the impact of Germany's ambition in Europe. In the face of that Britain chose to compromise with the United States. Perhaps no other choice was possible, but it was a fateful one. Germany was to perceive the obstacles to its realizing its potential as a world power as something of a conspiracy.

The argument in this book has been that Britain's power had in the days of its pre-eminence been exerted, not in pursuit of some larger imperial purpose, but to serve its economic interests and achieve its strategic objectives. The larger political view was of a world of states, not a world empire. In the phase of renewed rivalry, the larger view was not lost. The aim was to adjust British policy, to compromise with others, and even to win them to the British view. Britain's view of the world was easy to share. It was less easy to accept continued British leadership in the task of bringing it about and 'timetabling' it. Other powers put their rivalry in this form: neo-Rankeans in Germany spoke of a 'world balance of power'.[5] By contrast, Eyre Crowe at the Foreign Office pre-echoed Riezler and Churchill. A power supreme at sea 'should inspire universal jealousy and fear, and be ever exposed to the danger of being overthrown by a general combination of the world . . .'. An insular state could avoid such a danger only if its national policy is

so directed as to harmonize with the general desires and ideals common to all mankind, and more particularly that it is closely identified with the primary and vital interests of a majority, or as many as possible, of the other nations. . . . England, more than any other non-insular Power, has a direct and positive interest in the maintenance of the independence of nations. . . .[6]

Compromise as it might, however, Britain could not please everyone. If support were enlisted for British initiatives from some, the support of others might be lost.

Tariffs and Preferences

The further argument in this chronicle so far has been that Britain's economic interests held primacy in British policy, and that the British were in general clearing the way, but no more than clearing the way, for the operation of economic forces, believing that this would benefit all, but especially the most advanced economy, their own. The logic was that others would catch up, benefiting the British *en route*, and this was indeed what was happening in the later nineteenth century. How would that affect Britain's economy? How, if at all, should it change its policy as a result?

One logic was that Britain would stay ahead of others, moving into a second or third industrial revolution, while others moved through earlier stages. But industrialization did not quite work like that. It was possible for newly industrializing economies to join in at an advanced stage. Germany, for example, took the lead in the electrical and chemicals industries. It was also possible for the newly industrializing countries to adopt the latest methods and the high level of capitalization and cartelization that they implied.

The very scope of the German economic potential, but still more that of the United States, and ultimately of Russia, presented a challenge to the British, with a smaller domestic market, often smaller resources, and perhaps, even, less technological education. Moreover, the newer states, recognizing that they were competing with the British and in some sense with each other, adopted protectionist tariffs: the Germans in 1879, the Americans with the McKinley tariff of 1890, the Russians with those of Vyshnegradsky, while the Japanese, struggling to secure tariff autonomy, put state power squarely behind industrialization. 'British banks never penetrated Japan, which never really lost control of its banking (or its industry); it frustrated European expansion by a determination to minimize foreign trade until Lord Elgin's Unequal Treaties of 1858 had been revoked.'[7] And, of course, it borrowed technology from the West. If one nation had denied it, another would have supplied it.

A conceivable reaction to these developments would have been a drastic change in Britain's economic policy, and the adoption of policies like those of its new rivals, of subsidy and protection. No such change occurred. Britain's economic policy continued to be substantially based on the principles of the earlier period even though conditions had changed. For one thing, not all conditions had changed. Britain still benefited from the development of the German and American economies. Moreover, its finance capital benefited from the new opportunities it found in the modernization of other countries, in particular in the creation of communications and infrastructure. Protectionist arguments on behalf of industry could also be countered by the opposition to agricultural protection and the desire for cheap food. The Colonial Secretary Joseph Chamberlain's proposals for tariff reform were defeated. Finally, on the other hand, there was some insulation from the effects of decline in the old industries, because of the market and measure of protection in India afforded to British textiles. The policy thus survived by adaptation and by minor adjustment, perhaps above all because it suited capital. 'It appears', wrote Halford Mackinder in 1900, '. . . quite possible that the financial importance of the City of London may continue to increase, while the industry, at any rate, of Britain, becomes *relatively* less.'[8] London was to be the money market of the world while Britain was to lose its unique industrial leadership. Again Britain adapted rather than changed.

Chamberlain had envisaged a system of imperial preferences. A further conceivable reaction was, indeed, to rival the domestic markets of rivals by making the empire more integrated economically. But, given the kind of empire the British had built, or failed to build, that was not a realistic option. In many areas where Britain's economic writ ran, its political writ did not. Even where territories of settlement were part of Britain's empire, they had been held on a loose rein and, among the settlers at least, devolution and democratization had taken place. The power of control could not be resumed. Imperial preferences might have been acceptable, at least in the short term, but a *Zollverein* was a 'non-starter'.[9] Where Britain's political writ ran, there was talk of development. But it tended to mean self-development.

In the course of his voyage in the *Ticonderoga* in 1879–80, Commodore Robert W. Shufeldt, of the US Navy, concluded that the British empire had 'in itself no intrinsic strength. Its colonies and commerce would be helpless before any Combination of Power.' The navy could defend it only in home waters; otherwise it could no more protect it 'from an enemy than from a stroke of lightning or the shock of an earthquake'. In fact defence in home waters sufficed, and combinations of power were avoided. The United States was an ineffective rival, Shufeldt reluctantly admitted, though destined to become 'the centre of commercial power'. If he exaggerated Britain's weakness, Shufeldt's appraisal of its aims was also askew.

British rule in Asia and Africa is at present so aggressive in its character as to be more or less antagonistic to the interests of every civilized and semi-civilized nation of the Earth. Under pretext of suppression of piracy, destruction of slavery, protection of commercial routes and rectification of frontiers—it is really a mere grasping for Universal Empire—a usurpation of authority—an ill-concealed intention to become the 'Paramount Power' over the world at large, as it already styles itself in India.

But in this age another Roman Empire is impossible and I have faith that before it is too late—the sober second thought of England will rend this veil of imperial illusion and remand the Country back into the sisterhood of Nations, as the equal and not the Autocrat of other nationalities—otherwise someday not distant the British Empire will receive a shock from which it will not easily recover. . . .[10]

But sober second thoughts were always there: in fact they were more often first than second.

The Empire

The empire was, except in regard to India and to the Crown colonies, more of a collection of what James Stephen had called 'tacit alliances'[11] than a political entity. Such an alliance had its special qualities. Economic and financial ties were important in sustaining it. So were ties of common interest, of common inheritance, and of kith and kin. As Lord Granville put it, 'The ties which bind us together are loyalty to the Crown, goodwill between the Colonies and the mother Country, and a reciprocity of mutual advantages. When this state of things shall cease to exist, the idea of compelling by force any great and self-governing Colony to remain connected with this country is an idea which no statesman would entertain. . . .'[12] This, however, could only lead one to presume, or at the least hope for, common action in defence of common interests. Attempts to establish a more structured imperialism could not succeed: individual entities were encouraged to strengthen themselves singly or by federating. Imperial federation was again a non-starter. Some, like Chamberlain, argued for integration in a world of emerging super-states. 'The struggle for life, the struggle for existence in future will not be between cities or even between kingdoms. It will be between mighty empires; and the minor States will come off badly if they are left to be crushed between the gigantic bulk of these higher organisations.'[13] But the argument did not dislodge the preference for a world of nation-states, nor for an empire that was, in the Liberal Lord Rosebery's phrase of 1884, 'a commonwealth of nations'.[14]

The emerging dominions conferred and consulted with each other and with the British: they expected from the British protection but not instruction. Their political interests coincided: they preferred the *status quo*. But their economic interests to some degree diverged, and some sought to protect their own industries. Intra-imperial relations were a separate, if special version, of the international diplomacy through which Britain sought both to preserve and to adjust to changes in the *status quo*. But the British enjoyed considerable success in it; and that made them more optimistic about the still larger task they faced in the world at large. The British empire would lead to the British Commonwealth, even to a larger commonwealth of nations.

The period was thus marked by attempts formally to draw the empire together economically, which had little success, and by attempts, too, at more formal political integration, which fared no better. There were also attempts to avoid the incorporation of non-British territories into the protectionist systems of others, which would limit the opportunities open to British traders and investors. Sometimes this promoted counter-annexation: more often it invited delimitation, contributing to the move towards partitions of preponderance, as Salisbury called them,[15] rather than of territory. It was also necessary, of course, to preserve the strategic footholds from the threats of others, or to step in elsewhere to anticipate such threats. Often there was compromise. The British sought diplomatic solutions. That worked with and contributed to their failure to integrate their empire or to resort to protectionism.

The main aim was to preserve what could be preserved of the *status quo*. With some states, as a result, diplomatic solutions were easier to secure than with others. Moreover, compromise often meant contradiction. Making a deal with one state would damage relations with another. Even in the days of Britain's primacy, the patterns within its policy had not been wholly consistent with one another. Adjusting them might show up inconsistencies and expand contradictions that power had concealed or reconciled. Alliance with Japan might bring tension to relations not only with Russia, but to those with the Netherlands, as possessors of Indonesia, and with the Australasian dominions. Understandings with the United States would alarm the Germans. Better relations with France would also make relations with Germany more intractable, and encourage compromises with Russia. Even Britain's own limited imperialism could be seen as a threat by others, rather than a defensive reaction.

Adjustment was the more necessary not only because of the rivalry of other Western powers: it also reflected the disintegration of native Asian and African states, which indeed was provoked by that rivalry. The British had tended to assume in Palmerston's day that, with minimum aid and intervention, they might transform themselves. Some did, some did not, and others managed it to a degree insufficient to preserve their independence in the new context. That context was created by the political demands of the rival Europeans, but also by the changes brought about through economic forces and the revolutions in communications and technology, and by the appearance of concession-hunters and adventurers of all sorts. There was, too, one European empire that failed to transform itself, the remnant empire of the Spaniards.

Given all these factors, it may be that the changes in Britain's policy were not only limited, but reactive, and cautiously so.

Britain did not seem to be building an empire, but to be holding together what could be preserved of an earlier system. If its territorial frontiers were expanding, that was in a sense a result of a limitation of its economic prospects, and it was not intended as provocative. The impact of imperialism is difficult to measure. Its proponents were arguing for a more active policy, and in some areas that was pursued. But its role in the making of policy seems to be limited. It should be seen more as rather a rhetoric related to changes that were occurring in British society and apparently dissolving its coherence and sense of purpose; a rhetoric that could, however, argue for coherence and purpose if Britain were to survive in an increasingly competitive world. It was also a rhetoric which, heard in the world at large, could in fact be counter-productive, provoking or enhancing envy and antagonism. It may also have put a misplaced emphasis on empire rather than trade. But again that may be of domestic rather than external significance. Certainly, where India and its periphery were concerned, the impact of imperialism must be discounted against the long-term concern over its security, since the late eighteenth century a feature, albeit an exceptional one, of British policy.

The End of the Konbaung Dynasty

The concern for India's security affected the fate of Burma. There has been much controversy over the origins of the third Burma war. Clearly there were pressures from local British merchants; moreover, these were taken up at home, and some use of the issue was made in the 1885 elections. But the main thrust of an explanation lies elsewhere. India had always been concerned lest Burma should be too independent. An attitude of defiance on its part would undermine the reign of opinion that helped to sustain British rule in India itself. An association with a foreign power would be a still more direct threat. In the 1870s and 1880s the remnant Burman kingdom appeared, moreover, to be crumbling in the face of economic pressures. Concessionaires were active, and they came from an increasing variety of European nations. Still more threatening was the possibility that this 'disorder' would leave the way open to foreign intervention. This was the time when the French were securing northern Vietnam, and with it claims over Laos. These factors were important in combination, but the most important of them was surely concern for the security of British India. Commercial concerns were an occasion for action

more than a reason. The imperialistic urge was Indian and pro-
tective, rather than British and aggressive. 'If . . . you finally and
fully add Burma to your dominions before any European rights
have had time even to be sown, much less to grow up,'
Lord Randolph Churchill, the Secretary of State for India
declared, 'you undoubtedly prevent the assertion of such rights or
attempts to prepare the way for such assertion. . . .'[16]
Nor did the war merely end with the incorporation of the
kingdom or its assimilation into the Resident system: it precipitated its abolition. Again that was not the result of imperialistic
urge. Past history had given Lord Dufferin, the Viceroy of India,
little confidence in retaining the Burman monarchy after its new
defeat: but he rejected only reluctantly a 'fully protected' Burma
'with a native dynasty and native officials, but under a British
Resident, who should exercise a certain control over the internal
administration, as well as over its relations with foreign powers'.[17]
The breakdown of law and order, and above all continued Burman
resistance, seen as large-scale dacoity, were further arguments for
annexation, though in this respect it proved counter-productive.

The city people had not been fully aware that the King was to be taken
away until they saw our troops marching with Theebaw and the royal
family in their midst. Then they awoke to the fact and a great cry went
up from men, women, and children alike . . . an enormous crowd . . .
assembled, and . . . grew more and more excited, and at intervals their
lament rose up on the night air. . . . A few stones and clods of earth were
thrown by the crowd.[18]

Substantial opposition was to follow.

British Residents in Malaya

Outside the periphery of India's political concerns, Malaya may
have been affected by different factors in Britain's policy. Again in
the Malayan case, there has been much controversy over the
origins of British intervention. The various factors are not in
doubt—economic and commercial pressures, local initiative, strategic
considerations, concern over foreign intervention, and disintegration of native polities—but their relative weighting is. The
factors were all present in the 1870s. Perhaps the fear of foreign
intervention along the Straits of Malacca was decisive in producing a
change of policy, though other factors also operated.[19]
In the previous decades Governors of the Straits had vainly

urged a change of policy on their superiors. They had resisted. Only in 1873 were there signs of a shift, and Sir Andrew Clarke made the most of it. Even then it was a shift in regard only to certain states, and it did not amount to annexation. Intervention, it was thought, might be needed, not simply because of the disturbances that the development of tin mining had helped to bring about in the west coast states of Perak, Selangor, and Sungei Ujong. It might also be needed because those disturbances could lead to the intervention of another power in a region the security of which affected that of the Straits Settlements and the route to China. In states, however, where there were no such disturbances and no such risk, there was no need for such intervention.

The form of intervention, even where sanctioned, was not by way of acquisition; instead it was a form of protection. The British Government appointed 'Residents'—the title used in British India—to advise the Malay rulers, who were bound to accept the advice on all matters save religion and custom. The notion that this would suffice for the protection of British interests derived not only from the limited nature of those interests, but also from the belief based on an analogy with the rulers of Johore, who neighbouring Singapore had proved compliant, that, as collaborators with the British, Malay rulers unlike Burman would readily accept and could readily implement that advice. The belief, not accepted in Burma, was quickly shown to be erroneous in western Malaya and the analogy with Johore proved false. The sharp and forceful British reaction to the particular case of the murder of the first Resident in Perak made the general assumption that advice would be taken valid in the longer term. To carry it out, however, was increasingly to require the backup of British officialdom, particularly as the role of government expanded.

The establishment of the Resident system was not in the event achieved without a show of force. Thereafter, however, it worked, though practice was increasingly divorced from principle: the Residents ruled, and the Rajas advised. As Frank Swettenham put it, no Resident system had been conceived. 'There was an idea and that was all.' That was that a white man or two would 'reduce everything to order' by offering tactful advice. 'The greatness of the implied compliment did not reduce the difficulties of a task which was only possible when the native ruler was prepared to accept the advice offered him, and had authority to enforce his own commands. . . .' Force of arms accomplished in six months what would have taken twenty years.[20]

It does not follow, because the Resident is only the adviser, that the ruler may reject his advice when the peace and good order of the country are at stake. The advice which the Residents give is authoritative advice and may not be lightly rejected. . . . All the same the fiction (if such you prefer to call it) that the Residents are merely advisers must be kept up; and here is just where the adroitness and ability of the officer are so important. . . .[21]

Those qualities were important, though the demonstration of power had helped. The subsequent success of the system in some respects facilitated, in some ways inhibited its expansion. It provided revenue, and it provided an administrative example. But for other rulers it also provided a warning.

The 1880s saw moves to extend the system beyond Perak, Selangor, and their neighbours. Again the same factors prevailed, but perhaps in a somewhat different combination. In the case of Malaya concern over India had less significance than in the case of Burma; in neither was an imperialistic British thrust noticeable. But the local Governor, Sir Frederick Weld, was an expansionist— 'the further extension of Britain's civilizing influence over the peninsula' was his real goal'[22]—and his initiative had a role in the moves to bring Johore into a treaty relationship with Britain and to extend the Resident system to Pahang. So also did the inability of the Malay states to cope with the new pressures placed upon them by the expansion of concession-hunting, enhancing the risk of foreign intervention. It was significant that there seemed little need to put the Johore treaty into action, but that Pahang was thought to require the appointment of a Resident. The Sultan was less than willing to receive one, particularly one with extensive powers. Again some conflict ensued and this, together with the availability of the resources of the west coast states, was important in the establishment of the Federated Malay States in 1895–6. At that point, however, British policy in Malaya was affected by a larger imperial consideration. If the empire could not be consolidated as a whole, its individual parts could be consolidated. The Australian, if not the Australasian colonies could be pulled together, like the Canadian, though with a different title. The creation of the FMS, though a very different entity, was in line with this kind of thinking. It meant 'consistency and continuity of policy', Swettenham wrote. 'It meant the abolition of inter-state frictions and jealousies, and the power to conceive and execute great projects for the benefit of the partnership. . . .'[23] There were hopes in respect of Borneo, too.

The consolidation of the Malay states with Residents into the FMS bloc, however, did not make joining it more attractive to other rulers. For the present there was in any case another obstacle to the creation of British Malaya, whatever impulses there may have been towards it. The claims of the Thai kingdom over the northern states had always been an obstacle to any attempts to extend British protection over them. Those claims had been more or less recognized, and the conclusion of the Bowring treaty and the subsequent establishment of a British diplomatic representative in Bangkok had made them more difficult to challenge. Paradoxically, however, the recognition of the Thai position enhanced the opportunity for the exercise of British influence. That Governor Bonham had already seen back in 1839 when he had promoted the restoration of the Sultan of Kedah under Thai suzerainty. Now it was possible to provide for the protection of British interests through the appointment of a consul in Kedah, who was in fact also the Resident Councillor of Penang.[24]

The pressure to extend British influence, and even to create a British Malaya, was certainly enhanced at the opening of the new century as a result of economic changes. The creation of a world—and in particular a US—market for rubber as a result of the growth of the automobile industry gave Malaya an intrinsic economic importance that, even with the opening of the west coast tin mines, it had never enjoyed before. The physical conditions were encouraging, though labour was short. Initially the development concentrated in the west coast states which were also the focus of tin mining, since that had helped to create an infrastructure that could now serve the new plantations and their labour force. But the boom suggested there were prospects for other states that were not participants in tin mining, including Trengganu and Kelantan. It was still essential to recognize Thai supremacy, however: otherwise the British would only be encouraging other powers to challenge it. They therefore persuaded the Thais to appoint Britons as advisers with the Malay rulers, retaining the tripartite political relationships of northern Malaya, but adapting them to the new circumstances. This turned out, however, to be but a transition towards the assumption of British supremacy. By an agreement of 1909, the Thais transferred their claims to the British. But it proved more difficult for the British to bring the rulers under the Residential system, and they did not succeed in including them in the FMS. The allegiance of collaborators was not easy to shift.

Despite the pressures towards consolidation in the 1890s, British Malaya remained politically fragmented.

British Borneo

So did British Borneo. Some of the same factors again operated. The remnant sultanate of Brunei seemed unlikely to survive the pressure from its neighbours, and its turning to concessionaires seemed certain to precipitate its destruction. A further possibility was that a foreign power would intervene. Once it had been decided that this part of the Archipelago was not earmarked for the Dutch, that was always a risk for the British. The establishment of the French on the opposite shore of the South China Sea made it additionally necessary to keep northern Borneo free of a major power. The first Raja of Sarawak had seemed a rather uncertain quantity, and a gesture had been made to those who wished to keep him from turning to a foreign power, albeit the rather paradoxical gesture of so far recognizing his independence as to appoint a British consul in Kuching in 1863.

The chartering of the British North Borneo Company in 1881 was in part at least another means of keeping foreign powers out of northern Borneo by a measure short of British annexation, which the British themselves did not want to undertake and which they thought others would consider provocative. There had been doubts about the further extension of Sarawak, in view of its anomalous character, and a disposition as a result to rely on the treaty of 1847, so far as foreign powers were concerned, and even to operate it against the Raja. With the establishment of the Company, the British Government dropped its objection to the second Raja's further acquisitions. It seemed that the Company and Raj would share out the remnant of Brunei between them, and this prospect it was intended should be encouraged, rather than inhibited, by the establishment of the three British protectorates in 1888. The British did not want another power to step in, at the Sultan's invitation or otherwise, while the process was going on.

The process was, however, not completed. The Raj and the Company made some further gains, but their very pressure, and the apparent inevitability of Brunei's fate, led its Sultan to put up a last-ditch resistance. Charles Brooke's acquisition of Limbang in 1890 was decisive, not only in stiffening Sultan Hashim's resolve, but also in inducing doubts within the British Government about the policy of total partition. Colonial Office officials had indeed begun to think in terms of a future colony of British Borneo, but had seen it as based on the Raj:

if Labuan coal comes to naught, and the Colony is never to become worth having, the question will arise whether at no distant future it will not be wiser to try and do good in that part of Borneo by favouring the ambition of Sarawak, so that hereafter having absorbed Labuan and gained a predominant influence over the decaying Brunei Raja Brooke may found a sounder and more extended colony with better means of success than ever were within the reach of the little Island alone. . . .[25]

Now that seemed less attractive, and an alternative policy was opened up by the obstinacy of the Sultan. Might not a Residency be established in Brunei, be combined with the colony of Labuan, and become the nucleus of such a colony? With the establishment of the FMS, the impulse to consolidation that lay behind that, and the example it gave, the idea was transformed into the notion of a Borneo Federated States. 'I look in future', wrote C. P. Lucas at the Colonial Office in 1896, 'to an administration of North Borneo and Sarawak on much the same principles as the native states of the Malay peninsula, with a resident General at Labuan and residents on the mainland, the whole under the High Commissioner at Singapore.'[26] That might be a sounder basis for 'development' than the Brooke Raj. Again, however, it was not easy to change collaborators.

The very reasons for a Borneo federation were in some sense also the reasons why it did not come about. A Resident was established at the Sultan's court. But the Raja of Sarawak's urge to expand and finally to absorb Brunei was frustrated, and since he was angry at the outcome, the Colonial Office deferred any further moves towards setting up in Borneo the kind of regime it had partially set up in Malaya. How could Britain work with both Raja and Sultan? How could the British adjust their relationship even—or especially—with a British Raja?

French Indo-China

The establishment of the French on the further shore of the South China Sea had boosted Britain's determination not to let northern Borneo fall into the hands of a foreign power. Pressed by missionary interests, and by the pursuit of Bonapartist glory, Napoleon III had intervened in Vietnam in 1858, and in 1859 the capture of Saigon laid the basis for a colony in Cochin-China. It was nurtured by the autonomy of aggrandizing French admirals as well as by 'imperialism' at home under Second Empire and Third Republic. But, so long as French authority there, and in the Cambodian protectorate, did not trench upon the independence of Siam and Laos, the British thought there was no real strategic threat, since Siam would insulate their possessions in India and Burma from French influence. The French venture seemed menacing neither commercially nor politically. The fate of Cambodia and Vietnam could be viewed with equanimity. An eastern Cherbourg was not 'cause for serious anxiety'.[27]

The position changed in the 1880s and 1890s. Undoubtedly the general revival of Anglo-French rivalry was an important factor. The British were faced after the 1870s not only with the emergence of new would-be colonial powers, but with renewed activity by the French. This indeed was encouraged by one of the new powers. The revival of French colonial ambitions did not result from a burgeoning commerce or a wish to export men or money: it resulted rather from national pride. Following defeat in Europe, it seemed all the more essential to demonstrate, not least to Frenchmen themselves, the international standing of France under the new Republic. This disposition was encouraged by the victorious Bismarck. He wished to divert the French from any attempt at revenge, while also dividing them from the British. Colonial ventures fitted these objectives, and even allowed for the development of some congruence of aims between France and Germany. The Third Republic was thus active in parts of the world where earlier regimes had also been active, in Egypt, elsewhere in Africa, in the Pacific, and in Vietnam. The overall thrust of the enterprise added to Britain's concern about single parts of it.

Like other imperialisms, that of the French in Indo-China also reflected the inability of existing indigenous states to cope with the pressures of the late nineteenth century. That meant in this case not only Vietnam but China itself, which claimed suzerainty over Vietnam. The weakness of the Vietnamese realm owed little to Western economic penetration. Perhaps its greatest weakness was the insecure relationship between the Nguyen dynasty and the people over whom it aspired to rule. It certainly failed to rally popular resistance against the Western intruder, though such there was. Indeed it hesitated to try: '. . . the Emperor does not recognise us, but it is indeed our duty to carry on our struggle for the safeguarding of our fatherland.'[28] On the other hand the dynasty failed to compromise with the French. It attempted a diplomatic approach, but in particular it called upon its suzerain. The Chinese state was, however, in no position to afford it effective protection. True, it did try. The Chinese were increasingly determined in the 1880s to resist further encroachments from outside. The establishment of French control in Vietnam was indeed not achieved without a war with China. There followed a prolonged endeavour to put down patriotic Vietnamese resistance. In a sense the strength of that resistance only illustrated the weakness of the Nguyen dynasty that had failed to capitalize on it. There was a parallel with the collapse of the Burman dynasty. Unlike the British in Burma, however, the French retained the monarch as a puppet. He was, however, more or less powerless in Hué, and Cochin-China, a colony, and in effect Tonkin, though a protectorate, were ruled independently of him.

These territories, along with Laos and Cambodia, were to be thrown together into French Indo-China, the French sharing the consolidationist tendencies of the British in the 1880s and 1890s. Laos and Cambodia had, however, little in common with each other, or with Vietnam, hitherto in fact a state to be feared. In some sense indeed, the French were reasserting, but also limiting, the claims of the Vietnamese state over its neighbours. They were, as part of a federation, in one sense protected from the Vietnamese: politically they were all contained within the French structure. In another sense they lost what protection they had. Individual Vietnamese, for example, could move into Cambodia as settlers or as junior administrators.

Earlier the intermediate kingdoms had depended for their independence on sustaining a balance between the claims of the Vietnamese on the one hand and the Thais on the other. Indeed it was the claim of the French over Laos that brought about their major confrontation with the Thais. But the British had a strategic concern over Laos. They had been prepared to go along with French dominance in Vietnam only on the understanding that it did not stretch across the Peninsula, bringing the fate of Siam and the security of Burma and Malaya into question.

Siam

In the independence of Siam the British had had a long-standing interest, economic and political, which the Thai rulers had wisely decided to consolidate by agreeing to the Bowring treaty of 1855. Siam's policy remained one of making major concessions to the British as the major power, while attempting at the same time to retain real independence in a way that no other state in South-East Asia managed to achieve. In the previous phase, those concessions had been primarily economic rather than territorial. In the case of Cambodia, the concessions had been greater, but in Malaya the kingdom had at least retained a degree of control over the northern states and in some degree enhanced it by accepting a British envoy in Bangkok. In the new phase, more territorial concessions were required, as a result of heavier imperialist pressure. But the Thais' British backer did not entirely fail them, though it may have disappointed them, and they redoubled their attempts to consolidate the rest of their kingdom. It was in pursuit of that objective, indeed, that they were to concede to the British suzerainty over the northern Malay states in 1909.

Mongkut had accepted the loss of his claims over Cambodia. 'It is sufficient for us to keep ourselves within our house and home,' he said in 1867; '. . . it may be necessary for us to forego some of our former power and influence.'[29] His successor contested French claims over Laos. In pursuit of their objectives, the French mounted a naval expedition to Bangkok in 1893, and the crisis of the independence of Siam itself seemed to be at hand. The Thais turned to the British. They were interested in Siam's independence and they had their own reasons for limiting the advance of French authority. But British support was less extensive than the Thais anticipated: it did not uphold the Thais throughout the territory they claimed, but it kept the French out of Siemreap. Subsequently the British reached a compromise with the French, which put its emphasis on preserving the central core of the kingdom. Again the international pressures on the British were no doubt one reason for a performance that fell short of upholding the integrity of the Thai kingdom. The Germans had hoped that the British would be driven to seek their help at their price. But the British had never undertaken to uphold all the claims of the Thais. Their essential aim was to insulate their possessions from the French and to sustain an independent Siamese kingdom. Those aims they essentially achieved.

The fate of the outliers of the Thai kingdom had still to be settled, however. The Thais continued to modernize their state and endeavoured to make it more coherent.[30] 'The king himself . . . has seen, as have also some of his intimate counsellors, that if Siam is to preserve her independence—if, to use an Oriental expression, she wishes to "save her face" in the eyes of Europe—she must put her house in order, or at any rate keep up an appearance of doing so, whether she likes it or not....'[31] The Thais continued, too, to call upon their diplomatic resources. These included, of course, sustaining an international role without acting provocatively, and employing international advisers—'ready-made textbooks', as Chulalongkorn called them[32]—from a wider range of countries, including minor ones like Belgium and major new ones like the United States, but not Germany or Russia. They still looked to the British, too. An agreement of 1897 was designed to keep foreign powers out of the Peninsula. That was perhaps an undertaking by the Thais to the British more than vice versa. But the British themselves were also restrained from intervening even in the northern Malay states. Intervention there might only encourage the French to seek acquisitions at Siam's expense elsewhere. The 'buffer' principle was still of some effect.

In these ways the independence of Siam, which had been linked with the growth of Britain's power, was adjusted as that power was challenged. Greater challenge followed in the twentieth century, and more adjustment. The threat to British power in the world, particularly the threat of the Germans in Europe, led to understandings with France and even with Russia. The agreement that laid the basis for the *Entente Cordiale* in 1904 covered Siam. In effect the British were less likely than ever to resist further advances by the French in the peripheral regions of the Siamese kingdom, provided they did not clearly undermine British or British Indian interests. The Siamese made further territorial adjustments with the French. They also determined to reach a new settlement with the British. They surrendered their claims over the northern Malay states. But in return the 1897 agreement, which had obstructed their development of the northern Peninsula, came to an end, and they secured support for the development of the railway system that was one of their answers to the problem of holding their kingdom together.

A new colonial power, France, had been added to those in the region, one that the British accepted, but tried to contain within limits, one that added to the arguments for taking over Burma and for upholding the independence of Siam. The increased rivalry of the Western powers and their increasing penetration also affected the fate of old colonial powers and the peoples and territories over which they aspired to rule. Again the outcome was affected by the adaptations in British policy that had helped to keep them in being.

From Sabang to Merauke

The chartering of the British North Borneo Company in 1881 and the setting-up of the British protectorates in northern Borneo in 1888 had led to boundary agreements with both the Netherlands and Spain. Within their frontiers the sharing of power had been in a sense tripartite, as it had also been in the northern Malay states. As in that case, this relationship came under pressure in the new period. In Netherlands India—by contrast to the Philippines—the ruling colonial power remained. It responded to the changes in the outside world in a sense by replicating to others the response it had made to the British. Fearful of challenge to its political position—by a combination of foreign interference and the presence of 'disloyal' or 'inefficient' native states—it urged on the cumulation of colonial power, particularly after the Berlin conference of 1884–5. This the diplomacy of the Dutch had sought strictly to confine to Africa: they feared that 'the decisions—for example those about effective occupation—would be given a more general significance and be considered as applicable to the Netherlands Indies as well'.[33] And this fear their diplomacy could not altogether assuage. The challenge of the British North Borneo Company—as well as interest in coal—led the Dutch to consolidate their control on the east coast of Borneo. They restlessly pursued the subordination of Aceh, bloodily destroyed the independence of Lombok, and extended even to West New Guinea.

At the same time as they extended their authority—as earlier with the British, so now with other powers—they also liberalized their commercial and trading arrangements. There were no doubt arguments the other way: the opening-up of the Archipelago indeed had an economic urge as well as a political urge behind it. But the most powerful argument for a free trade policy in the case of the Dutch was the additional guarantee it offered against political intervention. The policy the Dutch extended even to the Japanese when they joined the ranks of the major powers, conferring most-favoured-nation privileges on them in a convention of 1912. The British lost the special position they had under the treaty of 1824 with the introduction of 'short contracts' between the Indies Government and the Indonesian rulers. But that was better for them than that other powers should challenge the

Dutch territorially. They accepted the adaptation of Dutch policy to changed circumstances.

In the latter decades of the century Dutch policies were affected by economic changes like the opening of the Suez Canal and the development of new markets and new products. They were also affected by political changes, including the emergence of other imperial powers like Germany. Essentially the Dutch reaction was to extend to other powers what Great Britain had secured—a fair share of the trade of the islands, an 'open door'—while redoubling the precautions that had been taken—intensifying political control over an empire still largely based, at least notionally, on contractual relationships. The relationship with the British remained of prime importance, uneasy though at times it was. A relationship with other powers was not without benefit. Investment by them, for example, was much smaller, but it afforded some balance against British predominance. Above all, however, in their case as in that of the British, the Dutch granted a share of the economic riches of the area as a hedge against political or territorial demands.

The Dutch nevertheless felt insecure, particularly after the turn of the century. Not only were Indonesians stirred and Netherlanders disturbed by pan-Asian propaganda, an ideology uneasily combined with the Japanese oligarchy's cautious imperialism. Britain's position in East Asia was, furthermore, no longer one of predominance, and its attempt to diminish its world-wide responsibilities by alliance with Japan from 1902 was by no means reassuring, since while an ally could be a source of restraint, it might be a source of encouragement. Moreover, Japan, which had already acquired Formosa and the Pescadores following the war with China of 1894–5, now fought a victorious war with Russia, and established its dominance in Korea and southern Manchuria. The war, which had involved the passage of a Russian fleet through the islands, had caused the Dutch some anxious moments; the victory excited their subjects. After it, Japan extended naval patrols as far south as Singapore. The development of oil in Netherlands India, too, made it of great interest to Japan, which was deficient in energy resources. Not only could the Dutch see reason to fear further Japanese moves—which helped to give rise to numerous spy scares—but also Japan was in renewed alliance with their nineteenth-century guarantor. The extent to which Britain could restrain Japan was unclear, given Britain's world-wide responsibilities and Japan's ambitions, and the Chinese revolution was indeed to test that aspect of the alliance. If there was misgiving among the British, there was mistrust among the Dutch. To the south, too, Australia and New Zealand, which had developed under the security system of the nineteenth century, viewed the new developments with a mixture of hope and fear. The relations between the British and the Dutch came under tension in this period of adaptation. The Dutch had to concede to others what Britain had secured from them, though that did not worry the free-trading British too much, but they also had to accept the compromises with others that Britain chose to make. Britain found in the Japanese a new collaborator in Asia, but they were distrusted by its older partners, and their commitment to the *status quo* was indeed less than complete. For the native Indonesian states the effects of the changes in this period were severe. Britain had not intervened in their favour even earlier, but its policy had in practice tended to restrain the Dutch. Now the Dutch pressed ahead, sometimes to the embarrassment of the British with their Muslim subjects. Nor could the Indonesians look to other powers: the latter, even the Japanese, dealt with the Dutch, and did not undermine the colonial pattern. Nor was it undermined in the Philippines, though the Spanish regime was destroyed.

The End of the Spanish Empire

With the Spaniards in the Philippines, the British settled a frontier in 1885. They abandoned their interest in the independence of the sultanate of Sulu, while the Spaniards agreed not to take up the sultanate's claims in northern Borneo. Within little more than a decade Spanish authority in South-East Asia had been eliminated. That was partly the work of the nationalist movement in Luzon. Its development and its revolutionary success were both new to Asia, but the triumph was short-lived. The Americans intervened and the Malolos Republic was destroyed, though they built their new regime in collaboration with the old élite. In the south the Spaniards had never fully established their authority, and the Americans made a special treaty with the sultanate of Sulu. This in turn they displaced, and proceeded to establish their control by military operations of considerable violence.

In these dramatic changes the British had little part. True, their economic enterprise had played a major role in stimulating the social changes that helped to bring about the Philippine revolution: it was not only Spanish education and Filipino enterprise that lay behind these changes but also British capital. The Spaniards had offered no positive response to the demands of the new élite. The Spanish littérateur and traveller Sinibaldo de Mas had offered his government the choice: to preserve the colony or 'to decide on its emancipation and prepare it for freedom'. If the latter course were chosen, he envisaged 'a popular assembly of representatives in Manila', and a Spanish withdrawal, leaving behind 'a constitutional form of government', perhaps headed by an Infante.[34] Spain chose neither. The new élite turned to revolution and sought independence. Confronted with a change that was novel in Asian terms, if not in Latin American, the British were not convinced that the new Republic could provide the stability they sought for their trade. Still less were they certain that the Republic could contribute to security in East Asia at a time of great changes like the decline of China, the rise of Japan, the growing power of Germany, and the advance of Russia in the Far East. The Sino-Japanese war, and consequent Japanese acquisition of Formosa/Taiwan, only added to the apprehension of change. A foreign power might step in when the Spaniards were dislodged. Indeed the movements of the German fleet in 1897–8 shortly after the acquisition of Kiao-chow added to the apprehension. The British preference was for the continuance of Spanish authority, that of their old collaborators. If that was impossible, the establishment of American control was more desirable than that of the Germans. That indeed was the outcome, though the Germans purchased the Marianas from Spain.

The episode illustrates the relative weakness of the British. There was little chance of their intervening on the side of the revolutionaries. Even if that had been the choice, it was not that of the revolutionaries themselves. At that time, they had no fellow revolutionaries to whom they could look, and they could only look to other powers, the Japanese, among whom pan-Asians offered sympathy and weapons, and the Americans, whose help had too high a price. The British found the Americans more acceptable than the Germans. They did not want a major European power in the South China Sea, and the American take-over at least foreclosed that option. In a larger sense it illustrated the growing tendency of the British to compromise with the Americans. In a South-East Asian sense it enlisted American sanction for the colonial system, diminishing, moreover, any challenge from the Japanese.

The Americans did not see fit to abide by the 1885 agreement so far as commerce was concerned. The British, however, did not go back on it politically. Some saw a possibility of reviving the independence of the Muslim regions and associating them with North Borneo. 'If . . . the United States in assuming a Philippine protectorate, should wish to relieve themselves of the care of these small islands, the North Borneo Company and State would be prepared to cooperate with the Sultan of Sulu in placing them under British protection. . . .'[35] But the wider implications of challenging the Americans ruled against this, once they had indicated their interest. Nor was it desirable to demonstrate any indication of British interest, lest that encourage Germany to seek a share. The frontiers remained as settled in 1885, though the commercial quid pro quo was lost. Spanish collaboration with Christian Filipinos had helped to make their relationships with Muslims negative. The British were, however, again unable to develop a pattern of collaboration with them. The American approach was even more forceful than the Spanish had become. But many Muslims were to prefer continued American control to that of the Christian Filipinos.

The British had not welcomed the emergence of the Philippine Republic despite the precedent Canning had set in the Americas in the 1820s. American imperialism, despite controversy at home, led to acquisition. In a sense the United States, by joining the imperialist powers in South-East Asia, helped to preserve the nineteenth-century pattern. 'Whenever a people have risen against another people that ruled them, a colony against the metropolis, the revolution has never succeeded on its own strength,' Ferdinand Blumentritt had warned José Rizal.[36] The Philippine revolution, unlike later anti-colonial revolutions in the mid-twentieth century, secured no overseas aid. 'In 1899,' Glenn May has written, 'it would have been almost unthinkable for any major power to come to the aid of Aguinaldo and his beleaguered army. The great powers bickered among themselves about treaty ports, spheres of influence, and other matters, but hardly ever to the point of assisting an army of upstart, dark-skinned colonials to defeat one of their number. . . .'[37] Aid was, perhaps, not quite unthinkable. Oi Kentaro and others thought of it[38] and some Filipino nationalists looked for such aid, either from Japan, the new occupants of nearby Taiwan, or from the United States itself. It was true, however, that international conditions were unfavourable; not only were major powers unwilling to sponsor their cause, there were no other liberated nations to give them fraternal support. The pattern of the greater part of the nineteenth century was not disturbed at the end of it: in some sense it was strengthened not only by the caution of the Japanese Government, but by the way the Americans used their new power. They were to deploy it vigorously within the Philippines, integrating the mountain areas of Luzon into the realm, as well as ruthlessly eliminating the autonomy of the Muslim sultanates.

Concluding Remarks

The late nineteenth century brought some new opportunities to the British, above all with the development of rubber in Malaya. But on the whole it was marked by challenge, and what was done in South-East Asia is best seen in the context of the rivalry of other economies and other powers. This at once tested the British, but also the parties with whom they had established their various compromises in the previous period. The framework in which they pursued their objectives was subjected to pressure. The reaction of the British was in South-East Asia as elsewhere to try to retain its essence while adjusting it in part. In Burma alone did they annex. In Malaya they sought to consolidate. In Borneo they half-heartedly tried to do the same. They compromised with France, even to some extent at Siam's expense. They put up with the displacement of the treaty of 1824, as of the Sulu protocol of 1885. They accepted the outcome of the Spanish–American war.

Perhaps the main challenge of the future was Japan. With that power, rather paradoxically, they made an alliance. That might not contain Japan's wish to shift the *status quo* to its advantage, but for the time being it generally behaved with moderation, at least outside Korea. The best guarantee of the *status quo* in South-East Asia was, however, the acquisition of the Philippines by the United States. That gave it an interest in the area over against Japan. It also made the United States a colonial power. That set back the nationalist cause in the Philippines and in a sense in South-East Asia as a whole. The United States was to shift its view of the Philippine advance to independence, but its patronage compromised Filipino nationalism fatefully and perhaps fatally. Others would look elsewhere for models and inspiration. The British would, too. They had not welcomed the Philippine Republic as once they had those in Latin America. Their model of the future lay in their dominions, as the Filipino leader Quezon was to recognize. To this model they were increasingly driven to assimilate India. If their growing weakness had constrained them in the

1890s, their involvement in the First World War prompted bolder policies in India. But the impact on South-East Asia was in general much less. Though the British would have preferred the *status quo* in the Philippines, they could not maintain it. The American take-over was, however, a guarantee of the *status quo* elsewhere and in effect was to help to preserve the colonial pattern till the Japanese invasion. In this sense South-East Asia provides once more a paradigm for the world at large. Britain's world-wide primacy was in decline. It was the United States that was to be its preferred successor. That was already evident at the time of the First World War.

1. N. Pelcovits, *Old China Hands and the Foreign Office*, New York: King's Crown Press, 1948, p. 128.

2. B. Porter, *Britain, Europe and the World, 1850–1982*, London: Allen and Unwin, 1983, p. 63.

3. R. G. Neale, *Britain and American Imperialism 1898–1900*, St Lucia: University of Queensland Press, 1965, pp. 91–2, 111.

4. Quoted in B. Porter, *The Lion's Share*, London: Longman, 1975, p. 102.

5. L. Dehio, *Germany and World Politics in the Twentieth Century*, London: Chatto, 1960, p. 60.

6. Memorandum, 1 January 1907, in G. P. Gooch and H. Temperley (eds.), *British Documents on the Origins of the War*, London, HMSO, 1928, Vol. III, pp. 402–3.

7. Quoted in Olive Checkland, *Britain's Encounter with Meiji Japan, 1868–1912*, Basingstoke: Macmillan, 1989, p. 39.

8. Quoted in B. Semmel, *Imperialism and Social Reform*, London: Allen and Unwin, 1960, p. 169.

9. M. Balfour, *Britain and Joseph Chamberlain*, London: Allen and Unwin, 1985, pp. 273–4.

10. Kenneth J. Hagan, *American Gunboat Diplomacy and the Old Navy, 1877–1899*, Westport and London: Greenwood, 1973, pp. 104–5; Frederick C. Drake, *The Empire of the Seas*, Honolulu: University of Hawaii Press, 1984, pp. 225–6.

11. R. Robinson, 'Oxford in Imperial Historiography', in F. Madden and D. K. Fieldhouse (eds.), *Oxford and the Idea of Commonwealth*, London: Croom Helm, 1982, p. 31.

12. Quoted in G. Bennett (ed.), *The Concept of Empire: Burke to Attlee 1774–1947*, London: Black, 1962, p. 252.

13. Quoted in J. Amery, *Joseph Chamberlain and the Tariff Reform Campaign*, London and New York: Macmillan, 1969, p. 538.

14. Bennett, *The Concept of Empire*, p. 283.

15. Salisbury to O'Connor, 25 January 1898, in Gooch and Temperley, *British Documents*, 1927, Vol. I, p. 8.

16. Quoted in C. L. Keeton, *King Thebaw and the Ecological Rape of Burma*, Delhi: Manohar, 1974, p. 243.

17. Ibid., p. 317.

18. Quoted in Muhammad Shamsheer Ali, 'The Beginnings of British Rule in Upper Burma: A Study of British Policy and Burmese Reaction 1885–1890', Ph.D. thesis, London University, 1976, pp. 43–4.

19. D. R. SarDesai's attempts to downplay it are not completely persuasive. See his book, *British Trade and Expansion in Southeast Asia 1830–1914*, Columbia, Missouri: South Asia Books, 1977, pp. 162–6.

20. F. A. Swettenham, *British Malaya*, London: Lane, 1907, pp. 214–15.

21. Robinson to Low, 9 June 1878, C.O. 882/4, Public Record Office, London.

22. Jeanine Graham, *Frederick Weld*, Auckland: Auckland University Press, 1983, p. 163.

23. Swettenham, *British Malaya*, pp. 273–4.

24. E. Thio, 'Britain's Search for Security in North Malaya, 1886–1897', *Journal of Southeast Asian History*, 10, 2 (1969): 287–8.

25. Minute by de Robeck, 25 June 1879, C.O. 144/52 [9624], Public Record Office, London.

26. Minute, 18 May 1896, C.O. 144/70 [10680], Public Record Office.

27. Memorandum by C. Alabaster, 1859, quoted in B. L. Evans, 'The Attitudes and Policies of Great Britain and China towards French Expansion in Cochin-China, Cambodia, Annam and Tongking 1858–83', Ph.D. thesis, University of London, 1961, p. 41.

28. Quoted in Truong Buu Lam, *Patterns of Vietnamese Response to Foreign Intervention*, New Haven: Southeast Asia Studies, Yale University, 1967, p. 11.

29. Quoted in A. L. Moffat, *Mongkut, the King of Siam*, Ithaca: Cornell University Press, 1961, p. 124.

30. See Likhit Dhiravegin, *Siam and Colonialism (1855–1909): An Analysis of Diplomatic Relations*, Bangkok: Thai Watana Panich, 2518 B.E. [1974].

31. J. G. D. Campbell, *Siam in the Twentieth Century*, London: Arnold, 1904, p. 171.

32. Quoted in Vivat Sethachuay, 'United States–Thailand Diplomatic Relations during World War II', Ph.D. thesis, Brigham Young University, 1977, p. 55.

33. H. L. Wesseling in S. Forster, W. J. Mommsen, and R. Robinson (eds.), *Bismarck, Europe, and Africa: The Berlin Africa Conference 1884–1885 and the Onset of Partition*, Oxford: Oxford University Press, 1988, p. 528.

34. S. de Mas, *Report on the Condition of the Philippines in 1842*, III. *Interior Politics*, trans. C. Botor, rev. A. Felix Jr., Manila: Historical Conservation Society, 1963, pp. 190–2.

35. Quoted in N. Tarling, *Sulu and Sabah*, Kuala Lumpur: Oxford University Press, 1978, pp. 293–4.

36. Quoted in L. M. Guerrero, *The First Filipino*, Manila: National Heroes Commission, Advocate Book Supply Co., 1963, pp. 311–12.

37. G. A. May, *A Past Recovered*, Quezon City: New Day, 1987, pp. 169–70.

38. Akira Iriye, *Pacific Estrangement*, Cambridge: Harvard University Press, 1972, pp. 48–9.

4

The Impact of the First World War and the Depression

IN the 'imperialist' phase South-East Asia had been divided up among mainly alien powers with a new rigidity and mainly alien governments established with a new level of capacity to penetrate society. Even the Siamese Government acted in many respects like one of the new colonial states. The frontiers, drawn originally to avoid conflict, now had a more positive connotation. Behind them, governments were securing a greater control over their subjects. Though collaboration with élites was still essential for the colonial regimes, they now acted with increased authority. Major changes took place within their frontiers, in some respects stimulated by them, in others restrained by them. They remained confident of meeting the challenges that emerged.

The Threats to Colonial South-East Asia

The colonial regimes were more concerned about threats from outside. Even in the First World War when Europe's divisions broke out in the first major conflict for a century those changes did not come, as in the past, from the intervention of other European powers. They came largely from other parts of the world. Nor were the threats merely military or political: they were ideological. To a considerable extent the colonial powers in South-East Asia—to which the United States was a recent recruit—saw common threats and acted in common to meet dangers. All but one of the colonial powers were or became allies in the war; all were opposed to Communist threats at the end of it and tended to act in co-operation. The colonial pattern had been established in the nineteenth century under the aegis of the British. Now, as their power declined, it nevertheless held together. The involvement of the United States and the threats from outside helped to preserve it.

In the previous phase, the imperial powers had been concerned with each other and with the states and territories that they claimed to dominate. The inability of the latter to cope with change had been one factor. But another concern was lest that might invite the intervention of a Western rival. The story of imperialism was not a one-sided one. The moves of the imperialists were conditioned by the moves of the indigenous peoples, by their resistance, diplomatic or violent, by their warfare or guerrilla opposition, and by the terms of their collaboration. Resistance was not always easily dealt with, neither the resistance of the Burmans to the British, of the Vietnamese to the French, nor the opposition of the Filipinos and the Moros to the imposition of American rule. But collaboration was easy to come by, if not always easy to modify once established. And once the colonial framework had been established, the rivalry of the colonial powers was diminished.

What they were now concerned about was challenge to the framework as a whole from outside, from a power or powers not already or not sufficiently part of the colonial pattern, or ideas that presented a critique of it. If the pattern could be upheld, they had little doubt they could sustain authority and collaboration within their territories. The greatest risk inside their territory, they were convinced, would also come from outside, from the spread of revolutionary religious or political doctrines. They were otherwise confident they could continue to handle their territories, if those territories were sufficiently insulated. But, while they had much in common, they differed as to the extent of the intervention or manipulation required. The French tended to resort to force, and the Dutch to diplomacy; the French, somewhat ambiguously, to spreading their culture, and the Dutch to sustaining Indonesian custom and tradition, though also pursuing a modernizing 'Ethical Policy'. The British remained more confident in the élites with which they dealt. They had not abandoned the attitudes and policies they had developed earlier, and this distinguished them from the French and the Dutch.

Generally, it is true, they preferred not to recruit armies from the majority peoples in their dependencies. 'A loyal and patriotic Malay nation, trained to arms might well prove in future a fitting guardian for the Western portal to the Pacific,' an Inspector-General of Overseas Forces suggested.[1] The FMS, however, maintained a battalion of mercenary troops, the Malay States Guides, wholly Indian in composition, not Malay. The idea was one for the future, and nation-building was not yet clearly on the Malayan agenda. But the British continued to envision future world politics in a multi-state pattern, slow though the evolution to it might be. They were all the more concerned about threats to the system as a whole in particular when international Communism emerged and took hold in Asia. It was not only necessary to sustain the old framework by conciliating or recruiting other powers; there was an ideological challenge to the whole concept to be faced. Sometimes the penetration of Communism complicated their relations with élites. Sometimes it made their policies more like those of other colonial powers. But their priorities continued to differ. The independence of action of those powers they patronized continued to be a problem for their own policy-makers.

The confidence with which the British viewed, or affected to view, the future was in a sense part of the policy itself. If it could be demonstrated that no major change was required, and that adjustment sufficed, there would be less argument for change, and less opportunity for those who sought change. If the framework as a whole were sustained, no revolutionary movement in one territory would win support in another, as Blumentritt had argued was essential. A weakness in one spot, if demonstrated, would suggest there were weaknesses elsewhere, and encourage those who wanted revolution rather than evolution, those who wanted to determine the timetable that the British kept in their hands. There were risks even so in such a policy. The British might neglect changes within a territory that were really necessary, fearing that their adoption would demonstrate weakness rather than strength, and their policy might be reduced to one of inaction. One of the greatest challenges—finding new collaborators and replacing old—might be bypassed rather than met.

The British assumption was that collaborators could always be found. The emphasis had always been on the framework within which their relationships were worked out, and it remained there. Adjustments were made so that such a framework might be preserved in its essentials. At times those adjustments were mutually contradictory. At times, too, they might be at odds with the relationship with collaborators. But the priority lay with the framework and the adjustments.

The world-wide framework the British had established suited their interests, and their aim, when challenged, was to adjust it rather than abandon it. That adjustment included consolidation, take-overs, surrenders, deals, and alliances. It increased the size of the territorial empire. But that remained only a part of Britain's interests, and its links with Britain were limited and dependent on economic and financial rather than political ties. In a way it was a defeatist view; in another way an optimistic one. Collaborators could always be found, and the British could always trade. They tended as a result to assume that international diplomacy and economic activity were enough. This was consistent with both the Palmerstonian and the Cobdenite views adopted at the height of Britain's primacy. It was, however, an assumption now made in a very different context. There was about it the vein of wishful thinking that Aaron Friedberg has detected in British policy at the turn of the century.[2]

One major change the British recognized, and perhaps exaggerated: the emerging threat, inter-war and even more after the Second World War, of international Communism. There were others. They had always been anxious to avoid the provocation of Islamic opposition, which they felt would fall upon Western powers as a whole, but Britain in particular. The Dutch tried to nip the revival of Islam in the bud, allowing the haj but trying to limit its effect, even attempting to counter it by a measure of assimilation in the form of the Ethical Policy. The British were more cautious, making religion, for example, a sphere in which a Malay Sultan was not obliged to accept advice from the Resident.

Another change was the emergence of a modern Japanese state. The impact of Japan upon the nationalists was considerable. 'Was it not from there,' asked Hatta of Indonesia, 'from the islands of the Japanese, that there first arose the idea of the freedom of Asian nations after centuries during which their lands had been surrendered to the white man?'[3] But the Dutch were more concerned about Japanese spies, and more about direct interference than example. They were also worried about the Anglo-Japanese alliance: their patron had joined a power that seemed to threaten them. There were indeed contradictions in Britain's policy. But the alliance of 1902 in some sense enlisted Japanese acceptance of the *status quo* at least pro tem. Some Japanese then and since have seen it as a kind of alliance against nationalism: 'one of the main intentions of the Alliance was to contain the aspiration of Asian people for freedom'. 'The main purpose of the Alliance was to suppress jointly the movement against the colonial interests of Britain and Japan. . . .'[4] That may exaggerate the strength and perceived threat of nationalism. But it has some validity. The alliance not only limited Japan's threat as a power; it emasculated pan-Asianism, another form of international challenge to the imperial framework, by supporting the 'realpolitikers' among the Japanese policy-makers. In any case, it was only when Japan attacked the colonial powers that the system collapsed. In that sense, their priorities were right; they could contain the internal threat. The nationalists could not liberate their countries without outside help. Securing that, they were to risk falling into an alternative imperial framework.

If the Japanese modernized in a particular way, and with a particular success, the Chinese revolutionized, but with a yet more ambiguous outcome. The dynasty was overthrown in 1911, but the revolutionaries were divided over the next steps, and civil strife ensued. That in itself was a challenge to the outside powers. Should the Japanese be guided by pan-Asian ideals and support the revolutionaries? British policy had aimed to uphold the integrity of China and the Open Door to international commerce, and leave the Chinese to work out their own destiny. But was their answer acceptable? China's independence had been an essential part of British foreign policy in the nineteenth century, but the British had limited its role overseas. There were many Chinese overseas, however. From them the revolutionaries had sought to elicit sympathy and support, and the pre-1911 government had begun to contact them, too. The post-1911 government was likely to continue along the same lines, if not go further. For the colonial powers, this was another international challenge, particularly but not solely, when it became involved with Communism.

If the colonial powers were in some sense right to emphasize the international threat, in another sense they were wrong. Their emphasis on threats from outside encouraged them to be too negative within their dependencies. Even the British, more committed than the Dutch and the French to the emergence of independent states, tended to avoid initiatives that might have suggested this was the prospect for the world at large and not for Europe only. Such failures were to give unearned ideological opportunities to the Japanese and the Russians.

The First World War

The Western powers had divided up the world among themselves; but they then fell out. The division they had reached did not satisfy all of them. That is not to say that the First World War was an imperialist struggle or even the result of there being no more of the world to split up. What was at issue was power in the world and influence, not merely nor even primarily territorial control, though it was often perceived and presented in that way. One of the difficulties was the definition of the issue. The Germans sought 'world power', but the phrase had many ambiguities. Did they want power over the world? Or power in the world? Where? What kind? Perhaps the best definition relates German aspirations to those of the British, the predominant nineteenth-century power, and those of the Americans and the Russians. The potential of the United States and Russia seemed so great that they were likely to dominate the world of the twentieth century, territorially and economically. The Germans could not wait for the achievement of economic success, which would certainly take them past Britain; it would not in any case take them past the United States. Thus Britain's open-handed treatment of trade they ignored: they visited on others their own disposition to protectionism and feared they would be 'shut out'. In order to be sure of a share of world power, moreover, Germany had to have a secure base in Europe, and since Europe could at most sustain only one power with world-wide influence, the British had to see the wisdom in stepping aside and accepting German leadership.

The programme, even so defined, was wildly impractical, but difficult to drop. There was no reason to expect that the Americans and the Russians would be prepared to ignore the emergence of a rival. Still less could the British be expected to exchange their independence for dependence on the Germans. They were prepared to make colonial concessions. But even these were limited by their concern to build up their friendship with France, at first seen as a power with which to reduce differences, then increasingly seen as a counterbalance to the growth of German power in Europe. In the case of Russia—seen also as a rather unfortunately necessary counterweight to Germany—the British themselves had to make concessions so as to diminish the tension in Asia and enhance co-operation in Europe. The British could make colonial concessions to the Germans, too, but the concessions could never in any case be sufficient for them. They did not want fragments of empire, but world power, and that they sought by means that threatened Britain's security, impatiently trying to alter the balance of power in Europe, rather than awaiting the outcome of economic trends that were in fact putting them ahead of Britain. The British were continuing with a policy of adjustment, of retaining, they hoped, the essence of the *status quo* while sacrificing the less important elements of it. The Germans wanted to change the *status quo.* This they were to achieve by war in 1914–18, but too drastically for their own good: power shifted more towards the United States and Russia, away from Europe, than they wanted. The British, as ever, fought with the support of allies, but expended their own manpower and financial resources on an immense and exhausting scale. The Germans did not pre-empt but precipitated an outcome they sought to avoid. But that was perhaps not fully revealed till the Second World War.

In their challenge there was an ideological element, as was to be in the case of other alternative world-systems, American, Russian, Japanese, and Islamic. To offer the world 'Germanism' was likely to mean little. The Germans did, however, claim to be speaking for other nations which, they argued, would benefit from the destruction of Britain's primacy and the system associated with it. Poland was a case in point. Such an approach was not new in aspiring empires—particularly after the French revolution and Napoleon I had set the example—though those liberated must always have feared that their new liberty was qualified by their position in a new order. The British argued that smaller nations had a fuller role in their world-system than they could in any alternative. The liberal approach they had adopted in the nineteenth century and more or less continued to sustain, even outside Europe, lent some support to their argument as Germans like Riezler conceded.

In the First World War itself, unlike the Second, there was no substantial conflict in Asia. The Germans had little to lose and could do little to attack others. But the war had dramatic effects, both on the framework within which empires were sustained, and within the empires themselves. In the pre-war period, the British had already withdrawn some of their naval forces from East Asia, relying upon their ally, Japan, to maintain the *status quo.* But the Japanese wished to change the *status quo* in their own interest; though restrained by their alliance partner, they were also encouraged. The absorption of Europe in the war gave them new opportunities in East Asia. Most obviously, they were able to take over German colonies, and also German concessions in China. 'When there is a fire in a jeweller's shop, the neighbours cannot be expected to refrain from helping themselves.'[5] Though this was far from welcome to the Chinese or the Allies, it was accepted, even by the Americans when they entered the war in 1917. The Japanese also prospered economically, becoming for the first time a creditor rather than a debtor nation. It was not certain that these opportunities would satisfy them. The appetite might grow with feeding. Official policy might become more ambitious, if not more ideologically pan-Asian. The war had its effect on India, too. The British, as ever, were concerned about subversion, and the Germans indeed became aware of the possibilities of Sikh extremism.[6] At the same time the British found it necessary to involve India increasingly in the war. The spread of the war into Turkey involved Indian interests, and Indian manpower was needed even in Europe. The involvement urged the British into new undertakings towards Indians. Towards the end they committed themselves to the goal of self-government along the lines of the settler dominions, the war precipitating a formulation so far only implicit. The policy for India, the Secretary of State declared, was 'the gradual development of self-governing institutions with a view to the progressive realization of responsible government in India as an integral part of the British Empire'.[7] The concept of extending responsible government to non-settler territories affected other parts of the empire besides India, particularly Burma. More generally India's example had less influence than might have been expected. Perhaps its political experience was too singular. Readiness to borrow from India was in some territories also qualified by the presence of Indian minorities.

The empire was itself undergoing a further transformation as a result of the role of the settler dominions in the war, so that it was to become in Zimmern's phrase 'a British Entente'.[8] Generations before, James Stephen had seen the relationship with the settler colonies as a series of 'tacit alliances': Jan Smuts of South Africa declared that

the British Empire, or the British Commonwealth of nations, does not stand for unity, standardisation, or assimilation, or denationalisation; but it stands for a fuller, a richer, and more various life among all the nations that compose it. And even nations who have fought against you, like my own, must feel that they and their interests, their language, their religions, and all their cultural interests are as safe and as secure under the British flag as those of the children of your household and your own blood.[9]

Indirectly the war affected the empires in Asia in other ways, in part again ideological. Despite their long association with the British, the Turks entered the war on the side of the Germans. It brought about the final breakup of their empire. And that had an impact throughout the Islamic world: the Sultan of Roum was no more, and the Islamic homelands responded in a variety of ways to the new challenges they faced. On the continent of Europe itself, three empires were destroyed, German, Austrian, and Russian. The collapse of the Tsarist regime in the course of the war left the way open to the Bolshevik seizure of power in 1917. That had a message for the workers of the world which the Comintern was to take up. 'And if our Soviet Republic should perish, others will carry the banner forward.'[10] Its initial aspiration was for revolution in Europe amid the post-war chaos. Failing to achieve that, it looked to revolution elsewhere as a means of undermining capitalism. In particular it looked, under Lenin's guidance, to the Asian world, 'seeking a temporary alliance with bourgeois democracy in the colonial and backward countries',[11] and its opposition was directed above all against Britain, the predominant colonial power and the power that benefited most from the unequal treaties against which the Chinese nationalists were struggling. The Indian revolutionary, M. N. Roy, found a home in Moscow. A traditional threat to the British-sponsored political system had come from Imperial Russia; now it had a new ideological dimension. Moreover, that crossed the frontiers in a way the old threat had not, and reduced the isolation of opposition movements in the colonial and under-developed territories, which had been so marked in the case of the Philippine revolution of the 1890s. Foreign powers had sponsored subversion before, but never in this all-encompassing way.

In a sense, however, the Bolsheviks had a rival. The United States entered the war in 1917, making it a world war, but also enhancing its ideological character. American power and ideals were now sure to play a larger part in the shaping of the world, and Wilsonian policies, with their emphasis on self-determination and nationality, were to some extent competing with Bolshevik ideology. His Fourteen Points were an answer to 'the voice of the Russian people . . . a voice calling for these definitions of principle and purpose which is, it seems to me, more thrilling and compelling than any of the moving voices with which the troubled air of the world is filled'.[12] Both ideologies opposed the old colonial system and gave the redemption of China a special emphasis. It was in these ways that the emergent superpowers, whose potential had been foreseen before the war, put forward their similar but competitive claims to establish a new world order. The fact that the Americans in the Philippines lagged a little behind their own pretensions—despite the Jones Act and Governor F. B. Harrison—did not undermine the impact of their ideas in general. The Chinese had set up a republic. What should happen next the revolutionaries found more difficulty in determining: strongman rule, warlordism, and civil war followed. If there was consensus, however, it had a focus in anti-imperialism, directed specially against the United Kingdom, the chief beneficiary of the unequal treaties, and Japan, entrenched in Manchuria. These changes affected South-East Asia in a number of ways.

Indirectly, China was a scene of international rivalry. Upholding its integrity, and looking to the reform of imperial rule, had been features of Britain's policy in the days of its primacy. The changes indicated Britain's inability to sustain its old policies, and it had some difficulty in adapting, even though the emergence of nationalism arguably fitted into its long-range concept of world politics. Abandoning one set of collaborators for another was never easy. China was important to the emergent superpowers, too, more particularly in an ideological sense. US interests were limited, but a new China seemed to fit in with the Wilsonian view of the world. Bolshevik Russia saw China as the leading 'backward' country, and Leninist policy had especial appeal to an élite that was searching to give its revolution a deeper meaning and a firmer political base. Japan, like Britain, had an economic interest in China, and like Britain, strategic interests of its own, particularly in the north, and a pan-Asian ideology, which its realism tended to play down. The fate of South-East Asia was bound to be affected by the competition of these forces in China.

China itself had other meanings for South-East Asia, too. The example of its revolution, dubious as its outcome was, had less impact in general than the successful transformation of Japan. But it attracted early Vietnamese nationalists, and China remained a base and at times a source of encouragement for later and more radical ones, despite the ambiguity of the historical relationship between the two countries. In relation to other South-East Asian countries, there was another ambiguity. Within these countries, there were substantial Chinese populations, particularly in Malaya and Singapore. Latter-day Chinese dynasts, reformers, and revolutionaries had all sought support among the Nanyang communities, and so did the leading parties in the new Republic, the Kuomintang (KMT) and the Chinese Communist Party (CCP), at first collaborators, then rivals. The overseas communities became more self-consciously Chinese. And that tended to alarm both colonial authorities and indigenous nationalists.

The ideology of the Americans, like that of the Russians, penetrated beyond the international framework into the territories which colonial powers aspired to rule. The successes of Japan and the revolutionary changes in China also affected the colonial peoples, direct or indirectly, and, to a greater or lesser extent, so did the successes of the Indian nationalist movement. It was more difficult for colonial powers to see their future merely in terms of trying to sustain an international *status quo*, within which they could expect to handle opposition movements isolated from one another and from the world. The changes that had taken place, coupled with greater sophistication in communications, had a direct effect on nationalist and other oppositional movements. Even the metropolises were themselves affected. In a war that saw the victory of democracies over monarchies, it was hard to deny that democracy could be exported. The Dutch monarchy was affected by the wave of post-war revolution, though the Netherlands had been neutral in the war. That, at one moment, seemed to open up the possibility of political change in Netherlands India. But the moment was brief.

South-East Asia in the War

In South-East Asia the war years themselves had shown some signs of the shifts outside South-East Asia and their impact on it and its rulers. The most dramatic, perhaps, was the mutiny in Singapore, though its importance was perhaps more symbolic than real. British power in South-East Asia was not overthrown. But a mutiny in an Indian regiment—however badly managed that regiment was—was disconcerting, even though it might be blamed on subversive Sikhs or Germans. Characteristically it led to the development of an intelligence service at Singapore concerned with spies and sedition, which was to focus on international Communism. The lack of British forces in the area was also shown up. Pan-Asians among the Japanese made rather more than the British liked of the assistance they afforded their ally. 'What is the significance to be attached to the fact that the flag of the Rising Sun was set up in the centre of Singapore?'[13] An alliance with the Japanese, though designed to maintain the *status quo*, always offered some threat to it. Now the Japanese seemed clearly to be supporting the British; almost too clearly since it showed they needed support and not merely in respect of a threat from another power, but within their own territory. Some Japanese would have preferred a direct break with the British alliance. But no such break ensued, and the alliance continued till 1921–2. The handling of the mutiny lends some support to the idea that it was an alliance against the colonial peoples. But the chief object of the alliance had been, and remained, that of enlisting Japanese support for a regional structure that, like the rest of the framework for the exertion of their influence, the British continued to see as threatened more from without than from within.

The British Government had no wish to see its ally expand its influence in South-East Asia even on 'realist' rather than 'idealistic' lines. Its Consul-General in Batavia at one point suggested that Japanese expansion was the logic of the situation. Neutral in Europe, the Dutch, he believed, were too supportive of German subversion in South-East Asia. Was there not a case, he argued, for splitting the Netherlands Indies? The Dutch could retain Java and the future of Sumatra, Borneo, and Sulawesi would be decided by Britain and Japan. W. R. D. Beckett saw this as at once satis- fying and appeasing an ally. But the British Foreign Office had no wish to encourage so large a change in the *status quo*: that was not the logic the British saw in the Anglo-Japanese alliance. 'If the Netherlands Indies are not too friendly, they are harmless. It would be quite another matter if the islands were in the hands of the Japanese and one would like to know whether the Admiralty would endorse Mr Beckett's views.'[14]

Blows at British prestige and at the territorial settlement would also react on the British position as a whole. In Siam, for example, the Government was sensitive to the decline of British power as it had been to its rise. British prestige was designed to uphold British influence there. The Siamese were as ever anxious to enjoy as independent a role as they could safely secure. They were sensitive to the rise of Chinese nationalism: their king, Vajiravudh, saw the Chinese as the Jews of the Far East.[15] Their response to the world war was to declare war on Germany too, but only in the year that the United States and China joined in, and they sent some troops to Europe.[16] They thus ensured themselves a place at the peace conference and acquired a new argument against the unequal treaties, renegotiated by 1925. They might shift further, if the *status quo* shifted.

Burma and the Philippines both belonged to powers that had taken part in the war. In Burma, part of British India, the British

finally came to make the same kind of concessions they felt necessary but also safe to make to India.[17] In the Philippines under the
Jones Act the United States committed itself more squarely to
ultimate independence even before entering the European war,
but it set no timetable. The French, of course, were also participants
in the war. But they characteristically made no concessions to emergent Vietnamese nationalism. Reactionary officials and the French
settlers added to the caution of the metropolitan government.
Britain's European enemies had not effectively brought the war
to Asia. Nor did it seem indirectly to affect the framework in
which Britain operated, nor even to enforce substantial change
within that framework. The territories that Britain ruled directly,
or were ruled by governments under its patronage, could, it still
seemed, be handled by a mixture, more or less judicious, of force,
conciliation, and co-optation. The international framework could
be sustained because, while the European powers were at war
with each other, Japan did not take the opportunity to sever its
connection with the *status quo*: only in China, with the twenty-one
demands of 1915, did it become more aggressive.

The ideological threat to the old system—from Bolshevik ideology,
Chinese and Indian nationalism, American idealism, and Japanese
pan-Asianism—was yet limited. Again the British believed it could
be handled. Communism they saw as a threat from the outside,
to be blunted by an intelligence operation. Chinese nationalism,
itself seen by some British officials as very much of Bolshevik
provenance,[18] was of ambiguous impact: the local Chinese might
identify with it and others be provoked by it. In any case it, too,
could be handled while there was no strong Chinese state to
take up the cause. Indian nationalism could be handled in South-
East Asia as in India: conciliating the moderates and eliminating
the subversives. American idealism could be conciliated, too: the
Americans were, moreover, themselves a colonial power, and
on that ground, and others, might sympathize with the British.
Pan-Asianism the Japanese themselves restrained: they were still
following the realistic policy of the Meiji oligarchy.

The Post-war Settlement

To win the conflict with Germany Britain called on resources
derived from both levels of its interests, the investments in the
Americas and the men of the empire and the dependencies, in a
stupendous but exhausting deployment of its power. The war

ended with British victory, but at monumental cost. That cost was represented in part by impoverishment and indebtedness, and it was also represented by a shift in approach. American ideas were in the ascendant, as the Japanese plenipotentiary in Paris recognized. 'Today it is a worldwide trend to honor pacifism and reject oppression. Everywhere in the world the so-called Americanism is advanced, and conditions have definitely altered from the days of the old diplomacy.'[19] These ideas, thrust into additional prominence by the need to compete with Bolshevik internationalism, affected both the aspirations of the peoples the empires ruled and the international attitudes to the framework of their power. But they did not at once transform them, and the Americans were unwilling to use the vast power they had accumulated to reorder the world according to the ideals they propounded. There was a chance, so the British thought, that the old framework could be adjusted, rather than displaced; the assumption continuing that it was the international framework that counted.

The war had produced no territorial changes in South-East Asia itself, despite Beckett's advocacy. On the periphery the German possessions and concessions passed into the hands of others; Shantung, the Carolines, and the Marianas into those of the Japanese, and New Guinea into the hands of the Australians. The empires destroyed in Europe had after all secured no actual possessions in South-East Asia, despite the apprehensions others had at times felt. The peace treaty, made in Paris, thus did not open up opportunities to new powers, or to old ones, as it did in the Pacific and in Africa. The League of Nations established formal trusteeship only in respect of the territories of the defeated powers: the concept of trusteeship, amplified by Frederick Lugard and other theorists of African empire, was characteristically outlined as a task for individual colonial authorities rather than for a world authority. The League agencies had a wider ambit, but, though their activities could impinge on colonial regimes and their collaborators, they did not dislodge them. The old framework was substantially undisturbed. Nor did it seem to be seriously threatened, from within or from without. The most insidious threat the British felt was an ideological one: Communism might penetrate to the colonial élites. The other threat was from the Japanese, seen less as an ideological threat than as a political or strategic one. The Communist threat seemed in the 1920s to be greater than the Japanese. The position was on the whole reversed in the 1930s.

The Washington conference provided an Asian counterpart to the Paris conference. Its decisions involved major changes, but the framework could even so appear to be relatively secure. The Anglo-Japanese alliance itself was displaced, but that had always had somewhat equivocal implications for South-East Asia, and while it had been displaced more because of American and Canadian pressure than because of that of Britain's Asian or Australasian allies or dominions, its abandonment did not appear to be a source of concern. The pledges of the four-, five-, and nine-power treaties increased the sense of security. They supported the territorial *status quo*, diminished the prospect of naval rivalry, and upheld the integrity of China and the Open Door. While the Netherlands was not directly involved in this security system, the powers, by identic notes, pledged to sustain the *status quo* in respect of Netherlands India too. 'The public announcement that none of the signatories of the treaty proposed to rob Holland of her undoubted possessions seemed embarrassingly superfluous', but the Dutch acknowledged it with 'une vive satisfaction'.[20]

The changes were, however, perhaps more important, at least potentially, than the continuity. The treaties were made in the Washington spirit, but it was only that spirit that would preserve them: they contained pledges, but there were no sanctions behind them. The Japanese had accepted the treaties, despite the blow that the loss of the old alliance seemed now to represent, and despite the limits on their naval building. The system provided security for Japan in East Asia: no other state could modernize its naval fortifications in the area, and the ratios in capital ships were such that, given the world-wide commitments of the United Kingdom and the United States, Japan could not be challenged by them in East Asian waters. But Japanese interests in China were less secure, and while the Washington powers envisaged a gradual accommodation between Chinese nationalism and outside interests, and thus the gradual dissolution of the unequal treaties, it was unlikely that this would satisfy an impatient Chinese nationalism, fuelled initially by a Communist alliance and later sustained despite or because of a break in that alliance. In times of prosperity, the Japanese might be content with the opportunities they still had in China. But if they determined to take more forceful steps to protect their interests, the international framework would provide few real obstacles in their way.

The displacement of the alliance with Britain meant that there were now even fewer restraints upon Japan than before. As a power, it might more easily challenge other powers, bound to them only loosely by the Washington agreements. To the limited extent that the alliance had also been a commitment to oppose nationalism, its displacement meant that the Japanese were freer than before to patronize that cause. It was to remain difficult to do so, however. First, the Japanese still could not choose squarely between the realistic and the idealistic options, and that undermined the effectiveness of the latter. Second, their approach to China had the same effect, even, perhaps, in cases in which other nationalities distrusted the Chinese. Third, the Japanese could after all be seen as another imperial power, couching its aspirations, as others had done, in terms of aspirations on behalf of others, which, however, it was hard to take at face value.

The war had made the United States the leading Western power. Would it use its power to uphold the settlement? That was quite uncertain. Hughes, the Secretary of State, had made it clear that its interests would not require it to intervene in China: the United States 'would never go to war over any aggression on the part of Japan in China'.[21] Its commitment to colonial South-East Asia was, at least superficially, still smaller. In fact, however, it remained in the Philippines, and under Leonard Wood's administration, it showed no intention of advancing, much less fixing the date of independence. The test in the Jones Act of 1916 was the establishment of a stable government. But what did that mean? The former Democratic Governor-General F. B. Harrison asked:

Must it be a government which under any circumstances can withstand aggression from without, and at all times be able to preserve its independence? If so, has there ever been a stable government in history . . . ? Must it conform exactly to American standards of government? If that is to be the test, must it conform to what we Americans would like to be, or to what we know of our institutions in actual practice?[22]

'If the United States carry out their expressed intention of granting independence to the Philippines, the tendency will be for these islands eventually to drift into the orbit of Japan, which would bring that Power appreciably nearer to Australia', it was observed at the Foreign Office in London in 1921. The then Republican administration was opposed to the 'surrender' of the Philippines. 'From the British point of view, this surrender ought not to be encouraged.' But it was true 'that the evacuation of the Philippines might eliminate a possible danger to the peace of the

Far East, inasmuch as they are strategically a source of weakness to the United States and a constant temptation to Japan'.[23]

The attitude of the United States to the Philippines was perceived by the British as a measure of its commitment to the *status quo* in the region. Characteristically they saw that as more significant than any risk that the Philippine advance towards self-government might be a disease that spread, though H. G. Chilton at the embassy in Washington suggested in 1924 that it 'would arouse our Indian agitators to a greater state of activity'.[24] 'It seems clear that an indication of the action to be taken by the United States Government one way or the other must affect the naval situation, not only perhaps in the Pacific Ocean but in general,' Sir Ronald Campbell wrote from Washington in 1929.[25] The capacity of the United States was of course limited in any case under the Washington treaty. The nearest naval base that could be modernized was in Hawaii at Pearl Harbor. The treaties may have been made in Washington; but Washington appeared to rely only on their spirit for their survival.

The British themselves did not have the power to support the new system should it be challenged. Their aim had been to avoid a naval race, because of its economic and strategic implications. But the accommodation of the United States and the United Kingdom, though desirable in itself, did not solve the security problems of East and South-East Asia. The British valued the American pledges to the system, but remained uncertain that they would be fulfilled. Yet they could not themselves undertake the whole burden. Their navy was now on a one-ocean standard. In order to meet a two-ocean commitment, they had determined to build a base in Singapore. That they could still do under the Washington treaty. But, unlike Hong Kong, which they could not modernize, it was remote from East Asia. Nor was building it easy to finance. And in any case the strategy had the essential weakness that its success depended on Britain avoiding a crisis in more than one part of the world at any one time.

These limitations were apparent. Yet, as elsewhere, the British combined a consciousness of them with a degree of optimism. Perhaps they thought, with their concepts of prestige, that they were stronger for thinking that they were, since others would have more confidence in them if they displayed confidence. There was always an element of presumption in their power; now they were coming to rely rather more upon the presumption than the power. At the same time, it was not easy to adjust their position. No power found it easy to come to terms with others; none found it easy to displace a given set of collaborators with another. Adjustments of the former sort were now more difficult than before. They had always run the risk of indicating weakness: now it was clearer than before that the interests of the ruled were involved, and not merely those of the rulers. Changing collaborators again became in a sense more uncertain even as it became in another more necessary. But it did not press. The fact that it did not seem urgent made it possible to avoid tackling problems the solution of which was far from clear. Too determined an attempt to tackle problems might show a desperation that might in itself undermine confidence. The framework could contain change, and change was implied by the view of international development implicit in it. But the timetable of that change was all-important. That should remain, the British thought, essentially in their hands, and they must not seem to be jolted lest they lost their grip altogether. They thus tended to take a cautious or conservative approach to the implications of their own world-view.

British Malaya and Borneo in the 1920s

In the colonial and pseudo-colonial territories, indeed, British policy appears in the inter-war period to be strikingly unconstructive. Malaya and Borneo were in some sense British Malaya and British Borneo. But no real changes were made to the pre-war political and constitutional structures. Burma felt the effect of Indian reforms, but Malaya did not. Sir Lawrence Guillemard, the post-war High Commissioner, sought to economize and rationalize, but the obstacles, both institutional and personal, were too great. Nor was there any clear perception of the future for the Chinese in Malaya. Chinese nationalism made an impact; the Communist element particularly worrying the colonial authorities.[26] The Chinese were becoming more domesticated. But at the end of the decade Sir Hugh Clifford, Guillemard's successor, could insist that Malaya was a collection of Malay monarchies which had to remain so.

These States were, when the British Government was invited by their Rulers and Chiefs to set their troubled houses in order, Muhammadan monarchies. Such they are today, and such they must continue to be. No mandate has ever been extended to us by Rajas, Chiefs, or people to vary the system of government which has existed in these territories from time immemorial; and in these days, when democratic and socialist theories are spreading like an infection, bringing with them, too often, not peace but a sword, I feel it incumbent upon me to emphasize . . . the utter inapplicability of any form of democratic or popular government to the circumstances of these States. . . .[27]

Such a view was in a sense convenient for the British; it would even attract the accusation that they divided and ruled. It might be better seen in another light. Malaya was of great importance to the British: their interest in it had increased, and they would need it in the future. They would also need to tackle the demands of modernization and democratization. Meanwhile, however, those demands were not urgent. Malaya was a land of different communities that lived apart: a plural society where they did not clash. It was tempting not to tackle the problems that were neither urgent nor tractable. Divide-and-rule is too positive a description. 'Sufficient unto the day' was again the watchword. British policy had been pragmatic in the nineteenth century: it did not deal too much in plans, it did what had to be done. Now the limited chance any new policy had of success was an argument against attempting one. It might stir up trouble and, moreover, make Britain's problems more evident. The attempts at reconstruction after the Second World War were to illustrate the difficulties.

In Sarawak, again, the 1920s suggested the need for change, but change was avoided. The Colonial Office had been increasingly unhappy with the old-fashioned rule of the second Raja, Sir Charles Brooke, and his unwillingness to promote development. But the hopes it had nurtured of influencing his son and successor, Vyner, were to be disappointed. He proved a master of evasion, and the Colonial Office was always awaiting a favourable moment for increasing its influence that never came. Too abrupt an approach, it recognized, might disrupt the Raj and undermine its authority. That made it difficult to reshape the role of this collaborator. So did his special position in British society: the Brookes were eccentric, but still had to be treated as gentlemen. The establishment of the League and its agencies urged the British Government to fulfil its responsibilities in Sarawak, but did not make it easier to do so. The Raja, as his brother Bertram put it, was in a very different position from a Governor.

With Sarawak, a pledge by the Government is a personal undertaking by the Raja, who is looked to by the whole community to honour it, and it is on his power to do this that the whole security of the present system of

Government rests. If he ever had to go back on his word because of 'high policy' at home it would be the beginning of the end of the present régime because it would be realized that matters of internal administration are not in fact, as they are in theory, in his hands.

Bertram Brooke added that 'the existence of the L. of N. and the idea that "high policy" may at any moment necessitate some criticism of local government makes one feel very wobbly . . .'.[28] No state could fully escape the consequences of the League's existence, a Colonial Office official observed. But Britain tried to limit its intervention, an objective entirely consistent with its approach to international affairs and its determination itself to monitor the development of states within the overall framework it sought to sustain.

One proposal, developed by the Colonial Office after consultation with Guillemard on his return to London, was to appoint a Resident or Adviser in the style of the Unfederated Malay States (UMS). 'I doubt', Sir G. Grindle wrote, 'whether it would be safe to go further for a generation but an arrangement on the above lines would secure all we really want—good government and a proper judiciary—without being in any way derogatory to the Brooke family.'[29] In fact Sir Lawrence's successor did not raise the issue. The Colonial Office itself displayed little interest in the Company's territory to the north, though inclusion of Sarawak and North Borneo in the Malay States confederation was, Grindle thought, 'no doubt their ultimate fate'.[30]

Netherlands India, the Philippines, and French Indo-China in the 1920s

Elsewhere in South-East Asia in the 1920s, it seemed that change could be avoided or accommodated. Dutch fears of Japan, Frank Ashton-Gwatkin reported to the Foreign Office, had died down. But they had not disappeared, and not many supported the current policy of 'hectic cordiality', designed to balance the power of 'conflicting rivals'. The long-standing Dutch 'envy and distrust' of the British at Singapore had, Ashton-Gwatkin felt, diminished, which was 'gratifying; for the interests of the British and the Dutch are essentially similar, and we are clearly concerned in the maintenance of Dutch rule and the prestige of the white races in the archipelago . . .'. At present, he concluded, the danger was not from Japan, but from the native and Communist movement. With

Netherlands India, the Philippines, and British India all on the way to autonomy, 'the future of South-East Asia is in an unsettled condition and requires careful and anxious watching. The result of a further upheaval, such as a Japanese–American war, might be most unwelcome both to us and to the Dutch. . . .'[31] Short of such an international conflagration, however, the fires of nationalism could be contained. The Dutch did so very effectively in the 1920s, snuffing out the 'Communist' rebellion, insulating the middle-class nationalists from the masses, and employing intelligence and police effectively. It was in a sense a new way of applying their traditional policy, using the minimum of force, but engaging in extensive manipulation.

For the Dutch, the British had indeed some responsibility, though perhaps exerting little control. In respect of the Americans in the Philippines, both responsibility and control were less. But under the Republican administrations of the 1920s, they seemed at least more likely to stay, thus insulating South-East Asia from worse threats. Within the Philippines the Republican adminis-trations conceded less than the Democrat F. B. Harrison to the nationalists led by Osmena and Quezon, while yet provoking no real challenge in response. Like other colonial rulers, the Americans were nervous about Communism, and in 1931 Governor-General Davis was to suggest formal co-operation among them to find out 'if the whole movement is headed up in one place'.[32]

In Indo-China the French remained fully in control, allowing too little scope for moderate or co-operative elements and so giving the élite a reason to turn to international Communism, and the Communists among them reason to organize the masses. Varenne, a Governor-General appointed by the Left Cartel, at-tempted to affirm 'the meaning of our civilizing mission'. In a speech in Hanoi in December 1925, he speculated about the future of Indo-China. 'If peace is kept, if the people of Indo China can develop freely . . . she can hope to attain one day the fullest and highest of existences, that of a nation. . . .'[33] But if the words were vague the actions were unhelpful: Pham Quynh, a moderate nationalist, sought recognition for a Vietnam People's Progressivist Union in vain.

In Siam the royal regime renegotiated the unequal treaties, but it was concerned to secure a status more equal with that of the Western powers, not to overthrow them, and the British found the adjustment easier to make than in China. The Thais still accepted Britain's leadership: more students went to Britain than elsewhere. But influence depended on power and prestige. The position was changed at the end of the decade by the onset of the depression and then by the Manchurian incident of 1931.

The Depression and the Manchurian Incident

The 1920s had seen change within China itself. The KMT and CCP had allied in order to reunify China and undo the unequal treaties, and had enjoyed success in the south and centre. Entrenched in the nineteenth-century system of unequal treaties in those regions, the British had borne the brunt of their attacks. But they characteristically if belatedly came to believe that they should try to accommodate Chinese nationalism and put their interests on a more collaborative basis. This was the purport of the Foreign Secretary Austen Chamberlain's policy of 1926, and it was in keeping with the general thrust of British policy in East Asia as elsewhere since the war, if not indeed since the beginning of the twentieth century. The essentials could be retained by adjustment within a more or less stable international system. That was in keeping with the Washington spirit, though the Washington powers had hoped for a longer time-span and looked for a less embattled approach from the Chinese.

With the Japanese the Chinese were to find adjustment less easy. While the focus of the nationalists and their communist allies was on central China, the Japanese did not feel threatened, and the Shidehara policy of 'China Friendship' could be sustained. It was in accordance with the Washington spirit and consistent with the policy of their erstwhile ally, the British. But when the Northern March reached the north, the Japanese became more anxious over the protection of their rights and interests. Nor was the break between the KMT and CCP that emerged with their very success likely to reduce Japanese anxiety: the KMT, anxious to show that the break would not mean that they would neglect China's status, sought the end of unequal treaties as demonstratively as ever, if not more so. The focus was Manchuria, and there the tension was apparent from 1928. Extremists in the Kwantung army had assassinated the Manchurian warlord and his son hoisted the KMT flag. But it was the onset of the depression that made the next incident decisive. This time Japanese troops secured control of Manchuria, and the government in Tokyo lost control.

The realism of the Meiji phase had been modified by the

internationalism of Shidehara. In turn this had given way to a more aggressive approach inconsistent with the Washington spirit and with the kind of adjustments the British envisaged. Increasingly it invoked, moreover, a Japanese nationalism that took up and reshaped early pan-Asian ideals and was conceived in terms of the reordering of the East Asian region. The states of the area would find their position within a Japanese sphere of influence. They would win a new status. They would not be colonies, nor would they be independent. The Japanese would reconcile nationalism and imperialism in a new way, by establishing puppet states. Their programme was, of course, designed to displace that of the British, as well, of course, as that of the Americans and the Russians.

The depression affected other powers involved in the fate of South-East Asia, including the British, the Americans, and the Russians. The opportunity for the last to take advantage of the capitalist crisis was limited by its own absorption in Stalin's revolution, though the planning that revolution claimed to involve was to prove an attractive example. The Americans, too, became more concerned with their own fate. The British finally shifted away from free trade towards imperial preference and made a modest start with colonial development. They sought, however, to protect their international financial position. A collapse of confidence in sterling they indeed saw as a threat to their whole position in the world.

The depression and the Manchurian incident affected South-East Asia in general and in special ways. South-East Asia was, of course, generally affected by the economic downturn that the crisis in America precipitated: many of its markets collapsed; hardship, unrest, and repression ensued. More generally, the depression can be seen as a major break in a phase of world-wide economic expansion that had lasted more than a century. That century had seen the shaping of many of the relationships of contemporary South-East Asia, social, political, and constitutional, and they were in that respect all challenged by economic collapse. South-East Asia was also generally affected by the Manchurian incident. It added to international insecurity. Whatever the rights or wrongs of the matter, it showed the weakness of the League and of the post-war settlements. They could not be upheld. But the South-East Asian *status quo* was still not directly attacked. Instead it was subject to new tensions. The overall framework remained, but came under new pressures, varying with the territory concerned.

The Extension of the East Asian Conflict

In East Asia, of course, the Manchurian episode became only one among others, and changes there interleaved with those in Europe, including the emergence of the Nazi regime in Germany in 1933. While complete success evaded them, the objectives of the Japanese continued to expand throughout the decade. In 1934, with the so-called Amau doctrine, they spoke in terms of a Monroe doctrine for East Asia, paralleling that doctrine the United States had more than a century before adopted in respect of Latin America. Adopting Fundamental Principles of National Policy in 1936, Japan committed itself not only to establishing a lasting peace in East Asia, by holding back both the Soviet and the maritime powers and, it was conceived, securing as a result its dominance over China, but also committed itself to taking 'footsteps' in South-East Asia, of particular interest because Netherlands India was a source of oil. This now all-important fuel the Japanese normally drew from American and Caribbean sources, and the supply was also dependent on the United States because its navy commanded the Pacific. The same year the Japanese enhanced their contact with Nazi Germany through the Anti-Comintern Pact, designed, so far as they were concerned, to make the Soviet Union more cautious in East Asia, and the colonial powers more ready to make concessions in South-East Asia.

The Japanese were indeed aware of, though perhaps slow to recognize fully, the magnitude of the tasks they imposed on themselves. But, despite the doubts of the general staff, the Marco Polo Bridge incident of July 1937 escalated into an undeclared war with China. By the end of 1937, the Japanese were attacking Chiang Kai-shek's capital, Nanking. The following year, the premier, Prince Konoe, was openly proclaiming that the aim was the establishment of a New Order in East Asia. He envisaged displacing Chiang Kai-shek with a puppet ruler, applying a model already developed in Manchuria to China itself.

The United States, deeply affected by the depression, was sympathetic to China's cause, but not convinced that it called for American intervention. The British, hugely overcommitted, from 1933 facing a threat in Europe, were unable to compromise with Japan for fear of losing US sympathy, but also unable to offer effective opposition. 'A threatening situation in Europe was capable of being multiplied in gravity by the difference between our present relations with Japan and those we enjoyed in 1914,' Neville

Chamberlain declared in 1937. 'There was now the perpetual danger that trouble in Europe might be Japan's opportunity to take some step to our disadvantage in the Far East. . . .'[34] The Brussels Conference of 1937–8 did nothing effective to stop the Japanese. But the West tended to depreciate Japan's chances of success in any case. They downplayed its determination and its capacity. Not only was it difficult for them to help the Chinese; the Chinese did not really need it. 'In the long run they will be more than a match for the Japanese and the extent of Japan's military dominion on the mainland will be the measure of her difficulties in the years to come,' Sir John Brenan wrote at the British Foreign Office.[35] Gestures of disapproval, China's endurance, and limited aid, these would suffice to bring the Japanese to a halt. That was a misinterpretation. The Japanese did not give up. Meanwhile, it was thought, their involvement in China might at least keep them from South-East Asia. But even that proved a mistaken estimate. Frustration there contributed to the move south, though that was not its main source.

The Japanese were seeking drastically to change the international order in East Asia. The British believed it might be sustained. They now had little power themselves to interpose. But they were aware of the strength of Chinese nationalism, which to some extent they had sought to accommodate, and believed that it would not reconcile itself to the vaunted new order of the Japanese. Japanese aggression helped to identify the Chinese with the Western powers and their view of the world. The Japanese overestimated the effect of Western support in keeping alive Chinese resistance. In a sense the British, who had once relied on Japan to stem the Russian advance, now relied on the Chinese to stem the Japanese. They challenged the British programme less. Indeed it seemed that they helped to blunt the challenge and to absorb the energies of the Japanese, whose determination the British were in any case inclined to depreciate.

South-East Asia in the 1930s

The fate of South-East Asia was seen to be connected with the conflict to the north. It might keep the Japanese occupied. If they triumphed, they would then be in a position to exert pressure on South-East Asia. There, too, they could benefit from the increased prestige they would have gained, while taking advantage of the humiliation their triumph would involve not only for the Chinese but for the Western powers in China. The Western powers did not expect them to triumph, but were anxious to avoid the loss of prestige their overrunning of coastal China and the foreign concessions brought. There was also the risk that frustration in China, coupled with events elsewhere, might after all prompt the Japanese to concentrate on South-East Asia more rather than less.

In South-East Asia the colonial structure indeed endured till the attack by the Japanese at the opening of the Pacific war. In some sense that justified the attitude of the British, that the threats within the system were less than the threats from outside, and that if the international framework were sustained, the system would not fall. Not surprisingly they were especially sensitive to links between outside opposition and internal opposition. They were concerned about the activities of the Chinese, Nationalist as well as Communist, more than with the penetration of the Japanese. In East Asia Chinese nationalism was in a sense co-opted into the defence of the overall framework, and it was thought likely to absorb and exhaust the energies of Japanese imperialism. In South-East Asia, however, Chinese nationalism could be disruptive, stirring up ethnic antagonisms, provoking counter-nationalisms, seeming to create states within states, and sheltering or giving a cause to the Communists. The British were still concerned, too, about Islam, though less than before, about India, about American opinion, and about opinion at home, where the new India Act provoked bitter debate. On the whole, even so, they felt that the situation could be handled, either by timely gestures or by maintaining the *status quo*. They were, however, generally unable or unwilling to carry through larger changes. Such were difficult. The fact that they did not seem essential made that less worrying. But inactivity was in a sense the result of weakness. Activity might show it up.

The Commonwealth of the Philippines

There were nevertheless alarming signs on the international front. The Philippines was not, of course, a responsibility of the British, but the presence of the Americans there, in succession to the Spaniards, had been a guarantee of the *status quo* in the rest of South-East Asia against Japanese penetration beyond Formosa, and also an indication of American interest in the future of East Asia as a whole. The depression was to reduce the American commitment to the Philippines at the very time that the Manchurian incident seemed to make it more desirable. During the 1930s, as the Japanese advanced on the continent, the American policies towards the Philippines gave the British little reassurance. The Filipino leadership was itself apprehensive. The Filipinos had long sought independence from the United States, though often nervous about their ability to sustain it, given their economic dependence and their fear of a Japanese threat to the *status quo*. American policy had committed itself to independence when the Filipinos were ready for it. No date had been set, and the Republican administrations were more inclined than the Democrats to argue that they were not ready for it. The depression introduced another factor and urged a decision. The privileged competition of Philippine sugar was politically unacceptable and independence would be a way to end it. In this somewhat unheroic style the Filipino dream began to come true, but it had its nightmarish side. Independence could not be refused. But would it come at the cost of not only poverty but of insecurity? A month after his non-recognition statement on Manchuria, Henry L. Stimson, the US Secretary of State, a former Governor-General, wrote that if the American market and American influence were withdrawn, 'it is the practically unanimous consensus of all responsible observers that economic chaos and political and social anarchy would result, followed ultimately by domination of the Philippines by some foreign power probably either China or Japan . . .'.[36] Granting independence now would further undermine the stability of the Washington system and encourage Japanese aggressiveness. 'It is like having your own people at home take off your pants when you are going out on parade.'[37]

The British Vice-Consul, L. H. Foulds, offered somewhat similar views. A Philippine Republic would be ruled by an oligarchy, against which the masses would have little protection. The Moros,

if they re-armed themselves, which would not be unduly difficult for a race of adept smugglers, . . . could easily become as great a thorn in the flesh of the Filipinos as they were of the Spaniards, and if trouble eventuated calling for repressive action from Manila, its repercussions in the Mohammedan world might be a matter of concern to Powers with Mohammedan subjects, particularly Great Britain. . . .

No doubt the Philippine Republic would be 'at least as good as some of the impecunious Republics of Central and South America', but the international context was different. That had been made evident with Japanese intervention in Manchuria and Shanghai.

The future would depend not only on the Filipinos and the Japanese, but also on the Americans. Stimson, and before him Governor-General Leonard Wood, had argued that withdrawal would encourage disorders within other colonial possessions and so contribute to instability in Asia. Such prognostications 'are usually made with India in mind, but one fails to see how the changed status of a small Oriental dependency could make any perceptible addition to the immensely complex problems of India . . .'. Withdrawal would, however, be unsettling in another sense. It

would be in effect a shirking by the United States of her share of the duty of maintaining the peace of the Western Pacific area and the influence of Western civilisation there, and it might be regarded also as a violation of the spirit underlying the agreements made at Washington in 1922. A feeling of unsafety might well be communicated to many authorities and peoples as for example in the Dutch East Indies and the British Dominions in the Antipodes. . . .

A 'politically weak state' might be the prey of Japan, or of 'communistic activity and intrigue'.

If there is any truth at all in the conception of Great Britain and the United States as the principal joint guardians of Western civilisation and of peace in the Far East, American withdrawal could not fail to impose a greatly added burden on the shoulders of Great Britain, whose Imperial outposts would then become if possible even more vitally important key positions than they now are. . . .

Foulds argued that if the United States left the British would have to return: he recalled their conquest of Manila in 1762.[38]

It was thought such a notion would provoke Filipino opposition; but Quezon himself took up the idea that the Philippines might join the British Commonwealth. 'The prospect of receiving a new Dominion into the fold', wrote Robert Craigie of the Foreign Office, 'will no doubt warm the cockles of the D[ominion] O[ffice]'s heart—but such a liability would cause less enthusiasm amongst the Service Departments!'[39] Britain did not want increased responsibilities, flattering though they might seem to be, and coincident with the notion of an emergent world-wide system of which the Commonwealth was a paradigm. What it wanted in this time of crisis was that an American guarantee of the Philippines should continue. The guarantee would be a reassurance over East Asia which they could not obtain directly. It would also directly contribute to the security of South-East Asia. Even more than in the 1890s there was reason not to entrust the future of the Philippines other than to a friendly great power.

'The Filipinos are not the only people who would like to be independent and yet defended by and at the expense of an altruistic Great Power who asked nothing in return....' 'One shudders to think that the day may come when the Philippines will be a member of the League, and their security become yet another obligation of the British navy....' So ran Foreign Office comment late in 1935.[40] But despite discouragement, Quezon did not abandon his hopes of British support till the Munich crisis finally underlined Britain's true position. Under the Tydings-McDuffie Act the Commonwealth of the Philippines was set up in 1935, as a step towards independence in ten years' time. It was not itself an independent regime, and in particular it had no power to conduct foreign policy. That, of course, made it hard for it to prepare for independence in the coming years. Complaining of 'the extremely unsatisfactory position of our Islands during the Commonwealth period because of their inability to properly provide for the future',[41] Quezon could make only the most indirect approaches to other powers, and the British, perhaps not altogether reluctantly, had a reason for evading them, though recognizing the need to keep on good terms with a man likely to dominate the Philippines when it did become independent. Their best hope was that the Americans would remain committed to the Philippines. Quezon could do little but work for that, too. Indeed their policy, both on the economic and security front, began to change. At least they had not abandoned the Philippines.

The policy that the British began to envisage towards an independent Philippines had some parallel with the policy they developed towards independent Siam. In China itself, the British had in the 1920s resolved that their interests could best be defended by coming to terms with the nationalist regime rather than insisting on the rights and privileges secured under pressure from the imperial regime. The alternative might after all be something more extreme, and more communistic. It was, as ever, better to adjust rather than to defy or to abandon, and better to take on new collaborators if they could be found. The same might be true of the Philippines. If a 'transfer of power' were successfully effected there, the British could work with the new power-holders, provided the international framework survived and provided British prestige was not undermined by obvious defeat. Showing that they would be prepared to do so would make it more likely that they would be able to do so. This they had sought to show in Siam.

Thailand and French Indo-China

There, Britain had long experience of working with an independent regime. It had accepted the terms the absolute monarchy had offered in the nineteenth century and it accepted the adjustments the monarchy had begun to make in the twentieth century. The depression precipitated a change of regime. The absolute monarchy had coped with imperialism; it could not cope with the depression.[42] With the coup of 1932, the monarchy was constitutionalized. In fact, power fell into the hands of the military and civilian Promoters. For a time they were apprehensive of foreign intervention. But the British had no such intention. They hoped to win over the new leaders. They also hoped to reduce any sympathy those leaders had for Japan. The new envoy Josiah Crosby, was determined to make it plain that Britain wished 'the new Siam all success in the process of working out her destinies. . . .'[43] He recognized that Japanese rivalry could not be taken lightly. With the fading of the idea that Britain and France might intervene, the Thais began to see that their independence might be threatened by Japan's predominance. But they would make Japan 'one of the pivotal points'[44] round which their foreign policy must turn, sending more students thither, and seeking advisers thence.

Siam had abstained from censuring Japan over Manchuria at the League of Nations. But, provided Britain's bluff were not called, nor its prestige destroyed by blatant revelation of its lack of power, the Siamese seemed unlikely to go beyond cautious adjustment, despite the pan-Thai urges espoused especially though not exclusively by the military Promoters. The British would not be called upon to appease this 'revolution' which once more they considered would be a threat only if the international framework were undermined by others. At the Foreign Office, A. W. G. Randall had commented that 'direct methods of counteracting the Japanese penetration are hardly possible but it may be suggested that if our general prestige in the Far East is clearly maintained, the danger of our influence in Siam being destroyed would be obviated'. 'It illustrates the kind of thing that will happen to an even greater extent,' C. W. Orde echoed, 'if we do not resist Japanese pretensions to behave as they like in the Far East.' Sir Victor Wellesley thought the Japanese held the 'trump cards. . . . They are determined to become, and will become, the dominant power in the Far East. I don't see how we can prevent it.' Lord Stanhope, the Parliamentary Under-Secretary, suggested Japan could be kept lean. 'Japan's finances are far from being in a flourishing condition. She depends on China for a large part of her trade, and China is not prepared to eat out of Japan's hand unless she is urged by other Powers to do so. . . .'[45]

Pan-Thai territorial aspirations were directed more at French Indo-China than at the British territories. There the French remained unyielding, even given (or perhaps because of) their deteriorating position in Europe. The depression had contributed to unrest in Vietnam, but, blamed on Bolshevism, that had been violently repressed.[46] The French were determined to contain opposition, rather than make concessions to it, and convinced that they could. Their measures continued to drive opposition left, and in effect to contribute to Communist leadership. In the longer term that was to prove a liability for the French: when they did become prepared to look for collaborators, they could find none of any standing. In the short term it secured them the assistance of the British in their contention with international Communism: Ho Chi Minh was arrested in Hong Kong in 1931.[47]

Japan and Netherlands India

Something of the same pattern was evident in Netherlands India. The uprisings of 1926–7 had already speeded withdrawal from the Ethical Policy of the early twentieth century, and the Dutch were effectively limiting contacts between the urban nationalists and the mass of the people. The depression increased the poverty of the workers and the peasants, though the collapse of the international sugar market was not an unmitigated disaster. The Dutch were driven, however, to reduce the inflow of cheap Japanese goods, abandoning the free trade policy which had been adopted as one of the means of winning international acceptance of their rule. Whatever effect it had internally, it could only worsen relations with the Japanese.

Together with the mutiny on *De Zeven Provincien*, Manchuria, furthermore, had already alarmed the Dutch. It marked a shift in Japanese policy which the Dutch feared might apply in South-East Asia as in North-East Asia, and challenge the identic notes as it had challenged the nine-power Washington treaty itself. Their possession of oil—in Sumatra and eastern Borneo—enhanced their feeling of vulnerability. A sudden strike by the Japanese say on Tarakan would be hard to resist, and they would be hard to dislodge once established. Nor could the British promise help with any assurance of delivery.

The 'essential motive' in Japan's policy towards Netherlands India, wrote R. Allen at the Foreign Office in 1934, seemed to be the need for oil. 'Without oil, her navy can neither defend her coasts nor protect the access of her raw materials on which, to a greater extent than any other country, her whole economic structure depends.' Ordinarily, Japan would be content to continue to buy and store oil. 'There will, however, always be the risk of a moment when from sheer nervousness, she may do something drastic, of incalculable consequences, in order to guard against what she conceives to be a menace to her supplies.' He thought that Japanese action might take the form of stirring up the nationalists, and then stepping in to protect their own interests. 'The Japanese have shown themselves past-master at this type of intervention in China, and it has never been easy to dislodge them from a position so acquired.' Moreover, it was hard to decide whether such intervention was to be treated as an act of war. Allen did not believe the Americans would in such a case assist the British, the Dutch, and the dominions: the trend in US policy was towards disinteresting itself in East Asia.

To console us for the fear that America 'will leave us in the lurch', there are two factors to be remembered. On the one hand, Japan will certainly not move against the N.E.I. as long as America retains any strategical hold, however nominal, over the Philippines. On the other, and paradoxical as this may sound, the more America keeps out of the Far East the less danger I think there is that Japan will ever do anything foolish in East-Indian waters.

Much depended on US attitudes. 'Much again depends on the commercial policy we pursue and the discretion with which Japan's trade is checked and hindered in foreign countries. . . .' And much depended on other factors—on Japan's success in Manchuria and on relations with Russia, for example.

Frank Ashton-Gwatkin thought a Japanese attack on Netherlands India 'a very remote contingency except in the case of a European war, or civil war in Great Britain and a collapse of British power'. To take all Netherlands India was a vast task; even if only parts of

Borneo were seized, the transport of oil to Japan would be subject to attack. Japan had guaranteed the inviolability of Netherlands India in 1922. Manchuria was a very different case. Indeed, the Japanese adventure there lessened the likelihood of pressure south. In the more likely case of war with Russia, Japan could get oil from the United States as well as Netherlands India.[48]

An approach from the Dutch Prime Minister, Hendrikus Colijn, in 1936 indicated a growing concern in the Netherlands, but also a presumption that, if Netherlands India were attacked, Britain would come to the assistance of the Dutch. The Chiefs of Staff were agreed 'that the integrity of the Dutch East Indies is vital to our security in the Far East, and the occupation of the Dutch Islands near Singapore by a hostile Power would be a most serious event'. But they did not recommend a guarantee of military support. It would cause the Dutch to rely on Britain and 'take little or no action to improve their defences', while the British, with a one-power standard, were in no position to undertake any additional commitment.[49]

Colijn had also asked for advice so that he might 'find out which form of defence would most usefully supplement British defence measures in these waters'.[50] While Britain had overall responsibility for sustaining the framework of power in South-East Asia as elsewhere, its relations with the territories under its patronage differed from its relations with the territories within its empire. The Chiefs of Staff commented:

If the Netherlands East Indies were one of our Dominions whom we were advising on defence, we should point out that their security must rest ultimately on the power of the British fleet to control sea communications in the area . . . and that their primary responsibility was to provide for their own local defence during the period before relief. We should therefore recommend that, after local defence requirements had been met, some form of naval contribution would be in the best interest of the Dominion.

But this line could not be adopted with the Dutch.

Apart from the technical difficulties of Dutch naval forces co-operating with our own, there is no agreement or alliance to guarantee our assistance in the event of war; and there is no Dutch fleet to send to the Far East. Hence the problem for the Dutch is essentially one of obtaining the most effective local defence for the money they are prepared to expend. Their object will be to oppose such resistance to the Japanese as will make aggression a difficult and risky operation. The Dutch, however, will realise that, unable as they are to face the Japanese fleet, their security must ultimately rest upon the intervention of the British fleet. In considering, therefore, proposals for local defence, the possibility of British assistance must to some extent be taken into account so that co-operation may be facilitated should the possibility materialise.[51]

The outbreak of the Sino-Japanese war revived the issue of collaboration with the Dutch. The Chiefs of Staff remained unwilling to take on a commitment to aid them in the event of a Japanese attack. At the Foreign Office there were rather different views.

We are losing prestige—for nothing. If war came, we should have to prevent a Japanese seizure of the N.E.I. Why leave it to the last moment and then improvise inefficient and expensive measures, when we could do the same now at less cost, and by doing so probably ward off the danger. We must show some spirit if we wish to retain the respect (and valuable support) of the small nations, and show the gangster Powers that we are 'a strong man armed'.[52]

Essentially the Dutch continued to rely, on the one hand, on the international *status quo*, and on the other, on their ability to contain opposition within Netherlands India. There was no attempt to win positive support for their regime among Indonesians and to identify them with it as external conditions became more adverse. The Dutch were second only to the French in their refusal to support or to offer realistic opportunities to moderate elements in the native leadership. No emphasis on internal peace and order, nor attempts to win the support of new élites, could have sustained Dutch rule when the Japanese overturned the whole colonial order in South-East Asia. The prime factor, as the British perceived, was the maintenance of the framework: they also saw how little power they had to maintain it, and how difficult it was to elicit and accept what co-operation their client could afford. The attitude of their client to its colonial charges—and the arrogance of Governor-General de Jonge contrasted with the doubts of Prime Minister Colijn—was something that, as ever, the British could do little to affect. But it was of more significance in the longer term than in the short term.

Clementi in Malaya and Borneo

The British themselves were somewhat more positive in Malaya, but too readily abandoned attempts at nation-building in face of evident obstacles. Those attempts did not relate particularly to the new problems created by the depression or by the Manchurian episode, though indirectly they were affected by them. They marked a new approach to the problem of creating a more unified Malaya, as a basis for future economic, political, and constitutional development. The depression may have played a part in stressing the need to enhance economic opportunity and effect government savings. The Manchurian episode and the subsequent Japan–China conflict helped at once to domesticate more Chinese in Malaya and to make the community focus its public attention on the fate of China itself. Both these trends affected British policy.

Pressed forward by the impatient High Commissioner, Sir Cecil Clementi, however, the policy, aiming at more, achieved less than might have been expected. Hoping to take the opposition by storm, he found that it overwhelmed him. The Settlements feared subordination to Kuala Lumpur, the UMS to the FMS and the Malays to the Chinese. The Colonial Office afforded him no support: he had only stirred up trouble. The visiting Under-Secretary of State, Sir Samuel Wilson, had to reassert the fundamental aims of British policy in Malaya:

It seems clear that the maintenance of the position, authority, and prestige of the Malay Rulers must always be a cardinal point in British policy: and the encouragement of indirect rule will probably prove the greatest safeguard against the political submersion of the Malays which would result from the development of popular government on western lines. . . .

The aim should be a genuine federal system, which all the Malay states might join, but the interests of non-Malays must not suffer by decentralization.[53] Clementi's successor could make only cautious advances towards decentralization, stopping well short of the recentralization that was the ultimate objective, one consistent with the long-term overall imperial policy of establishing larger units that could largely fend for themselves.

The policy is difficult to appraise. Were the British only too happy to revert to a pro-Malay policy, allying with the weak, making themselves indispensable as an arbitral power among Malays and immigrants, and curbing a population that seemed too prone to KMT/CCP enthusiasms? Was it divide-and-rule? Or was it that a change of policy provoked so much opposition that it did not seem worth pressing ahead, especially as it did not appear to be essential immediately to do so? There was still no threat internally. The Malays and Chinese and Indians lived apart; they did not clash nor jointly oppose. Nor was the external threat immediate enough itself to urge a problematic change in Malayan policy. Such an attempt at change might not succeed. It might only display the weakness of the British and their incapacity to carry change through: better to leave alone.

The confidence of the British in the international situation was in fact limited. The base in Singapore was gradually completed, but their capacity to reinforce it effectively diminished, and its ability to defend itself while the reinforcement was on the way diminished also. They were unwilling to make promises to the Dutch, though aware that Netherlands India and Singapore stood together, and alarmed lest the Americans left the Philippines. They appeared to have persuaded themselves that there was a chance that the Japanese would not act, especially if they concentrated on China. They also seemed to have thought that a business-as-usual policy had its own validity. Not only would it boost Britain's depleted economic resources, the sinews of war in Europe or elsewhere, but the very failure to make change would demonstrate a confidence in the future that was itself, they conceived, of political value, while an attempt at change would risk failure and show weakness.

Though conscious that the regimes there were out-of-date, the British effected little change in British Borneo. Clementi wanted action there, too, but again he failed to secure it. He hoped to drive the four Borneo territories together, and to this end he needed to assert a more effective British control in Sarawak and North Borneo. The Company's territory seemed the easier target. Its venture had never been very profitable, and the depression made the Directors more ready to contemplate being bought out. But the very fact that made the bargain possible on their side made it impossible on the Government's side. It was not prepared to spend money buying out the Company. Nor was the Singapore Government, which Clementi also tackled. 'I can't understand Sir C. Clementi's mentality!' the Under-Secretary exclaimed. 'If there was ever a more inopportune time to make a suggestion of this kind I don't believe he could have found it. . . .' He indicated what the Directors hoped to get; '. . . but he does not refer to the additional expenditure which would be necessary if the Malayan Government were to take over the administration; when everyone would expect about twice as much (I mean in the way of roads, schools, hospitals etc.), if not more, than they now get from the Company!'[54]

Clementi's hope of establishing a stronger influence in Sarawak got nowhere. The Colonial Office had sought it earlier particularly as it became aware of the gulf that appeared to exist between the third Raja's standards of government and the standards expected of British dependencies in the inter-war world. But they had not found a way past the Raja's evasiveness, and doubted, too, whether the realm would survive the deflation of the prestige of its ruler produced by placing him under a system of advice and guidance. The same point was eloquently made by the Raja's brother in response to Clementi's moves. It would be better to bring the Raj to an end than to engage in half measures: 'the paragraph in British history representing the Brooke association with Sarawak should be a clean-run one, rather than . . . depict a gradual decline in authority, or a sudden cessation' as a result of incompetence in the hereditary rulers.[55]

The inter-war British Government was not in the business of taking such risks in respect of its collaborators. Attempts at change might only reveal its impossibility. Britain would have weakened its position rather than strengthened it. In the 1930s, in Borneo as in Malaya, it did not altogether abandon reform, but it pursued a very modest degree of change. The main Sarawak initiatives came, as the Colonial Office had thought they must, from within the Raj itself. The result was that the centenary of the Raj was celebrated by the introduction of a constitution, which modified the Raja's autocracy by imposing bureaucratic constraints and procedures upon him. The same year the Raja agreed to receive an adviser from the Colonial Office. But his role was to be less extensive even than that of advisers in the UMS. The year was 1941. The British Government had taken a step towards increasing its influence in Sarawak on the very eve of the destruction of its capacity to exercise it.

The Burma Constitution

In Burma the British Government had, thanks to Indian precedent and Burman pressure, already embarked on a programme of reform. To this it adhered. The impact of the depression was considerable and helped to bring about the major Saya San rebellion. But that did not deflect the British from their course, while it gave the Burman nationalists a new occasion for pressing constitutional change upon them. The Manchurian incident, and the subsequent Japanese expansion in China, seemed to have had little impact on British thinking in respect of Burma. The building of the Burma Road was, however, to reduce its insulation and heighten Japanese interest in the area. It also helped to keep KMT resistance alive.

In the meantime it was perhaps easier in the Burman case to stick to the path of constitutional change already started on, rather than abandon it, just as elsewhere it was easier not to start. The same consideration of prestige might also apply. To abandon reform once started would show weakness and incapacity. If in Malaya and Borneo it was better not to take the risk, in Burma the course was already set, and the risk of abandoning it might be greater. Burma thus secured a constitution of its own. Separated from India, it began to govern itself from 1937, though the Governor still retained substantial powers and controlled the non-Burman Scheduled Areas. Indeed the development of participatory self-government showed up a further problem in shifting away from a colonial structure. Adjusting the terms of collaboration with one group could damage relations with another. San C. Po wrote:

The Karens ... have not appreciated the advantage of the Reforms Scheme at all. In the first place it was with difficulty ... that Karen interests have been safeguarded by Communal representation. Communal interest should not enter into Democratic institutions, but are the members or communities of the embryo democratic institutions really sufficiently broad-minded to deal fairly with all communities and races? It is very doubtful. . . .[56]

Burma showed no greater capacity to defend itself against the invader than the other colonial territories. For too many Burmans the constitution of 1937 was only a step towards independence, and the British Government declined to promise even dominion status as the price of eliciting support. Perhaps the Burma case showed that the British had their priorities right after all. The preservation of the international framework came first. Creating loyal and integrated communities was far behind because it was a difficult if not impossible task the benefits of which were at best long-term. But that was the objective they selected during the war as the basis for their post-war policy.

Concluding Remarks

By September 1939, when war began in Europe, the old pattern had apparently not changed in South-East Asia, though the frivolity of Singapore social life seemed to some forced and fragile. An Australian was critical of British 'tidapathy'. Why worry?

It makes them content with the past, repugnant to change, impervious to the present, however repellent . . . they still think in terms of Kipling and Waterloo, and talk of Home and leave and football and bridge and make high-sounding but mostly meaningless speeches on birthday parades. But they refuse to see that down below them in Chinatown, among the squirming mass of Chinese and Indians and Javanese and Thai people and other racial mixtures, within a day's plane range of their pleasant homes, the crust of blind acceptance is bubbling.[57]

There were stirrings within the South-East Asian countries, but none seemed seriously to threaten the governments they faced. The challenges from without were, as the British at least had always thought, more significant. How would the Japanese, who had been associating themselves more closely with Germany under the Anti-Comintern Pact, react to the Nazi–Soviet pact of August? Would they remain absorbed in their conflict with China? Frustrated there, would they use the European war to undermine the colonial powers in South-East Asia?

Like the war itself, and in response to it, their policy was to go through a number of shifts. Its climax, reached only at the end of 1941, was the attack on American and British possessions that turned the European war into the Second World War. The Japanese triumph was astounding: colonial South-East Asia, already damaged by the compromises made by the Vichy French, was destroyed. The British, dominant since the early nineteenth century, were turned out: their own regimes and those of their allies and clients eliminated. But they determined to return.

Defeated so humiliatingly, the colonial powers were all nevertheless determined to make a comeback: perhaps all the more so. But, while some were optimistic, the task was impractical. And those among the British who thought the hesitations of the interwar period could now be brought to an end came to see that the prospects of the colonial powers were diminished post-war rather than expanded.

1. Quoted in Nadzan Haron, 'British Defence Policy in Malaya, 1874–1918', in K. M. de Silva et al. (eds.), *Asian Panorama*, New Delhi: Vikas, 1990, p. 443.

2. Aaron L. Friedberg, *The Weary Titan: Britain and the Experience of Relative Decline, 1895–1905*, Princeton: Princeton University Press, 1988, p. 298.

3. M. Rose, *Indonesia Free: A Political Biography of Mohammad Hatta*, Ithaca: Cornell Modern Indonesia Project, Cornell University, 1987, p. 74n.

4. Sho Kuwajima, *First World War and Asia: Indian Mutiny in Singapore (1915)*, Osaka: University of Foreign Studies, 1988, pp. 80, 128.

5. Quoted in Jerome Ch'en, *Yuan Shih K'ai*, London: Allen and Unwin, 1961, p. 192.

6. Don Dignan, *The Indian Revolutionary Problem in British Diplomacy 1914–1919*, New Delhi: Allied Publishers, 1983, pp. 50 ff.

7. R. J. Moore, *Liberalism and Indian Politics*, London: Arnold, 1966, p. 112.

8. A. Zimmern, *The Third British Empire*, London: Milford, 1934, p. 46.

9. Quoted in G. Bennett (ed.), *The Concept of Empire: Burke to Attlee 1774–1947*, London: Black, 1962, p. 390.

10. Quoted in L. Schapiro, *The Origin of the Communist Autocracy*, London: Bell, 1955, p. 109.

11. 'Communism and the East: Theses on the National and Colonial Questions', in R. D. Tucker (ed.), *The Lenin Anthology*, New York: Norton, 1975, p. 624.

12. Quoted in P. Dukes, *October and the World*, London: Macmillan, 1975, p. 96.

13. Quoted in N. Tarling, 'The Singapore Mutiny, 1915', *Journal of the Malaysian Branch Royal Asiatic Society*, LV, 2 (1982): 26.

14. Minute by Langley, n.d., F.O. 371/2691[235431/31466], Public Record Office, London.

15. W. F. Vella, *Chaiyo! King Vajiravudh and the Development of Thai Nationalism*, Honolulu: University Press of Hawaii, 1978, pp. 193 ff.

16. Vikron Koompirochana, 'Siam in British Foreign Policy 1855–1938: The Acquisition and the Relinquishment of British Extraterritorial Rights', Ph.D. thesis, Michigan State University, 1972, p. 206.

17. John F. Cady, *A History of Modern Burma*, Ithaca: Cornell University Press, 1958, pp. 199 ff.

18. Cf. C. F. Yong and R. B. McKenna, *The Kuomintang Movement in British Malaya, 1912–1949*, Singapore: Singapore University Press, 1990, pp. 51, 67–70.

19. Makino Shinken, quoted in Akira Iriye, *Pacific Estrangement*, Cambridge: Harvard University Press, 1972, p. 232.

20. Quoted in N. Tarling, '"A Vital British Interest": Britain, Japan, and the Security of Netherlands India during the Inter-War Period', *JSEAS*, 9, 2 (September 1978): 192.

21. Quoted in C. Thorne, *The Limits of Foreign Policy*, London: Hamish Hamilton, 1972, p. 51.

22. F. B. Harrison, *The Cornerstone of Philippine Independence*, New York: Century, 1922, p. 197.

23. Note on Memorandum by Ashton-Gwatkin, 10 October 1921, F.O. 371/6678[F2839/115/23], Public Record Office, London.

24. Chilton to Macdonald, 12 February 1924, 211, F.O. 371/9619[A1198/436/45], Public Record Office, London.

25. Campbell to Henderson, 28 November 1929, 2214, F.O. 371/13550 [A4849/3133/45], Public Record Office, London.

26. C. M. Turnbull, *A History of Singapore, 1819–1975*, Kuala Lumpur: Oxford University Press, 1977, pp. 134–5.

27. Quoted in R. Emerson, *Malaysia*, New York: Macmillan, 1937, pp. 174–5.

28. Bertram Brooke to Paskin, 29 January 1925, C.O. 531/18[8273], Public Record Office, London.

29. Minute, 1 December 1927, C.O. 531/20[31729], Public Record Office, London.

30. Minute, 8 April 1927, C.O. 531/20[31717], Public Record Office, London.

31. Memorandum, 8 September 1921, F.O. 371/6696[F3600/901/23], Public Record Office, London.

32. Quoted in T. Friend, *The Blue-Eyed Enemy*, Princeton: Princeton University Press, 1988, p. 46.

33. W. H. Frederick, 'Varenne and Indo-China 1925–6', in W. F. Vella (ed.), *Aspects of Vietnamese History*, Honolulu: University of Hawaii Press, 1973, p. 115.

34. Quoted in R. J. Pritchard, 'Far Eastern Influences upon British Strategy towards the Great Powers 1937–1939', Ph.D. thesis, University of London, 1979, p. 38.

35. Quoted in W. R. Louis, *British Strategy in the Far East 1919–1939*, Oxford: Clarendon, 1971, p. 249.

36. Stimson to Bingham, 15 February 1932, *New York Times*, 5 April 1932.

37. Quoted in Armin L. Rappoport, *Henry L. Stimson and Japan, 1931–1933*, Chicago: University of Chicago Press, 1963, p. 123.

38. Report, 31 August 1932, F.O. 371/15877[A6810/312/45], Public Record Office, London.

39. Minute, 1 November 1933, F.O. 371/16611[A7649/89/45], Public Record Office, London.

40. Minutes, F.O. 371/19822[A533/34/45], Public Record Office, London.

41. Hodsoll to Figueras, 27 February 1937, F.O. 371/20650 [A2079/20/45], Public Record Office, London.

42. N. J. Brailey, *Thailand and the Fall of Singapore*, Boulder and London: Westview, 1986, p. 51.

43. Crosby to Orde, 18 August 1934, F.O. 371/18207[F5730/21/40], Public Record Office, London.

44. Crosby to Foreign Secretary, 25 September 1934, 200, F.O. 371/18210 [F6575/3035/40], Public Record Office, London.

45. Ibid., Minutes.

46. Huynh Kim Khanh, *Vietnamese Communism 1925–1945*, Ithaca: Cornell University Press, 1982, pp. 156 ff.

47. D. Lancaster, *The Emancipation of French Indo-China*, London: Oxford University Press, 1961, p. 83.

48. Minutes on Dickens to Orde, 22 May 1934, F.O. 371/18186 [F2996/652/23], Public Record Office, London.

49. CID Paper, 8 July 1936, 1245-B, CAB 4/24, Public Record Office, London.

50. Montgomery to Sargent, 22 April 1936, F.O. 371/20507[W3583/498/29], Public Record Office, London.

51. CID Paper, 27 July 1936, 1256-B, CAB 4/24, Public Record Office, London.

52. Minute by Henderson, n.d., F.O. 371/22172[F545/487/61], Public Record Office, London.

53. Report of Brig. Gen. Sir Samuel Wilson, March 1933, Cmd 4276, p. 12.

54. Minute on Clementi's letter of 24 December 1931, C.O. 531/24[92503], Public Record Office, London.

55. Bertram Brooke to Clementi, 9 September 1930, Clementi Papers.

56. San C. Po, *Burma and the Karens*, London: Stock, 1928, p. 73.

57. R. C. H. McKie, *This Was Singapore*, Sydney: Angus and Robertson, 1942, p. 21.

5

The Second World War:
Plans and Potential Partners

JAPAN'S attack on Pearl Harbor in December 1941 brought the Americans into the war and ensured its ultimate defeat. But meanwhile it destroyed colonial South-East Asia and placed it in the Greater East Asia Co-Prosperity Sphere. The Americans themselves were turned out of the Philippines. British Malaya was quickly overrun, and the Dutch defeated in Netherlands India. The British contested in vain the invasion of Burma that the Japanese had launched with Burman allies. Only the French remained, their regime compromised but not finally dislodged by the Japanese till March 1945.

The Future of South-East Asia

Mary Turnbull, the historian, has suggested a comparison between the return of the British to Malaya in 1945–6 and their intervention in the 1870s.[1] The comparison can be developed and extended to the rest of South-East Asia. At first sight the approach the British took to their return provided a dramatic contrast to their earlier approach. They were, after all returning and, starting anew, not starting completely afresh. The most obvious contrast was, of course, the intermission of their political control and their commercial contacts, and of most contacts other than with guerrilla forces. Now they had to renew them. And they had to assert their right and duty to do so. The British must win the war, and regaining the empire they had ignominiously lost must result.

The intermission of their contacts and their determination to renew them somewhat paradoxically provided a further area of contrast. The imperialism of the British had been marked by so much pragmatism as to cast doubt on their employment of the term to characterize their activities. In the plenitude of their power, their policy had been one of sufficiency unto the day, of doing no more than seemed necessary to meet their interests, and of ruling only where there seemed to be no satisfactory alternative to doing so. Now they began to plan, and to plan in some detail. Perhaps that was a reflection of their weakness, though much of the planning seemed to presume a greater strength than they had, and to proceed on the basis that their freedom from the immediate problems of the territories concerned meant that little change was occurring within them, and that the prime issue was their own change of policy.

There was a third contrast, more particularly with the inter-war period. Then indeed there had been plans for change. In most cases they had been deemed too problematic to carry out, for fear they might reveal problems that the British could demonstrably not deal with, and so reduce their prestige. Better to do the minimum and enhance the chance that the Japanese would as a result be discouraged from challenging a *status quo* that could thus appear the more impregnable. The policy had in the end not stopped the Japanese, and the territories, weakly defended by the British, had put up little resistance of their own. The dislocation of the *status quo* suggested the need to concentrate and the possibility of concentrating more on the reforms within the territories concerned. Both the framework and the territories themselves had to be rebuilt: the latter must be stronger in themselves, but also part of a system of regional collaboration, centred on Singapore, that linked and reconciled imperial and nationalist interests.

The contrasts may in fact be less than at first sight appears. First, the earlier policies of the British, pragmatic though they were, were also set within a series of understandings about the future that looked forward to a world-system of independent states, trading and dealing with each other on a theoretical basis of equality. Though there had been a striking lack of formal planning in the making of the empire, the disposition now to plan was not entirely novel, prompted though it might be by the example of other states, post-1917 and post-depression; prompted, too, by the practice of war; and by the determination at the end of it effectively to resume the imperial task. Characteristically the lesson that the historian Margery Perham drew from the fall of Singapore was that the British needed to alter their timetable. 'A revision of the time factor is needed for all aspects of our colonial policy. . . .' In the nineteenth century, she wrote, '. . . we set ourselves to bring change by gradual development from the old order rather than through rapid imposition of the new. . . .' But now 'the whole tempo of human affairs' had changed.[2] In a sense the British were led to define what they had assumed, to state the principles upon which they had been acting, and to make their objectives more explicit. The world-wide nature of the struggle, and the involvement in it of the emergent superpowers, led them, too, to insist that what had applied to Europe applied also to Asia. But, as the British argued, the Atlantic Charter of 1941 was there in some sense superfluous, though the Colonial Office could not find the pledges that Prime Minister Churchill declared already existed.[3]

That does not mean, of course, that the British did not recognize that circumstances had changed and that their policies must as well. But the emphasis was on adaptation rather than abandonment. In the longer term a world of independent states was still envisaged. The merely imperial stage in that development was over. But if empire could no longer provide the security it had in South-East Asia, other sources must be found. The British tended to seek it in a regional approach. In this they at once hoped to harmonize their approach with that of the other colonial powers and with the United States, and with the developing interests of the nationalists in South-East Asia themselves.

The former was an ambitious task. It had always been difficult to prompt other colonial powers, even given their dependence on Britain, to follow the lines of policy the British wanted them to follow. Now the United States was relatively far more powerful than even in the inter-war period, and it had its own policies to follow in the Philippines and in respect of Thailand. The French and the Dutch were more dependent on the British. But they had their own post-war objectives and their own special determination to restore their position. The difficulty of influencing them was increased by the relationship with them in Europe. Even in the imperial period, European considerations had limited the British in dealing with the other European empires in South-East Asia. The same was true in a period in which the British had an interest in restoring the states of Western Europe as a testimony of victory and a guarantee of security.

Harmonizing British objectives with those of the nationalists in South-East Asia was complicated by the European connections, but it was also difficult in itself. Again tradition in British policy was in one sense in its favour. The aim had been to seek collaborators, and in a sense that was still the aim. But pursuing the aim was hedged about with greater difficulties. First, it might not always be safe or feasible to jettison past collaborators, and to take account of new conditions or new aims. Changing collaborators had never been easy, and the dramatic events of the war did not in fact make it easier. Was loyalty to be rewarded? Was collaboration with the Japanese to be punished? That might relate to the treatment of minorities, problematic in any case. Second, the nationalists might not be able to fit their objectives, even if they were capable of harmonization with those of the British, into the same timetable or the same international structure. Should they not have independence now? Should their state be part of an intermediate structure or entirely independent? Should emerging states develop armies of their own? How would that affect national stability or international security? Such questions could no longer be deferred.

The British were, third, inclined to be more ideologically selective about their collaborators than pre-war. Even then their doubts about the Communists had been intensified by the recognition that they did not look towards the same kind of international structure that the British did but gave their allegiance to an alternative view of the world. These doubts were not overcome by collaboration with the Soviet Union in the war and were redoubled after the war when the Soviet Union seemed to be taking up Leninist overseas policies in a new form. Their unwillingness to accept Communist elements among their collaborators sometimes meant that the British tried to rely on reactionary elements that had little popular support, even though their essential assumption remained that the élites with which they collaborated must and would have effective backing within their own countries. Alternatively, those who might have collaborated with them on an acceptable basis were driven to emphasize that they were no less radically anti-imperialist than the Communists. The élites, not numerous nor strong, were in fact not quite so useful to the British as the latter had hoped they would be. Moreover, the British drew from their experiences before and in the war a renewed dislike for totalitarian and one-party states. They believed new élites with which they could collaborate must be democratically inclined, willing to contemplate a multi-party system as well as a legitimate opposition, British-style. The British were more exacting about their potential collaborators than in the days of their plenitude of power. The new states would have, after all, a greater role to play, and their dedication to democracy was seen as a further guarantee of security and stability in the newly emerging international system.

Their new emphasis on nation-building presented other problems for the British. Politically, it meant fuller surrender of their arbitral position as a colonial power. Even pre-war some of the effects of this had become apparent. How would peoples from the Scheduled Areas fare in a future Burma? What were the implications of majority rule for minority peoples? Economically, nation-building presented another, not unrelated, problem. Some of the differences might be bridged by substantial economic and social investment. That was really a break with British colonial policy, the prime emphasis on which had been on self-development, and only a small breach had been made in tradition by colonial welfare and development acts passed in the inter-war period. It was a break difficult not only because of tradition. It presumed that colonial territories could absorb the development proposed. It also presumed that Britain could finance it. In fact the second war, even more than the first, deeply damaged Britain's economy: its resources were insufficient unto the day. It became more than ever dependent on the United States. 'Do you want me to beg, like Fala?' asked Churchill at Quebec in October 1944.[4] It also became in a measure dependent on the colonies that could earn dollars for the sterling area. Another complication was introduced into the question of their political advance.

The Impact of the War of 1939

The Japanese did not at first perceive the need to conquer South-East Asia. As a result their own plans for so doing, and for governing the territories conquered, contained a great deal of improvisation. But, even though it did not dislodge the *status quo*, the pressure they exerted on South-East Asia before they turned to conquest was not without its effect, particularly after the outbreak of the war in Europe in 1939.

For many years they had demonstrated an interest in the area, to the alarm particularly of the Dutch. What concentrated their attention in the 1930s was indeed their interest in the energy resources of Netherlands India. There were other reasons for looking to South-East Asia. The depression underlined the sense in which the world was being divided into economic units. The failure to bring the China war to an end paradoxically invited its expansion. The help afforded the Chinese by the West and by Chinese communities in the Nanyang, mistakenly seen by the

Japanese as the main reason for their continued resistance, invited Japanese attention to South-East Asia.

The outbreak of war in Europe was initially a shock for the Japanese. After failing to secure a definite Japanese commitment against the maritime powers, the Germans had made a non-aggression pact with the Soviet Union. Hitler hoped thus to find a different route to the reordering of Europe on which he was bent. At once the Japanese felt more exposed to the north and hastened to come to terms with the Soviet Union over their bitter border struggle. But at least they seemed to have new opportunities in South-East Asia while Britain and its partners were threatened by the changes in Europe. The example of China itself seemed not unhopeful. Britain removed most of its remaining troops, though the United States indicated its continued opposition to Japanese hegemony. In South-East Asia the Japanese believed that they might gain by exerting pressure on the existing framework rather than displacing it. They could make demands on the colonial powers without the risks involved in conflict, and without, for example, inviting the intervention of the United States, or indeed the Germans. Faced also by local opposition, the colonial powers might prefer to yield to Japanese pressure rather than risk a whole-sale onslaught. But while the phoney war continued in Europe, the Japanese made little headway in South-East Asia. The Dutch were quite unyielding.

The major changes in Europe in the middle of 1940 gave the Japanese new opportunities in South-East Asia. 'This is a great opportunity such as comes once in a thousand years. It must not be lost.'[5] Their aim was still to exert pressure on the existing framework, rather than to displace it, and to some extent they succeeded. In Europe Hitler had ended the phoney war by dramatic moves into Denmark and Norway, into the Low Countries, and into France. The French defeat was the most striking of these events. Britain now stood alone in Western Europe, while its position in the Mediterranean was further weakened by the Italian entry into the war. The French in Indo-China, anxious to preserve the continuity of their rule, adhered to the Vichy regime, but, despite this breach in imperialist unity, still hoped for collaboration with the Allied powers against Japanese pressure. Deprived of a metropolis, the Dutch colony was also exposed to Japanese pressure. The outcome depended on the British, but their attitude and their capacity to act largely depended on those of the Americans. The British sought to encourage resistance to Japanese demands in Vietnam, and took care to avoid precipitating further destruction of the *status quo* by sponsoring Gaullism.[6] Their support, however, could in any case be little more than verbal. Even in regard to the Netherlands India, where, thanks to the existence of a Dutch government-in-exile in London, the political position was clearer, the British would still make no promises of support in the event of a Japanese attack.

The attitude of the Americans was crucial, in Europe as well as in Asia. This the British recognized, and as before the war, so in the war, their policy was regulated accordingly. If there were a war in the East, their help would be essential. Increasingly, however, it was apparent that their help was already essential in Europe. The chances of continued British resistance to the Germans were limited, unless US aid were forthcoming. Even direct US involvement might be required. It was necessary, therefore, not to pursue a policy that would alienate the Americans. The British had to avoid appeasement, but at the same time they must not appear to be drawing the United States into a conflict. The Americans indeed increased their aid during 1940. Once the Battle of Britain and the Presidential election were over, they could be more forthcoming. Destroyers for bases was followed by lend-lease.

The British ambassador in Washington, Lord Lothian, had argued in November 1939 that the United States would enter a war if the Japanese expanded south. True, if Japan concentrated on British and Dutch possessions, American reaction would, he thought, be slower than if it attacked the Philippines.

But partly because the Central Pacific is now regarded as a kind of American reserve, partly because the expansion of Japan overseas would eventually threaten the Monroe Doctrine and partly because a war with Japan would probably not involve sending abroad vast armies of conscripts, I think that long before Japanese action threatened Australia or New Zealand, America would be at war. This probability is probably enhanced by the fact that the army and navy and a great many publicists, though not yet public opinion, recognise clearly that the present form of American security and the Monroe Doctrine is, in the long run, just as dependent upon the British as on the American Navy. If the United States is to rely upon Great Britain to prevent totalitarian Europe from entering the Atlantic through the Straits of Gibraltar and the exits from the North Sea, the United States must themselves underwrite the security of the British Empire in the Pacific because they cannot afford the weakening of Great Britain itself which would follow the collapse of her dominions in the Pacific.[7]

This viewpoint President Roosevelt came to share.

We are faced with the danger of Japan's continuing her expansion in the Far East especially toward the south, while the European issue remains in the balance. If Japan, moving further southward, should gain possession of the region of the Netherlands East Indies and the Malay Peninsula, would not the chances of Germany's defeating Great Britain be increased and the chances of England's winning be decreased thereby?[8]

In the perception of the Americans, South-East Asia thus had an important role to play. Their aim was to keep British resistance alive, so avoiding German dominance of Europe and the consequent threat to the Western hemisphere. Keeping Britain's resistance alive did not depend on American aid alone. Britain, it was believed, also needed the manpower and resources of its empire, of India, South-East Asia, and Australasia.

If the Nazi power is to be defeated, the United Kingdom must not be overwhelmed. British military power mans the gate which holds back from the Americas the flood of German military strength. The supports of British power extend to all parts of the world.... A particularly important, possibly an essential part of that structure is Singapore, which, with the Philippines and the Netherlands Indies, furnishes great quantities of the raw materials required for the success of the American and British defense effort.... Were Japan established in Singapore or the Netherlands Indies, the security of the British Isles themselves would be endangered, and thus the security of the United States threatened....'[9]

That did not lead the Americans to commit themselves till the last moment to supporting the British against a Japanese threat. It did lead them to take a stronger attitude towards the Japanese, expressed in words as before but now also in deeds. Those deeds, they believed, could be confined to the economic field: this, with a demonstrated Anglo-American stand, would suffice to deter the Japanese. The British, on the whole, shared this judgment. There was in fact little else they could do. They could not risk provoking the Americans into stronger action: it might be counterproductive, as well as unnecessary. Some thought it might divert them from Europe. In the event the route to their direct participation in the European war was after all through South-East Asia.

That was, in fact, however, the result of another outcome of the German victories in Europe in mid-1940. The United States began to take other steps to provide for the security of the Western hemisphere. In particular they resolved to build a two-ocean fleet. Though they had tried to insist on limiting Japan's naval building and on preserving a margin, in fact, beset by isolation and economic problems, they had not built to the limits they had secured for themselves. Now they resolved to catch up. At last the vast US potential would be activated. Though this fundamental decision was taken in response to the European crisis, it affected the situation in Asia. In turn that was to bring them directly into the European war.

The Japanese had also reacted to the defeat of France, not only by exerting more pressure on the French in Indo-China, but, under the guidance of Konoe, by conceiving a new diplomatic thrust, designed to take advantage of the weakness of the British. This was the notion lying behind the Tripartite Pact. But it had the same weaknesses as earlier diplomacy. The unity of Germans and Japanese remained less than complete. It merely added a further strain to the relations between Japan and the United States. The euphoria with which Konoe's concept had been surrounded was succeeded by a gloom equally unfounded. The Dutch remained unyielding. Only the border conflict between the French in Indo-China and the Thais seemed to give the Japanese an opportunity for increasing their influence.

A new means of exerting pressure seemed to be necessary. Initially the aim was to strengthen Japan's position in the north, so that it could be more exacting in the south. The Foreign Minister, Matsuoka, accordingly secured a neutrality pact with the Soviet Union in April 1941, while negotiations with the United States were commenced. The United States was far from yielding, however. Indeed it formulated its stance in the form of principles, which seemed to challenge not only Japan's hopes but its achievements so far. Insisting at this stage on the principles of the 1920s was to require the Japanese to abandon what they had secured in the 1930s.

This unpromising situation was changed again by a move in Europe. Fatefully Hitler determined to break with the Soviet Union, and the German invasion began in June 1941. The Japanese had now to decide whether they would persist with their southward strategy, or, abandoning the recently concluded neutrality pact with the Soviet Union, join their wayward partner in attacking it. Should they seek the resources of Siberia and insulate China from the Communist menace? Or should they use the opportunity of Russia's involvement in the west to exert further pressure to the south? Matsuoka, though the maker of the neutrality pact, favoured the former course. But, dropping him, Konoe's cabinet resorted to the latter. As the panzers swept over the Russian plains, Japanese eyes were still trained on the south. 'Regardless of whatever changes may occur in the world situation, Japan will adhere to the established policy of creating a Greater East Asia Co-Prosperity Sphere and thereby contribute to the establishment of world peace.'[10] New demands were put to French Indo-China. The opposition of the Americans was the more serious for the Japanese in view of their consciousness of the growth of the American navy. If diplomacy, even when more forcefully managed, could make no progress, then the Japanese might have to resort to force, the success of which, never likely to be complete, would be greater in the short run than in the long run. In the coming years, as the American building plans were fulfilled, Japan's margin would diminish. If forceful action had to be taken, it must be taken soon.

The American reaction to the new move on Indo-China indicated that Japanese diplomacy was unlikely to be successful. Believing that a determined attitude could stop the Japanese, the Americans froze Japanese assets and imposed an oil embargo. The British and the Dutch followed suit, though apprehensive that Japanese wrath might fall on them, and still without a promise of American help. Some felt that the Japanese would not dare attack both the United States and Britain. In fact that was what the Japanese determined upon. They acted in no spirit of confidence, but more in one of desperation. If they did not act, they felt they could be reduced to dependence on an America that controlled the Pacific, that was activating its power, and that had indicated its interest in the future of South-East Asia. Faced with the failure of his diplomacy, Konoe resigned in October. Tojo vainly tried a time-limited diplomacy, then went to war, leaping into the unknown, jumping, eyes closed, from the verandah of Kiyomizu Temple.[11] 'We have some uneasiness about a protracted war. But how can we let the United States continue to do as she pleases, even though there is some uneasiness? . . . I fear that we should become a third class nation after two or three years if we just sat tight.'[12]

The Fall of Singapore

The initial successes were dazzling. Psychologically and physically ill-prepared, the Allies could do no more than make gestures, and the greatest of those was ineffectual, resulting in the loss of two great British battleships. Striking at Pearl Harbor and at the Philippines, the Japanese also attacked the big British base at Singapore, approaching overland and attacking by air. Its fall in February 1942 was the Yorktown of the British empire in Asia. Churchill found it hard to believe.[13]

It fell, however, not merely because of the vigour and deter-mination of the Japanese, nor even because of the miscalculations and weaknesses of their opponents. The empire had an intrinsic weakness in a context of international struggle. Britain had relied on diplomacy and naval and economic strength to sustain its influence in the world, whether that was expressed in formal or informal empire. In the territories with which it was in contact, it sought collaboration, whether or not it was ruling. It made no real attempt to turn its influence, nor even its dominance, into a unified and centralized political structure. It continued to see the world as on its way to a system of independent states, in the progress towards which formal imperial control was only a stage. But there were defects in the model. How should or could the transition be made? Could you, in the civilian sphere, provide useful experience for the would-be self-governing without granting full self-government? And, in the defence sphere, could you pro-vide military experience without risking the security of imperial control? Within the territories imperial power was in general sustained, not by recruiting armies from the majority peoples, but from minorities, from 'martial races', or by recruiting them in a balanced way that accorded more with the principle of divide-and-rule than with any national principle. It was in fact difficult to build nations within a framework of dependence, as the Japanese, trying a different formula, also found. The forces created were essentially constabularies rather than armies. The resistance they could be expected to offer an outside invader would be limited. If the outside invasion could not be met by other outside forces, the regimes would collapse. This was what happened in 1941–2.

The same applied as much, if not more, in territories under the lesser European powers. A visiting New Zealander had pointed out that his dominion hoped to raise 75,000 men out of 1.5 million: he thought Netherlands India could raise more than 100,000.[14]

The *De Zeven Provincien* mutiny had done nothing to show that a colonial power could rely on its subjects against an invader: Consul-General Walsh referred to 'the uncertain value of much of the human material available. . .'.[15]

Meanwhile, however, the Americans had been drawn directly into the war against the Germans, speeded by Hitler's declaration of war. Initial defeat was thus sure to be ultimately redeemed, and Churchill recognized that.[16] Perhaps, however, he did not recognize the cost. The disruption of the imperial hold on South-East Asia was a fatal blow to the future of empire, as the French had foreseen that it would be. Deprived of prestige, dependent on the United States, the British would find it difficult to return.

The Japanese Empire

The success of the Japanese invaders in South-East Asia, in utter contrast to China, was a testimony not only to the weakness of the opposition, but to the effectiveness of their military preparations, undertaken though they were at relatively short notice. Their civil plans, even more improvised and at the outset of the war still very short-term,[17] were much less successful. It was true that their moment of power in South-East Asia turned out to be no more than that. Their empire never reached beyond an early stage and was always under the emergency pressure of war. But what plans there were lacked realism and their implementation lacked conviction. That did not mean they lacked effect. To some extent they dislocated the boundaries within which the colonial powers and their collaborators had worked. Even more they displaced those collaborators or set up rivals to them.

It might at first sight seem that their plans were random. But if they were improvised, there was something of a pattern, as in the earlier ventures of the British. They had a model of colonial development, drawn from their own Meiji experience, and applied in earlier acquisitions, Formosa and Korea.[18] A newer pattern derived from their experience in Manchuria and to a lesser extent in China. In Manchuria the conflict had been between their entrenched 'imperial' rights and Chinese nationalism. Their answer was to construct a puppet regime, which they hoped would at once elicit political support and yet follow Japanese policy. Failing to destroy the KMT regime, they tried to apply the model in China, too. From 1938 onwards Konoe began to contemplate setting up, within a new regional framework, a regime in China

with which the Japanese could deal, and in subsequent years
Wang Ching-wei agreed to head it. The paradox of such a regime
was soon to be revealed. If it was to elicit popular support—and it
would not counter the appeal of the KMT otherwise—it had to
have real power. But if it had real power, it was unlikely to follow
Japanese policies.[19] The Japanese answer to the problem of
nationalism was in fact no more successful than the Western:
there was no real way in which nationalism could be reconciled to
any regime that offered less than effective political independence.
The British had sought to do so by sustaining a gradualist timetable. That was not an option for the Japanese. Their gestures had
to be more dramatic. That could elicit support, but only a short-
term basis. 'Independence seems like a marriage,' Sukarno declared. 'Who shall wait until the salary rises, say to 500 guilders
and setting up house is complete? Marry first!'[20]

It was nevertheless the puppet model that seemed to be in the
minds of the Japanese authorities in South-East Asia. But even
this model, faulty as it was, they applied only to two of the
acquired colonial territories, Burma and the Philippines, in 1943.
Elsewhere they faced colonial polities that were less politically
developed. But their policies were also determined by other factors.
Their interest in the resources of Netherlands India helped to
make them less ready to envisage the setting-up of even a puppet
regime there. They were also divided among themselves. The
divisions among the authorities in Tokyo were reflected on the
ground in South-East Asia and different policies were pursued in
different parts of Netherlands India. Thailand, of course, provided another exception to their rules, as it had to those of the
European system. There the Japanese sought to win Thai support
by territorial concessions, redeeming the losses the kingdom had
sustained in the British period, at the expense, of course, of
alienating some support in Burma, Malaya, and Indo-China, the
territories concerned. At least till 1945, Indo-China was an
exception as well. Sponsors of pan-Asianism, the Japanese nevertheless allowed the French regime to continue to administer Indo-
China. It saved troops, but it limited the practical impact of the
Japanese in Indo-China and, with their arbitrary views on frontiers,
undermined the impact their idealism made elsewhere.

The French were finally dislodged in March 1945. By then the
Japanese, pressed by the successes of their opponents, had made a
number of adjustments in their policies. They had announced the
prospect of independence for Java/Netherlands India, and albeit

slowly the military authorities began preparations to that end. There was not much chance now of setting up an effective puppet regime. But setting up a regime that gave the nationalists some opportunity would help to obstruct the return of the Allies and their advance towards the Japanese homeland. The Japanese, too, could appear as sponsors of independent nation-states.

At the very least they might, as George Kerr suggested, lay the groundwork for further struggle, though losing the war, by counting upon 'the awakened race consciousness of the Orient. . . . If the Japanese can make their forced withdrawal seem to be a further invasion of Asia by imperial white powers, they can leave behind them the foundation for another effort some time in the future.'[21] The Gaimusho argued that

the Greater East Asia war is fundamentally a struggle against the Anglo-American world order—in essence a war between two world outlooks. Even if America and Great Britain, with their utilitarian outlook, do not comprehend the significance of the present war, regardless of whether or not the war is viewed as a clash in terms of the old concepts of national interests, and no matter whether circumstances are even now enabling the complete restoration of the old order, the ideological foundation developed through the war of liberation in Greater East Asia by the Empire is, regardless of the course of the war, an eventuality which even the enemy must follow and accept ... even if the independence of Indonesia finally fails in being upheld by diplomatic negotiations after the termination of the war and is temporarily left in abeyance as a future problem even the enemy will not be able to deny the fundamental truth that independence inevitably follows the formative development of a people; if so, and if independence is granted by us, then half the victory can be acknowledged by us.[22]

In fact the war ended in a different way, not by advance through South-East Asia, nor by negotiation, but by island-hopping, by Soviet entry, and by atomic bombs dropped on Hiroshima and Nagasaki. Only Burma and the Philippines, where puppet regimes had been set up, were fought over. In Malaya and Indonesia, where they had not, and in Vietnam, where they had enjoyed only a brief existence, the interregnum between the Japanese surrender and the arrival of the Allies was arguably more important than their latter-day puppetry.

The impact of the conquest itself was in any case considerable. The colonial powers had to recognize it, and they made some attempt to take account of it in their planning for the future. But, resorting to planning in a way for which their earlier history offered no real precedent, they now perhaps lacked a sufficient measure of pragmatism. Conscious of their signal defeat, and the loss of prestige it involved, they failed fully to estimate the effect they had. Despite their recognition of the issue, they thus took too little account of the impact of the Japanese phase. However inapt their programmes were, and however inept their execution, the Japanese stirred ambitions and hopes and fears; they created new élites, new military forces, and new social balances and imbalances; they elevated politics over administration; and they shook, though rarely destroyed, the colonial frontiers. Where they fought over the territories, the Allies came reluctantly to recognize the changes that resulted. Elsewhere they discovered them later. Their plans were lacking in realism and they had to adapt them, often too slowly for their success or too rapidly for their credibility.

The concept of a puppet regime the Japanese applied most clearly in the Philippines and in Burma. These were the countries under Western control that had attained the greatest degree of political autonomy. Not only were they therefore the most apt for this treatment: it was hard to afford them anything else. But the impact of Japanese policy differed even in these cases. The Philippines, while placed under the interim 'Commonwealth' regime, yet had a promise of independence and a deadline for it. 'I give the people of the Philippines my solemn pledge that their freedom will be redeemed and their independence established and protected', Roosevelt had declared.[23] Politically the Filipino leaders had less to gain from Japanese offers of independence than the leadership of any other colonial territory in South-East Asia. Al McCoy, the historian, downplays the impact of Japanese rule in the Philippines.[24] Working from the example of one province, he perhaps overdoes his generalization. In any case the impact of the Japanese was not negligible. But it was true that the élite could see no great new opportunity in the Japanese occupation, and, as McCoy argues, it was for the most part a matter rather of deciding whether or not to accommodate to a regime that had little to offer. The question of accommodation to a foreign power had faced the Filipino élite before. But now the gains seemed uncertain. Furthermore, the Americans were likely to return, as they promised, and the regime would thus be temporary. It was, however, desirable to diminish the harshness of the occupation, and also to avoid the social disruption and revolution that would result. Collaboration could be supported by the argument that it would preserve not only the position of the élite but its capacity to protect its clients. The faction-ridden nature of the élite introduced another factor. The occupation might last long enough for one faction to gain decisive advantage by collaboration. However, collaboration might give opponents a decisive argument with the returning Americans. It was not surprising that in Iloilo factions kept a foot in both camps, and it may be that the kind of arrangements that, as McCoy says, emerged there were replicated elsewhere. Only in Central Luzon were the patron–client patterns seriously disrupted and the Hukbalahap movement thus able to secure the loyalty of the peasantry.

What happened in the Philippines was, as before the war, or even more so, beyond the ability of the British to determine. The decision would lie with the Americans. But the outcome would be important for the British on their return to South-East Asia. As before the war, it would be an indication of the American stance and the extent of American commitment in the region. The example of the Philippines would also afford an example, cautionary or otherwise, to other South-East Asian territories. The British, too, would have to deal with a new Filipino regime, as they had seen that they would in the early years of the Commonwealth phase, and perhaps both sides would be freer than at that point to negotiate with each other. Considering the Philippines is in any case a basis for a comparison with other territories in South-East Asia.

In Burma the position was quite different. There, too, the political arrangements under the 1937 constitution allowed substantial autonomy, and in fact wider popular participation in the political process. But there was no promise of independence. Despite the requests of Premier U Saw before the invasion, the British Cabinet would not substantially add to its pre-war promises on constitutional advance. 'We were engaged in a struggle for our very lives,' Churchill told Saw, 'and this was not the time to raise such constitutional matters.'[25] The programme of the Japanese was certain therefore to make a bigger impact than in the Philippines. They secured support from the radical Burman Thakins in the course of their invasion in a way that has no parallel in the Philippines and the nucleus of a Thakin-led army was created. Together with Ba Maw and other older leaders, the Thakins were also given new political opportunities at the centre and locally. Not all the Thakins agreed that it was right to pursue these opportunities. Indeed the independence the regime was granted fell far short of reality, though even its symbolism was not without effect. The evident turning-of-the-tide against the Japanese was, of course, more decisive in shifting the viewpoint of the collaborators. What Burma had to secure from the war among the great powers, the Thakins concluded, was its independence. If it could no longer be done under Japanese patronage, it had to be done in a different way: by a measure of collaboration with the Allies against the Japanese, coupled with a strengthened local control and a political challenge. This was the course that the Thakin leadership pursued during 1945. It challenged the plans of the returning British.

In a sense the puppet model was also applied in French Indo-China, but in a very different way. For most of the war, the Japanese allowed the French regime to continue under Admiral Decoux. Rather paradoxically, it pursued policies that at times were not unlike those of the Japanese, though their origins lay at once in the ideology of the Vichy regime and in practical considerations. The French saw the importance of sustaining the continuity of their rule: once that was interrupted, it would be difficult to resume. They also wished to secure greater support for it. Hitherto they had been the power least accommodating to moderate nationalism, and their approach had left its leadership to extremists, whose violence they had met with violence. Now they sought a limited and controlled mobilization and promoted a *mystique Indochine*. But, a kind of puppet themselves, they could not go too far without provoking the Japanese. Leaving the French in occupation was one thing; a politically active French regime was another. The British had found it difficult to direct or control the colonial regimes they had patronized. The Japanese faced a similar problem.

What led them to destroy the regime, however, was a number of changes outside French Indo-China. First, there was the impact, once more, of the European war, and the approaching liberation of France. In that, of course, the Americans played a major role, and it was certain that they would play a major role in Asia, too. They were deeply critical of French colonialism, particularly President Roosevelt, who had indicated that he thought French rule in Indo-China must end. 'The President said that the Indochinese were people of small stature, like the Javanese and Burmese, and were not warlike. He added that France had done nothing to improve the natives since she had the colony.'[26] Participation against the Japanese might be a useful argument against that view, and as the French re-established themselves in Europe, they tried also to re-establish their credibility in Asia. But that presented a major difficulty: doing this, as had been seen in 1940–1, might undo the Decoux regime and so interrupt the continuity of colonial control. The Japanese showed the incompatibility of the two French objectives by finally eliminating the regime in March 1945. To this they were also driven by the deterioration of their own position. While they could ill afford more occupation troops, they needed to set up more effective barriers to Allied advance than were afforded by a Decoux regime that now showed signs not only of autonomous action but of accommodating to Gaullism.

The result was the setting-up of new puppet regimes. By contrast to those in Burma and the Philippines, those in Indo-China were not only belated; they were also in the hands of old-style authorities. Their chance of enlisting popular support was thus much less. Furthermore, the Bao Dai regime in Vietnam was not given control over the whole of the country; Cochin-China being kept apart from it. Effective opposition to the French return was to come from an element which the Japanese could tolerate no more than the French, the Communist-led Viet-minh. But they were not the only actors in the field, and were weaker in the south than in the north. It was in the south that the British forces were to land after the Japanese capitulation.

While puppet regimes made only a belated appearance in Indo-China, they were not in fact set up at all in the Malaysian–Indonesian area. In Indonesia in particular, the Japanese certainly engaged in political mobilization, and their rule had some of the features of a puppet regime such as an army drawn from the majority people. They hesitated, however, to surrender even the measure of political power that the creation of a puppet regime required, and moved in that direction only as defeat approached.

Netherlands India was a prime object of the Japanese venture, above all because it was a source of oil. The aim was, however, to secure its resources rather than to promote its political advance, and the new imperialists aimed initially to incorporate the territory into their empire. They had to mobilize support, but they did this rather as if the territory were directly part of the empire than a separate state within the Co-Prosperity Sphere. Indonesian leaders sought to expand the latitude they were allowed and to turn mobilization to their own account. Their task was not easy. Japanese intervention promoted alternative leadership, from the army, from the Muslim community, and from youth groups. Though their goals might be generally similar—at least in the sense that they sought independence of external control—their concepts of strategy and timing differed.

Under the impact of approaching defeat, the Japanese Premier Koiso announced in September 1944 that the goal was independence for Indonesia. Preparing for that was to be a slow process, since the Japanese military were unwilling to press ahead with it. But it did expand the role of the nationalists, who by mid-1945 were planning the future constitution, frontiers, and ideology of an Indonesian state. The process was not quite completed when the Japanese capitulated in 15 August. But, with some covert Japanese patronage, and at the prompting of impatient youth leaders, Sukarno and Hatta proclaimed independence on 17 August. The returning colonial power was to face an opposition that was stronger than its divisions made it appear.

The Indonesians in mid-1945 contemplated a state larger than Netherlands India. The arbitrariness of the Japanese in the island area had extended to their treatment of its frontiers under the old framework, and to those of Malaya. The nationalists in turn sought to undermine the previous colonial pattern, and there were those in Malaya who saw advantage in an association with Indonesia that would counter the influence of the Chinese. The challenge to the frontiers was unsuccessful, but the idea did not altogether disappear from post-war politics.

In Malaya, the Japanese had been even more arbitrary than in Indonesia; the northern states, for example, being returned to Thai suzerainty in 1943. But the overall effect of their policy was to boost the role of the Malays by comparison with the Chinese, who were the main sources of resistance in the Malayan People's Anti-Japanese Army (MPAJA). Within the Malay community they relied as had the British on the traditional rulers. More radical Malays looked to an Indonesian association. No effective steps were taken by them, the rulers, or the Japanese to build a pan-Malayan state. But what had happened did not leave the British as free to create one as they had expected.

The transfer of Malay sultanates to Thai suzerainty was an indication of Japanese policy not only towards the Peninsula, but also towards Thailand, to which, furthermore, they transferred some of the frontier territory of Burma. There were rewards for the Thais in associating with the Japanese, but there was also a price to pay. The transfers of territory were gratuities for a loyal member of the Sphere, and, while it was not reduced to puppet status, clearly Thailand's dependence on its patron was increased. Listening to Premier Tojo, Premier Phibun 'displayed a joyful countenance. But it was not to the point of a broad smile.'[27] There was another risk. The Allies might seek to punish Thailand for its collaboration with the Japanese, and make it difficult for it to revert to the fuller international status it had preserved in the nineteenth century and enhanced in the early twentieth. The existence of an underground movement was an insurance against this and helped to ensure Thai independence. The hankering to undo the territorial concessions that had originally bought that independence remained.

In Thailand and elsewhere, it was not only the Japanese that made calculations about the return of the Allies: so did the South-East Asian peoples themselves and their leaders. Those calculations naturally varied, as had the calculations of those that had faced the earlier advance of imperialism. In Burma, where a reconquest took place, the option chosen by the leading Burman nationalists was to change sides, so as to help the British against the Japanese, but also to increase the chance of then successfully challenging the British. In the Philippines, there was good reason to think that the Americans would return, and also that they would stick to their promise to grant independence. In Indo-China there was by contrast no real hope that the French would offer political advance. The tasks were to maximize local strength and to appeal to the other Allies. Much the same applied in Indonesia, while in Malaya reconquest was expected, and the Chinese there hoped to take the opportunity this would afford. But their calculations, like others', were affected, not only by the way the war was fought, but by the way it ended.

The South-East Asian peoples were, of course, not united, either across the colonial boundaries, or even within them. The Japanese had done little to bring them together and much to divide them. That was perhaps particularly true in ethnically divided Malaya. The Chinese, a source of resistance to Japanese power in China itself, were a particular butt of their policies. The Indians, by contrast, were given a new sense of importance. Though the conquest of India had been no part of their plans, the Japanese sponsored an Indian National Army (INA), recruited in part in Malaya. To Subhas Chandra Bose, their client nationalist, the Japanese theoretically transferred the government of the Andaman islands, which they had occupied in 1942.

There, though the native population had been decimated, a homogeneous Indian settler community had developed out of heterogeneous convict antecedents. 'You give me blood, I will give you independence,' Bose told them on a visit at the end of 1943.[28] In fact the regime in the islands remained Japanese. It was a reign of terror for the Indians and the Nicobaris, and the Japanese bombed the Jarawa areas of South Andaman. The Allied blockade also fell heavily on the Andamans.

Allied Propaganda

In fighting and in planning to fight, the Allies tried to increase the support they were likely to receive from the local population. While some countries were fought over, some in the event were not. The surrender of the Japanese in August 1945 came before the counter-attack was complete. But even those countries that were not fought over were affected by the propaganda designed to prepare the way for the Allied counter-attack.

Burma and the Philippines, the two territories most politically advanced both before and during the war, were also the two most thoroughly fought over. To retaking the Philippines the United States was committed both by the island-hopping strategy it initially adopted for defeating the Japanese, and by its concern to redeem the impact of the defeat of 1942. The victory of the Americans had never really been in doubt, and their return was a calculation that all members of the Filipino élite had to reckon on. American wartime propaganda did not complicate their future commitment: they felt bound to abide by the programme they had set out when the Commonwealth was set up. They did, however, have to drive the Japanese out. In the process, the Philippines underwent another phase of destruction. It also involved adjustments among the élite and attempts in some areas both on the one hand to break its hold and on the other hand to reassert it. The Americans were able to fulfil the objectives of their propaganda. But the Philippine government that emerged was a weak one and a heavily obligated one. That formed one part of the new South-East Asia with which the British had to deal.

Driven out of Burma, the British had to fight their way back, like the Americans in the Philippines. This again they were anxious to do, not only because of the importance of Burma, in itself and in respect of India, but also because of the need to demonstrate that their power in Asia was not at an end. True, the reconquest or liberation of Burma could not be accomplished by Britain unaided. Not only was it a matter, as with the initial conquest, of employing Indian troops. The British depended heavily, too, on American air power. The attitude of the Burmese was also important to them. They elicited considerable support from the frontier peoples, among some of whom they had been thrust by the invasion. But the attitude of the Thakin-led Burmans themselves was different. They did not consider the return of the British as either inevitable or acceptable, as the Filipinos saw that of the Americans. Their rationale was simple expediency. Independence had to be secured from the war. As the fortunes of the Japanese waned, they might do better to turn to the Allies, and offer them help at a price.

The British differed over the proper response. The civilians feared to make over the future to the Thakin-led Anti-Fascist People's Freedom League (AFPFL). But the military argument suggested that any help against the Japanese was better than none, and propaganda suggested that it would be difficult to refuse the offer. A strengthened guerrilla movement would assist operations behind the enemy lines, Force 136 argued, pointing out that a policy of supporting left-wing resistance was being undertaken in Malaya. Admiral Mountbatten, the Supreme Allied Commander in South East Asia (SACSEA), concluded he could do with additional help: he could certainly not risk a conflict with the Burma Defence Army. 'Moreover, I considered that armed intervention on our part, to prevent the Burmese from fighting the common enemy and helping to liberate their own country, could not fail to have unfavourable repercussions in the United Kingdom, in the United States and in other parts of the world....'[29] The risk was that military policy and civilian policy would diverge. The risk was enhanced by the approach Mountbatten adopted. Rightly, he saw that the two were connected. But he was not really prepared to accept the civilian policy, even though the British Government in essence adopted it.

There was no reconquest in the case of Malaya, but one was planned, even as the liberation of Burma got under way, and the same kind of divergence was becoming apparent as the expedition was being prepared. Military considerations suggested the value of encouraging political pronouncements that would help to win support for the Allies or neutralize opposition to them and allegiance to the Japanese. But the policy that the civilian government deemed appropriate might not do this. If, for example, it seemed to favour the Chinese, would not the Malays make the task of the Allied forces more difficult? And if the policy were announced too far in advance, there would be more time for criticism of it to develop. The dilemma was not really resolved when the war came to an unexpectedly early end. But that produced its own difficulty. It meant that the military were not ready and that the civilian policy was inapt. There was an interregnum that was damaging for race relations, which also roused Malay political consciousness in an altogether unprecedented way that made the policy still more inapt.

Propaganda for the regaining of Indonesia had not been prepared. The extension of SACSEA's task to the whole of South-East Asia (excluding northern Indo-China) took place only in July 1945. Little information was available about the political situation in Netherlands India.[30] Moreover an interregnum was again to follow the capitulation of the Japanese, and of it the Indonesian leaders were to make considerable use. The simple tasks the military had been set—to accept the surrender of the Japanese and to release prisoners of war—turned out to be far from simple. The implicit assumption that the Dutch were to return was challenged, all the more effectively because they were not ready to do so, partly thanks to their commitment to the Allies in Europe. Faced with an unwanted problem, the British were to urge compromise on the Dutch.

Indo-China was not wholly made over to South East Asia Command. In the north, a gesture was made to the status of the Chiang Kai-shek regime. It was in the south that General Gracey inherited the same kind of tasks that faced General Christison in Netherlands India. But he was more responsive to the French than his counterpart was to the Dutch. Though the French, too, had scant forces available they were able to establish themselves effectively in Saigon.

Plans for the Future: American, French, and Dutch

The day-to-day demands of the campaigns, whether fought as in Burma and the Philippines, or prepared for but precipitately ended as elsewhere, affected the political programme of the returning powers and the execution of the plans they had developed for the future. Such plans generally sought to make some provision for change. But if they sought to remedy the defects of the pre-war period, they invariably took too little account of what had transpired during the war. The demands of war might point up the gap, but did not necessarily lead to appropriate adjustment. Where there was no real fighting, it was tempting to proceed with the plans without any adjustment. In the Philippines, the Americans made only a limited adjustment, though they fought a campaign. Their plan called for independence for the Philippines, and for the early restoration of civil government. If they made an adjustment that allowed for the social tension unleashed by the war, it was only in the direction of seeking in Roxas a strong-man successor to Quezon. Frank Hodsoll, a British merchant confidant of Quezon, noted that Roxas had been put on MacArthur's staff and concluded that 'he is being primed for much more important work—perhaps the leadership of the Filipino people . . . a very good friend of mine . . . the best qualified to follow the late President Quezon; indeed, ten years ago the late President told me confidentially that he hoped M. R. would succeed him.' He was 110 per cent pro-American. President Osmena's Cabinet was composed of 'men of either mediocre attainments or guerilla proclivities', unlikely to enjoy the confidence of native and foreign bankers and industrial leaders, though such was necessary for rehabilitation.[31] The Americans did not envisage a government other than by the élite. Their postwar security needs further committed them to seeking a compliant government in the Philippines. In that sense, indeed, they adjusted their programme for the Philippines: it was to be more closely bound to the United States than the Tydings-McDuffie Act had envisaged. It was not the form of dominion status that Quezon had sought, and which he again spoke of in the war: '. . . he still would not have had a single American in uniform in the parts of the Islands which is government administered,' he told Harrison, 'but he would be willing to give the United States such small islands as they needed for their own bases, etc. . . .'[32] The effect of US policy was in fact to provoke division among the élite at the national level.

The acting British Consul-General, D. F. MacDermot, commented not altogether unfairly on the impact on Filipinos of sympathetic speeches from American politicians and on the prospects of rehabilitation. Filipinos, he said, were expecting 'a shower of gold'. Their belief in Santa Claus

reduces Filipino political interest to two questions: how much is America going to pay, and who is going to control the money? . . . Independence . . . is seen as an advantage in that it will limit outside interference with the disposal of the loot; as a disadvantage by those who fear that even a generous America may not adequately cushion the shock of separation from American economic protection.... Collaboration with the Japanese régime, of which practically no prominent Filipino is entirely guiltless, is regarded not so much as having been a reprehensible action in itself—it was to some degree inevitable if these people were to survive—but as a stick with which one clique may belabour another when the time comes to scramble for the gold....[33]

For the British, the attitude of the Americans in the Philippines had long been a signal of their interest in the region. In that sense their insistence on retaining naval bases in the islands could be welcomed: 'the republic is a buttress to the South-East Asian Bastion', as Lord Killearn, the Special Commissioner, put it in 1946.[34] But the dominance of their position tended to set the Philippines aside from the rest of South-East Asia. It would become more difficult to pursue a policy for the whole region. Nor did the Filipinos set an example other nationalists would be anxious to follow. First with independence, they received it with heavy qualifications. There was a penalty for promptitude, as well as for pecuniary considerations.

The building up of the Philippines by American propaganda as a model for European Powers attaches a special importance to what happens there. The achievement of full independence must have its moral effect all over South-East Asia. On the other hand, the difficulties attending independence and the obvious American tendency to resume controls which were expected to be given up are also likely to have their effect on observant Asiatic opinion.[35]

Killearn added:

When they discover that the trappings of sovereignty of themselves avail little, it would not be surprising if the Filipinos were to chafe at the restrictions they have now so blithely accepted. If that happens, is American mentality sufficiently sensitive and responsive to meet changing conditions? Looking far ahead, I confess to some doubt whether the Philippine experiment in its present form will continue....[36]

The position of the United States was, of course, quite different from that of the other powers and that of the Philippines differed from the position of the other South-East Asian territories as a result. The immense power of the United States meant that it had a greater chance of carrying out its policies, whether or not they were apt or well-conceived. The French and the Dutch were in quite a different position. Defeated in Europe and anxious to restore their fortunes, they had no intention of abandoning their role in South-East Asia. But that role had to depend on the United States and also on the United Kingdom. The United Kingdom itself was even weaker than before the war. Its American ally set limits on what it could achieve, while it had many commitments at home, in Europe, and elsewhere in the world. The Americans also set constraints on the French and the Dutch. But their direct intervention in the SEAC area was limited—their concern was with China and Japan—and their example in the Philippines somewhat ambivalent.

In 1941, the Dutch Colonial Minister had declared that 'the traditional policy towards the Indies must be continued, and . . . one should continue to work . . . towards the gradual preparation of the Netherlands Indies for self-government within the context of the kingdom'. In the present circumstances there could be no reforms.[37] But by mid-1942, the colony lost, H. J. van Mook was telling Lord Cranborne that a new relationship between Holland and Netherlands India would be necessary after the war, with a Netherlands Government and an Indies Government, and an imperial government responsible for defence, foreign policy, and matters of general interest. An announcement to that effect would give the people of the Indies

some attractive alternative to the propaganda which was being daily pumped into them by the Japanese. And secondly he wanted to counter the vigorous propaganda which was going on in the United States and in China to the effect that recent events had shown the Dutch—and the British—not only to have been Imperialists but bungling Imperialists at that, whose day was now over. . . .[38]

Queen Wilhelmina delivered a major address on 6 December, alluding to the Atlantic Charter, and envisaging a post-war commonwealth for the Netherlands and its overseas territories, and convinced Roosevelt that the Philippines would be the example followed in Netherlands India. 'And it means a sharp break away from the leadership of the British.'[39] The Dutch designed to interest the United States in the continuance of their regime. They thus promised a greater measure of political participation. But their declaration, prepared only after considerable controversy within the government-in-exile, was couched in vague terms.[40] It may have served a propaganda purpose in the United States during the war. It could mean little to Indonesians at the end of it. But it was with it that the Dutch were to return, after the interregnum, late in 1945. They made little attempt to adapt it, either in order to meet Indonesian demands, or in order further to internationalize the issue, which the Indonesians turned out to be better at doing. British pressure and Indonesian opposition tended to produce tactical rather than strategic changes on the part of the Dutch. Their policy, too, lost what idealism it had, and provoked so much distrust that sound concepts were discredited along with unsound ones.

The French had been still more grudging than the Dutch in their plans for the future of their colonies. They had produced no rhetoric for American consumption. Early in the Pacific war, of course, the Vichy regime still remained in occupation of Indo-China. Later, the French found that President Roosevelt was opposed to their return in any case. But no French regime could envisage simply abandoning the overseas possessions. The French attempted to play a role in the Pacific war, only to precipitate Japan's destruction of the Decoux regime. They also made a characteristically vague commitment to a changed future for Indo-China. It fell far short of what the Viet-minh wanted. The latter consciously echoed American ideals in an attempt to appeal to the United States.

All men are created equal. They are endowed by their Creator with certain inalienable rights, among these are Life, Liberty and the pursuit of Happiness.

This immortal statement was made in the Declaration of Independence of the United States of America in 1776. In a broader sense, this means: All the peoples on the earth are equal from birth, all the peoples have a right to live, to be happy and free. . . .[41]

By this time, however, US policy had changed. The French, the State Department recognized in April 1945, would not assent to 'any program of international accountability which is not applied to the colonial possessions of other powers'. To put pressure on France would 'run counter to the established American policy of aiding France to regain her strength in order that she may be better fitted to share responsibility in maintaining the peace of Europe and the world.'[42] French adjustment to reality was further delayed by the assistance received from the British.

British Planning

For their own territories, and also for Thailand, the British had developed quite elaborate plans for the post-war period. In a sense that was out of character. In the days of their power, their policies had been more pragmatic. The change was no doubt associated with the greater emphasis on state planning already generally appearing during the pre-war period, and spurred on by the war itself and the military approach it fostered. It was associated, too, with the determination to return to South-East Asia to complete what was seen as a mission, a task, a job, and with the need to persuade the Americans and others of their bona fides. It was also associated, perhaps paradoxically, with the diminution of Britain's resources. While the plans at times called for unrealistic expenditures, the concept recognized a need to allocate and ration what was scarce, to establish priorities, and to enlist support from the private sector and from international organizations.

It is tempting to suggest that Britain might have planned more effectively when it had resources that might have made it possible to carry out the plans devised. Plans, however, do have drawbacks, as the British were to discover. The more elaborate they are—and it was true that the greater role of government meant that they had to be more complex—the more inflexible they are. The investment of so much effort made the plans difficult to abandon. Yet the political situation was never quite what was expected. A broader strategy might have been more effective.

In the earlier period, a broader strategy existed, though rarely spelled out, and now again the plans for post-war South-East Asia contained common concepts and had an overall rationale. There seemed to have been few formal occasions in which the overall direction of Britain's policy was discussed. But, though it was conducted in more than one department of state, it had a general thrust. It envisaged a new kind of British empire, in which trusteeship gave way to partnership, and which, at least in the longer term, would consist of dominions expected to behave in the autonomous but loyal way the settler dominions had behaved. That empire would be held together, no longer by ties of kith and kin, but still by economic, commercial, and financial ties, by constitutional links to the Crown, by common democratic and participatory concepts of government, and by defence collaboration.

While these were concepts designed to deal with the future of the British empire, they were also in a sense designed to deal with the whole of the dependent world, the fate of which had so largely been determined in the past by the decisions of the British. It was not, of course, intended to increase the frontiers of the empire, other than formally where required, but it was thought that

British policies pointed the way to other colonial powers. Regional approaches indeed depended upon this, while, the British thought, also making sense in themselves. In a way, such policies were successors to the imperial approach in providing for a stable and orderly world. That was the irreducible aim of the British. It was, as ever, difficult to get the Dutch and the French to proceed along what the British conceived as the right lines. They had never been easy to control; nor, needed in Europe, could they be put under pressure in Asia in the post-war period any more than in the nineteenth century. They had their own agendas in South-East Asia: mere stability was not enough for them, and never had been.

In the event the fact that their basic aim was stability made it easier for the British to drop their plans when they proved impractical than for the French or the Dutch to alter their objectives when they proved unattainable. There was more than one way, it seemed, to attain the minimum objective of the British. The Dutch and the French, involved with fewer territories, more concerned with prestige, and under greater pressure to ensure recovery in Europe, had less room to adapt. Not only their need to reassert their power but their own experience of collaboration in Europe made it difficult to come to terms with nationalists. That, of course, not only affected their approach to the territories to which they were endeavouring to return. It affected their expectations of the British and their readiness or otherwise to follow the British example. It also affected the fortunes of a regional approach such as the British advocated.

The old framework had been dislodged. Within that the British had thought it necessary, even desirable, to avoid political intervention wherever possible. Now a new framework had to be created. It would require more intervention and more resources. It would even at times require a step back in order to march forward, undoing the previous pragmatism or inter-war inaction: renewed direct rule in Burma, and 'Clementification' in Malaya, the colony of Sarawak, and North Borneo, rejected earlier. But the essence of it was decentralization, devolution, regionalism, and collaboration. The aim was still a world of nation-states, as stable as possible within and among themselves. In a sense the old principles were reinterpreted rather than replaced. The framework and the timetable were adjusted. But Britain's power to determine them had in fact diminished. It would be something of a *tour de force*.

The Burma White Paper

British wartime planning for post-war Burma had been a pro-longed process. That had not made the plans more realistic, and the commitments undertaken during the battle for Burma in 1944–5 were to be so much at odds with the plans that Britain seemed in effect to have two policies for Burma at the end of the war. Planning had begun back in 1942, at the initiative of the government-in-exile. The very existence of that government was a function in part of Burma's pre-war political advance, and it had no counterpart in respect of the Straits Settlements. Keeping it in existence was also an indication of Britain's determination to return to Burma. It felt all the more committed to prepare the way. The Governor, Sir R. Dorman-Smith, his staff, and some exiled Burmans were, like others, anxious to justify so doing, and, conscious of the deficiencies of pre-war Burma, wanted to take the opportunity they believed would exist to build a better Burma. At the same time, they recognized that Burma's constitutional advance must continue. They shared the common concept that the empire must evolve into a family of nations, and believed that a new-model Burma would be a willing and effective family-member. In a sense, both these views expressed new forms of British imperialism. They were, however, somewhat at odds with each other. Building a better Burma required intervention on a scale that Britain had not previously attempted, and that would require not only investment and subsidy on an unprecedented scale but also a high degree of compliance and co-operation on the part of the Burmans. But this hardly accorded with the degree of political advance the Burmans had already achieved, let alone with the political advance they had sought and must now expect to achieve. The Simla planners hoped to reconcile the two object-ives by phasing and promising, by a fixed timetable, and a firm undertaking. There would be a phase of direct rule on the return of the British, during which extensive reconstruction would take place. This would be made acceptable to Burmans not only by its generosity but also by an understanding that, after a set period of time, constitutional advance would be resumed; the goal being the dominion status within the empire that the Burman premier had vainly sought in 1940–1.

The solution, never perhaps very convincing, met difficulties in Britain, even before it met difficulties in Asia. Some objections were more realistic than others. The Treasury, for example, was increasingly aware of Britain's bankruptcy. Vast sums could not be promised for the reconstruction of Burma, particularly as there was no guarantee that Burma would be able to sustain the infrastructure it created once it was left more to its own resources, running, in Saw's phrase, 'a Rolls-Royce administration on a Ford income'.[43] There were also more emotional objections. Not all shared the forward-looking view of empire that Dorman-Smith and his colleagues shared with officials in the Colonial Office. Moreover, Burma, as ever, was still seen more in an Indian context than in a South-East Asian one. Churchill echoed a phrase from a poem Arthur Bennett had written on hearing the results of the Canadian election of 1911: 'What we have we mean to hold'.[44] With India in mind, the Prime Minister declared in 1942 that he had not become Prime Minister in order to preside over the abandoning of the empire. He condemned the approach to Burma Dorman-Smith recommended: it seemed that Britain was to pour money into Burma only to give it away, to spend in order to be 'kicked out'.[45] There was no doubt some good political sense in avoiding, in the midst of the war, the notion that Britain was to lose its empire at the end of it. But the idea could have been presented more constructively, and have made a positive contribution towards Britain's war effort. It would have made it easier to meet the criticisms of the Americans, on whose air support the battle for Burma must largely depend, and to solicit the support of the Burmans as that battle developed.

In the face of opposition from the Treasury and the Prime Minister, Dorman-Smith persisted with his planning. Perhaps that prevented the preparation of a scheme that might after all have been more practical in other respects. Neither the Treasury's criticisms nor even the Prime Minister's were altogether without foundation. Britain was bankrupt, and a programme of political restraint, followed by promised political advance, might well be impractical. The planning continued, however, to be based on these ideas. As a result, though it had begun in 1942, no plan had actually been approved by the end of 1944, when the reconquest was getting under way. Pressed even by Conservatives in the House of Commons, Churchill referred the matter to the Cabinet Committee on India. It was there that new proposals were hammered out, which Dorman-Smith accepted on a visit to London in March 1945.

These plans, finally embodied in a White Paper of 17 May,

envisaged a phase of direct gubernatorial rule with the prime purpose of reconstruction, and the Governor had secured from the Treasury rather more generous allocations that it had at first offered, though they were less generous than he had at first sought. No set timing was given for this phase. But it was envisaged that the 1937 constitution would be restored within three years, and that steps would be taken, through a constituent assembly, to set up a new one, with which Burma would advance to dominion status, though, as a Burmese correspondent pointed out in *The Times*, no date was fixed as by President Roosevelt for the Philippines.[46]

To Dorman-Smith's disgust, the White Paper was couched in what one of his colleagues called 'Whitehallese',[47] ill-suited to arouse any Burman enthusiasm. What it offered fell in any case far short of what the main Burman leadership now sought. The same month it set forth the aims that had been conceived back in 1944: Burma must become an independent republic, and a provisional government must meanwhile be set up. A further gulf appeared in June. In Burma the Thakin-led AFPFL dominated political life. Yet the White Paper committed Britain to seek a pluralistic democratic system, and there was bipartisan support in London for this approach. At the end of the war Britain could not readily accept the concept of one-party states. Dorman-Smith, returning as Governor, was to be committed to a task that was all the more difficult to achieve, even apart from the problem of the hill peoples, who were still set aside from parliamentary Burma.

The difficulty of the task was seen by Mountbatten, the Supreme Commander, though his reaction only added to the difficulty. The failure to develop a satisfactory plan for post-war Burma had meant that wartime propaganda had no such basis. But, as the campaign got under way, wartime propaganda there had to be, and it fell all the more into the hands of Force 136 and those who were trying to rally support for the military tasks Mountbatten and General Slim had been set. To speed their advance, they accepted the proffered collaboration of the Burma Defence Army (BDA) in March, and with that they boosted the position of the AFPFL. Speaking often of the South African settlement, Mountbatten also played down any prospect of political vengeance or the punishment of collaborators. 'He said that he wished the problem of Burma to be treated in a sensible manner as we had done in South Africa after the Boer War and that we should not use a heavy hand which might result in disaster as it had in Ireland.'[48] The commitments were so extensive that the White Paper became all the more unrealistic. But Mountbatten had no confidence in this policy in any case. He believed that Burma might still remain in the empire as South Africa had, but only if the British dealt with Aung San and the AFPFL leaders. In effect he was arguing that Britain must compromise: it must accept a one-party state if it wanted that state in the empire. There is no certainty that his policy would have worked. But his adhering to it dealt a final blow to Dorman-Smith's chances. Two policies are not better than one.

In the case of Burma, the obligations assumed in and the realities of the war of reconquest, and the commitment of Mountbatten to a programme with political as well as military overtones and purposes, pointed up the irrelevance of the policies developed in London. The adjustments belatedly made to the policy Dorman-Smith had promoted by no means kept up with what was really needed, and the White Paper he himself was disappointed with. But the Government in London failed either to restrain Mountbatten or to alter the policy prescribed for Dorman-Smith. For that failure there were no doubt a number of reasons. First, there was more than one government in London: the wartime coalition was succeeded after VE day by a purely Conservative Government, in turn overthrown in the elections of July. Those changes did not make changes of policy overseas easier. For one thing, the Governments were busy with other tasks. Perhaps, too, they were unwilling to appear to jettison programmes agreed upon during the coalition; and Labour did not wish to be accused of imperial abandonment or scuttle. Moreover, it was as committed as the Conservatives to avoiding one-party states. 'We do not want to see, in Burma or any other country,' Sir Stafford Cripps had told Parliament, 'the rapid seizing of power by any particular group of people in order [to] improvise some form of Government. . . .'[49]

If, however, Labour would not alter its policy, and indeed retained Dorman-Smith, a one-time conservative Minister of Agriculture, as its executant, it made little attempt to control Mountbatten. Again that was difficult. He was Supreme Allied Commander; he was on the spot. And in any case he was intrinsically difficult to restrain. To find a satisfactory policy would no doubt have been extremely difficult in the case of Burma, as it was to prove in the case of French Indo-China and Netherlands India. But that does not perhaps entirely excuse the failure of the Government to do so. Dorman-Smith was to be used in the end as something of a scapegoat, and Hubert Rance, the successor Mountbatten suggested, was given instructions that only pretended to aim at continuity. At least, however, the British did adapt their policy more quickly than the French and the Dutch, and perhaps that is the main point.

Malayan Union

Malaya did not undergo reconquest or liberation. There was an imposing, if belated, surrender in Singapore, damaged a little in Mountbatten's eyes by the action of one of the representatives who pulled out a camera: 'Not even Hollywood, had they been called upon to stage such a ceremony, could have thought up the idea of a Chinese delegate taking pictures.'[50] But the interregnum made the return of the British a less than imposing event. The plans had all the same been drawn up with reconquest in mind, and to those plans, again, the Government initially adhered, even in circumstances that were unanticipated. Pre-war discussions of Malaya had shown that the Colonial Office was divided, as were its officials on the spot. That reflected what was in origin a dual commitment on the part of the British—to the Malays, and to development—the duality of which had been emphasized by the increasing permanence of the immigrant community involved in development, and the need to provide for constitutional advance. Some had almost welcomed the destruction of the ramshackle political system by the Japanese: '. . . a God-sent chance,' said Sir Roland Braddell.[51] Dissolving that framework, such people seemed to think, would enable the British to start anew. For them, Malaya was seen as *tabula rasa*. They took too little account of what had happened in Malaya during the war. The plans developed then became even more irrelevant when the war itself ended in an unexpected way.

The destruction of the old Malaya gave Edward Gent and his colleagues in the Colonial Office and the War Office the opportunity to propose a new structure that would accord at once with the general imperatives of post-war imperial planning and with the particular needs of Malaya.[52] Malaya, like other units in the empire, needed in itself to be stronger, more integrated, and more able to defend itself, so as ultimately to become one of the family of nations that the Commonwealth should become, though, as the Colonial Secretary pointed out, dominion status was not to be the stated aim.

We have been very careful hitherto, in view of the wide divergencies in the Colonial Empire and the obvious fact that many areas will never be suitable for Dominion status, to confine the statement of our objective to that of self-government within the Empire. Malaya and Borneo, with their appalling problems of mixed racial populations, are certainly not territories about which it would be wise to make rash promises about Dominion status.[53]

To reach even the goal of self-government it was necessary in Malaya's case to create a political entity that would involve the immigrant communities as well as the Malays, and the core of the planning at the Colonial Office was the virtual dissolution of the Malay states into an all-Malayan Union. In this fuller Chinese participation would be both possible and desirable, though Singapore, predominantly a Chinese city, should be kept apart, at least for the time being, because of its special strategic importance and because its inclusion might tip the demographic balance against the Malays too provokingly. There was another reason for the Union approach. If the Chinese were not offered the chance of citizenship, they might be exposed to the claims of the KMT regime in China, difficult to deny now that, under the sponsorship of the United States, that regime was taken to be one of the Big Four, and a new treaty on extraterritoriality had been made. 'This gives the Chinese Government power for great intervention in Malaya. It would be intolerable if they could exercise this on behalf of all persons of Chinese race.'[54] Inter-war it had been possible to work with the KMT in China and limit it in Malaya: it could no longer be done, at least not in the same way. Finally it was thought that the Chinese especially would see the war of reconquest as one of liberation. They would be likely to assist the British forces, and for that reason could now hardly be denied a full role in Malaya's political future. In any case, Gent argued, squaring the circle, the British were not abandoning the Malays, but challenging them to develop.[55]

These plans, endorsed by the Cabinet, were to be pursued late in 1945, even though the situation they had envisaged did not in fact eventuate. There was no war of liberation. On the contrary, following the Japanese surrender and given the delayed formal capitulation and the lack of British forces, there was an interregnum in which interracial tensions, provoked in part by the MPAJA, produced a stiffening of Malay resolve and steps towards peninsula-wide Malay political organization. If the sultans could still be bullied, other Malays were unlikely to accept the outcome.

By contrast, the plans the British had adopted were difficult to drop. Though they had not been formally announced before the surrender—partly because the propaganda losses might have been as great as the propaganda gains—the Government was conscious of the connections Force 136 had made with the MPAJA and of the 'collaboration' of some of the Malay élite. The left-wing Malayan Democratic Union had, moreover, published proposals for the future which, not unlike the Government's own, would make modification of the latter difficult to achieve. Again, however, the Government gave the impression of being too busy or too unwilling to change its plans. It would have been difficult. But would it not have been preferable to the kind of volte-face to which it was in the event to be driven?

Borneo Colonies

Borneo was perhaps an exception to the rule. There Britain's plans were in some sense a counterpart to those in Malaya, and it wanted to work towards greater co-ordination between Malaya and British Borneo. The expression of this was in the appointment of a Governor-General, who would co-ordinate the policies of the Union, the new colony of Singapore, and the Borneo territories. Sarawak and North Borneo were formally to become colonies. This was in itself a striking anachronism. But it was argued for on the basis of immediate development and ultimate political participation. Not only was it anachronistic: it would be practically difficult to secure, particularly in the case of Sarawak. In Sabah, which had suffered great destruction, the Company might readily be bought out, and the inhabitants were unlikely to organize opposition. Opposition, if such there was to be, would come only from the Philippines, which was conscious of the old claims of Sulu, and it contemplated, though finally decided against, a protest against the creation of a formally colonial frontier. Sarawak was rather different. The Brookes could be made to abandon the Raj; the old Raja far more willingly than his heir, Anthony Brooke. The leading chiefs could be persuaded to agree. That, however, did not suffice. Borneo was an exception to the rule only in that Britain's policy was to be carried through even in the face of opposition. Adjustments were made elsewhere, but not in Sarawak. It was not that it was *tabula rasa*, but that opposition there could be overridden. Not, however, without the assassination of a Governor.

Thailand

The return of the colonial powers meant readjustment for Thailand. The British wished to fit it into their new framework, not, as some said, as a dependency, but certainly on conditions that were seen as diminishing its independence. They did not go so far as the former minister in Bangkok, Sir Josiah Crosby, had advocated during the war. He had argued for self-government in South-East Asian countries, but did not consider they should have strong armies. 'It will be futile at one and the same time to favour the growth of democratic institutions and to help forge the instrument by which they are likely to meet their doom. What occurred in Siam might just as well take place elsewhere. . . .'[56] The British did not attempt to resolve the problem. What they did attempt did not help the cause Crosby favoured. Their proposals, long-planned, were ill-judged, and the attempt to carry them out, even in a limited way, probably helped to provoke the revival of the military faction that had been discredited at the end of the war. Moreover, the limits of British power were emphasized when the Thais turned to the Americans for support. The old boundaries were restored, but the old independence was regained. While, moreover, the pre-war pan-Thai policy was dropped, the civilian leader Pridi and his colleagues displayed an interest in the nationalist cause in Indo-China. 'Pridi had had the idea of a South East Federation for a long time . . . a Federation consisting of a Free Laos, a Free Cambodia, Burma, Siam, and possibly the four Southern States of Siam to form a separate State. . . .'[57] None of this was at odds with the fundamental aims of British policy. But its strategies had to be modified.

Concluding Remarks

The imperial framework of South-East Asia had been dislodged by incursion from outside. But the powers it turned out determined to return even though, as the French had seen, the discontinuity in authority might well be fatal. Within the territories, the dislocation of colonial authority, the policies the Japanese pursued, and the initiatives the élite and masses seized, all promised great challenges to the old powers. They would have to carry out their objectives, moreover, in a different world context. The ideology of self-determination and nationality had been promoted by the war. The superpowers both in their different ways endorsed it.

Moreover, independent states were now no longer alone in the world as once the Philippine Republic had been.

To meet the challenges of the future in South-East Asia, the British had new plans, albeit they were in keeping with old principles. But, though they prided themselves on their realism, their plans were not realistic enough. They took too little account of what had taken place during the war, and their schemes for going back if only to go forward were unacceptable. Internationally, too, they were over-optimistic, neither able sufficiently to carry along with them the French and the Dutch on the one hand nor the United States on the other. The long-standing principles of their policy were, however, to stand them in good stead. They were able to adapt to what they found in the territories they aspired to rule. Their idealism outlasted that of the Americans.

The Dutch and the French were less able or willing to adapt than the British. The former attempted to fit the independent Republic, proclaimed on 17 August 1945, into a federal state in which they would retain significant power, but undermined the chances by the force they applied to achieve it. The French characteristically resorted more readily to force and made a political solution ever more remote. American intervention was determined by the impact of the cold war, in particular of the 'fall' of China. They were to endorse the Indonesian nationalist cause but afford the French support.

1. C. M. Turnbull, 'British Planning for Post-war Malaya', *Journal of Southeast Asian Studies*, V, 2 (September 1974): 254.

2. Quoted in W. R. Louis, *Imperialism at Bay: The United States and the Decolonization of the British Empire, 1941–1945*, Oxford: Clarendon Press, 1977, p. 136, and D. A. Low, *Lion Rampant*, London: Cass, 1973, p. 71.

3. J. M. Lee and M. Petter, *The Colonial Office, War and Development Policy*, London: Maurice Temple Smith, 1982, pp. 127–8.

4. Quoted in C. Thorne, *Allies of a Kind: The United States, Britain, and the War against Japan, 1941–1945*, London: Hamish Hamilton, 1978, p. 388.

5. J. W. Morley (ed.), *Japan's Foreign Policy 1868–1941: A Research Guide*, New York and London: Columbia University Press, 1974, p. 88.

6. N. Tarling, 'The British and the First Japanese Move into Indo-China', *JSEAS*, XXI, 1 (March 1990): 49–50.

7. Telegram, 10 November 1939, 747, F.O. 371/23562[F11933/456/23], Public Record Office, London.

8. Quoted in G. R. Hess, *The United States' Emergence as a Southeast Asian Power, 1940–1950*, New York: Columbia University Press, 1987, p. 21.

9. Draft message to Congress, 29 November 1941, quoted in D. Miner, 'United States Policy towards Japan 1941: The Assumption that Southeast Asia

Was Vital to the British War Effort', Ph.D. thesis, Columbia University, 1971, pp. 385–6.
10. Morley, *Japan's Foreign Policy*, p. 94.
11. Mark C. Michelson, 'A Place in the Sun: The Foreign Ministry and Perceptions and Policies in Japan's International Relations, 1931–1941', Ph.D. thesis, University of Illinois at Urbana-Champaign, p. 138.
12. Quoted in N. Ike (ed.), *Japan's Decision for War*, Stanford: Stanford University Press, 1967, p. 238.
13. W. S. Churchill, *The Second World War*, London: Cassell, 1954, Vol. IV, pp. 41 ff.
14. Walsh to Foreign Secretary, 31 December 1940, 190, F.O. 371/27786 [F1091/141/61], Public Record Office, London.
15. Walsh to Eden, 23 December 1940, 187A, F.O. 371/27846 [F4291/4291/61], Public Record Office, London.
16. Churchill, *The Second World War*, 1950, Vol. III, pp. 539–40.
17. Akira Iriye, 'Wartime Japanese Planning for Post-War Asia', in Ian Nish (ed.), *Anglo-Japanese Alienation 1919–1952*, Cambridge: Cambridge University Press, 1982, p. 177.
18. Cf. Mark R. Peattie and R. H. Myers (eds.), *The Japanese Colonial Empire*, Princeton: Princeton University Press, 1984.
19. J. H. Boyle, *China and Japan at War*, Stanford: Stanford University Press, 1972.
20. Quoted in T. Friend, *The Blue-Eyed Enemy*, Princeton: Princeton University Press, 1988, p. 110.
21. Quoted in Akira Iriye, *Power and Culture*, Cambridge: Harvard University Press, 1981, p. 166.
22. Quoted in H. Benda et al., *Japanese Military Administration in Indonesia*, New Haven: Southeast Asia Studies, Yale University, 1985, p. 242.
23. Radio broadcast by Roosevelt, 28 December 1941, quoted in Hess, *The United States' Emergence*, p. 217.
24. In his '"Politics by Other Means": World War in the Western Visayas', in A. McCoy (ed.), *Southeast Asia under Japanese Occupation*, New Haven: Southeast Asia Studies, Yale University, 1980, pp. 191 ff.
25. Quoted in Robert H. Taylor, 'The Relationship between Burmese Social Classes and British–Indian Policy on the Behavior of the Burmese Political Élite, 1937–1942', Ph.D. thesis, Cornell University, 1974, p. 627.
26. Quoted in Allan B. Cole (ed.), *Conflict in Indo-China*, Ithaca: Cornell University Press, 1956, p. 47.
27. Quoted in E. B. Reynolds, 'Ambivalent Allies: Japan and Thailand, 1941–1945', Ph.D. thesis, University of Hawaii, 1988, p. 505.
28. Quoted in L. P. Mathur, *History of the Andaman and Nicobar Islands*, Delhi: Sterling, 1968, p. 295.
29. Report to Combined Chiefs of Staff, London, 1951, paras. B489–92.
30. John A. L. Sullivan, 'The United States, the East Indies, and World War II: American Efforts to Modify the Colonial Status Quo', Ph.D. thesis, University of Massachusetts, 1968, pp. 140–1, 192 ff.; P. Dennis, *Troubled Days of Peace: Mountbatten and South East Asia Command, 1945–46*, Manchester: Manchester University Press, 1987, pp. 75 ff.
31. Hodsoll to Sansom, 14 May 1945, F.O. 371/46463[F3394/1127/23], Public Record Office, London.
32. M. P. Onorato (ed.), *Origins of the Philippine Republic: Extracts from the*

Diaries and Records of Francis Burton Harrison, Ithaca: Cornell University, 1974, pp. 182–3.

33. MacDermot to Eden, 31 May 1945, F.O. 371/46463[F3822/1127/23], Public Record Office, London.

34. Telegram, 7 July 1946, 28 Saving, F.O. 371/54344[F10678/10035/83], Public Record Office, London.

35. F.E.(O)(46) 52, 16 April 1946, CAB 134/280, Public Record Office, London.

36. Telegram, 7 July 1946, 28 Saving, F.O. 371/54344[F10678/10035/83], Public Record Office, London.

37. Quoted in C. L. M. Penders, *Indonesia Selected Documents on Colonialism and Nationalism, 1830–1942*, St Lucia: University of Queensland Press, 1977, p. 148.

38. Conversation, 12 June 1942, F.O. 371/31751[F4533/90/61]; printed in *Documenten betreffende de Buitenlandse Politiek van Nederland 1919–45*, C, The Hague: Nijhoff, 1984, Vol. IV, pp. 640–1.

39. Quoted, with some doubt, by Robert K. Wolthuis, 'United States Foreign Policy towards the Netherlands Indies: 1937–1945', Ph.D. thesis, Johns Hopkins University, 1968, pp. 372–3.

40. Cf. 'background' issued by Dr Van Mook, 5 December 1942, *Documenten* C, 1987, Vol. V, pp. 727–9.

41. C. Kiriloff and R. Rathausky (eds.), *Documents of the August 1945 Revolution in Vietnam*, Canberra: Department of International Relations, Australian National University, 1963, p. 66.

42. Quoted in Iriye, *Power and Culture*, p. 247.

43. Quoted in E. C. V. Foucar, *I Lived in Burma*, London: Dobson, 1956, p. 208.

44. Quoted in R. G. Myles and Doug Owram, *Imperial Dreams and Colonial Realities*, Toronto: University of Toronto Press, 1988, p. 19.

45. Amery to Dorman-Smith, 15 April 1942, L/PO/236, India Office Library, London.

46. Ma Hla Ye, *The Times*, 25 May 1945.

47. Waight to Dorman-Smith, May 1945, R/8/11, India Office Library, London.

48. 6th Misc., 2 April 1945, W.O. 172/1757, Public Record Office, London.

49. The debate is in Hansard, House of Commons, Vol. 411, cols. 495–550, 1 June 1945.

50. P. Ziegler, *Mountbatten*, London: Collins, 1985, p. 303.

51. Quoted in A. J. Stockwell, *British Policy and Malay Politics during the Malayan Union Experiment 1945–1948*, Kuala Lumpur: MBRAS, 1979, p. 17.

52. Albert Lau, *The Malayan Union Controversy 1942–1948*, Singapore: Oxford University Press, 1991, Chaps. 2–4.

53. Stanley to Eden, 6 January 1944, Secret, F.O. 371/41726[F126/126/61], Public Record Office, London.

54. Loose sheets, n.d., found in C.O. 531/24 [92503], Public Record Office, London.

55. Stockwell, *British Policy and Malay Politics*, p. 33.

56. J. Crosby, *Siam: The Crossroads*, London: Hollis and Carter, 1945, pp. 152–3.

57. Memorandum by John Coast, 12 January 1948, F.O. 371/69686 [F1216/286/61], Public Record Office, London.

6

Decolonization and Independence

BRITAIN'S plans for post-war South-East Asia were unrealistic. There was a gap between the resources it could apply and those it needed. The planning took little account of Britain's growing indebtedness, and the plans envisaged were more suited to the kind of prosperous metropolitan power Britain had once been than the impoverished one it now was. At the same time Britain's aims had expanded well beyond those it had normally adopted when it was comparatively more powerful. The British appeared to envisage substantial restructuring of the societies with which they were connected, Burma, Malaya, and Borneo. And that—if it could be done at all—required far greater resources than they had at their disposal. The Colonial Secretary told the House of Commons on 13 July 1943 that he considered 'the real test of the sincerity and success of our Colonial policy is two-fold. It is not only the actual political advances that we make, but it is also, and I think more important, the steps that we are taking, economic and social as well as political, to prepare the people for further and future responsibilities.' As the historian of colonial development suggests, 'a truly tremendous obligation was undertaken',[1] a deeper and more explicit obligation to the future than Britain's principled pragmatism had ever previously suggested.

Additionally, the planning the British undertook involved more substantial intervention than they had previously attempted. It may have marked a continuity in their thinking that misled them. Increasingly the British had to recognize that it was no longer quite so much a matter of establishing a framework for the exercise of power. But there was a sense in which their new ordering of South-East Asia did not go much beyond that. They spoke characteristically of a transfer of power. What was needed, as they saw it, was a further adjustment. An educated élite could take over, and somehow be in a position at once to satisfy the demands of the outside world and those of its own people. The British engaged in a process always difficult for an imperial power to undertake, shifting from one set of collaborators to another: it was not surprising, perhaps, that some of them saw the Japanese interregnum as a godsend. Given that new collaborators could be found, it was not certain they had or could acquire or sustain the necessary popular support. The power the British had to transfer was limited. The holding of power had always been a shared activity in any case. The new élites did not have force at their disposal, any more than wealth; nor did the British. The plans of the British had been predicated on the impact of a military victory. In most places, they were victorious without fighting. Even where they fought, as in Burma, the effect was reduced by the participation of nationalists or by commitments to minorities. They were rarely in a position to force through their policies, particularly as the demobilization programme reduced the number of British troops in the East. Moreover, Indian troops, on whom increasing reliance was placed, could be used only if due account were taken of the susceptibilities of the Indian leaders, whose allegiance the British were also seeking to retain.

The Other Colonial Powers

In another way, too, realism was lacking: that was in relation to the other European colonial powers. Once their patron, Britain was not now in a position to enforce their return. That might not have elicited their gratitude in any case, though doing it would certainly have provoked nationalist opposition. But it could not stop their trying to make a comeback, pressed as they were both to restore their prestige and to respond to the interests of Europeans resident in their colonies. Nor could Britain greatly influence the nature of their assertive attempts to do so, or even avoid its own involvement in them. That was partly because of the way the war ended and of the obligations to rescue prisoners of war and internees and receive the surrender of the Japanese. But the British had also to take account of European interests that affected their treatment of Holland and France. History might have indicated the past impact of European considerations on British policy in South-East Asia. But too little account was taken of the interconnection in the plans for the post-war period. The British could not compel the French and the Dutch to come to terms with the nationalists. That limited, too, the possibilities of a regional approach. So, too, did their failure to recognize the potential of nationalism in

Indonesia and Indo-China. Yet the success of their policy for their own dependencies—their desire to build them into a new post-imperial framework and defend them from Communism—partly depended on that.

'We must not appear to be ganging up with Western Powers against Eastern peoples striving for independence,' Esler Dening told a Foreign Office meeting early in 1947.

Rather should our aim be to contrive a general partnership between independent or about-to-be independent Eastern peoples and the Western Powers who by their past experience are best able to give them help and, in our case, to some extent protection. Owing to political conditions in the N.E.I. and Indo-China, this process of consultation and cooperation with these areas must be a gradual one.[2]

These problems the British continued to recognize as the independence struggles went on. Guibaut, the French Consul-General in Singapore, advocated a common policy among the colonial powers, the Brussels treaty being reflected in South-East Asia, as P. S. Scrivener, of the Special Commissioner's office, put it in April 1948. The difficulty was that the peoples of South-East Asia were not yet conscious of the threat of Communism that had united those in Western Europe: their concern was with imperialism and colonialism. 'We have consistently pursued a more liberal Colonial policy in South-East Asia than either of the other two Metropolitan powers concerned,' a Foreign Office comment ran. 'There is a great danger that, if our alliance with the other Western Powers in Europe were to be correspondingly reflected in our behaviour in the East, we should lose the sympathy of the Asiatic peoples. . . .'[3] The persistent Frenchman tried again the following year. The response was

that the UK cannot offer to underwrite the colonial policies of either the French or the Dutch in South East Asia. Our only hope lies in their finding respectively some settlement of their own problems with the people of Indo-China and Indonesia. If and when that is done, the possibility of a closer association, not only between them and us, but between the Western and the Asiatic powers, may become a practical proposition. . . .[4]

Whatever their defects, Britain's plans had an element of realism which the plans of others did not share. Though their making seemed uncoordinated, they can be seen as a positive attempt to deal with a post-war problem. They were not merely an attempt to give Britain a place in the world, but also an attempt to deal with what was later called the 'Third' or 'developing' world by providing there an 'order' that would 'succeed' the 'imperial' one. Empires of the old sort, the British recognized, were at an end. But what was to replace them? This question they were seeking to answer.

The ideology of this new world was plain enough. The Wilsonian concepts of nationality and self-determination were accepted in the Third World itself and in the United Nations (UN), and were a focus of rivalry between the emerging superpowers. Accepting such an ideology, the bases of which were akin to their own thinking, the British wanted to ensure that the nations that emerged could survive. They should be viable in themselves; their governments should be orderly and responsive. In turn that would make them less the focus of international conflict, affording the rival superpowers less reason to intervene, and requiring less intervention of the British, too. All the same, the British saw themselves as having a key role in this transition, and perhaps indulged themselves too much, either in contemplating the joyously long time it would take, the constructive employment it would offer, or the influence it would confer. But the burdens would be great, whatever the rewards.

The Colonial Office was, as in Africa, 'attempting no less than to build "nation-states" which would not only be self-governing but democratic and economically self-supporting'.[5] The First World War had intensified the commitment to self-government in India. The Second World War redoubled the urge to create a world of nation-states. The British had to speed the process, but still intended, partly by that means, to play a determining role in it.

Self-government must be an orderly growth, and be designed to meet local conditions (e.g. plural communities). We cannot, in the name of liberty, allow territories which we control to fall into chaos and general unrest, nor into such weakness and instability as to create political danger spots. This might mean, however, that we should have the appearance of resisting legitimate claims. It is therefore important that action and publicity should go hand in hand. We have not only to decide the proper tempo for political advancement, but also to convince the peoples concerned and the world at large that we are not yielding step by step to pressure, but are sincerely following out an enlightened policy.[6]

The British also saw that they would need to retain a number of regional *points d'appui*, from which their influence might be exerted at least in the transitional phase. The concept of a framework remained. Within it, however, substantial adjustments were to be made. The concept in some ways recalled the days of Cobden and Palmerston. A world of independent states could be set up. The imperialist framework would prove to have been nothing more nor less than a prelude to it and a preparation for it. It was here, perhaps, that the British showed themselves at their most optimistic or unrealistic. The old framework had this objective remotely in view; but the transition to it was cautious, determined, the British hoped, by the power they could apply, as well as by the influence they could educe, by the mutuality of their relationship with the world. The new order was now to be brought rapidly nearer. But that still required not only adjustments in the collaborating élites, but the application of power during the transition. That Britain hoped to supply, eking it out by building regional structures which it trusted would be more, not less than the sum of their parts, and also by trying to maximize the coincidence of their aims with those of others, the United States, the United Nations, and even the Soviet Union, without diminishing their own role or abandoning their definition of the world of nation-states. Sometimes they were precipitate in implementing policy or, again, in abandoning it. The haste was sometimes justified. Others might have the opportunity in the post-war world to advance worse options. And the British were no longer sure of determining the timetable.

In one sense, therefore, Britain's wartime plans for post-war South-East Asia were realistic: they attempted to look forward. But both the commitments undertaken during the war and the circumstances faced at the end of it indicated that the plans had to be adjusted. Not only were they too optimistic in terms of the resources at Britain's disposal; they were unrealistic given what had happened in South-East Asia during the war and what the position was in South-East Asia at the end of it.

The Adjustment of Britain's Policies

The policies of the British were adjusted during the immediate post-war years 1945–7 in respect of British territories, in respect of those of the other European colonial powers, and in respect of Thailand. In some cases it seemed that implementing the policies should never have been attempted in the first place, and that adjustment should have begun immediately, if not sooner. In others, it could certainly be argued that Britain adhered to the prescribed policies for too long, failing to improvise or to develop satisfactory alternatives. But perhaps the overall impression that should properly be derived is that of prompt and extensive adjustment, and it may be that rather than inflexibility that needs to be explained. The contrast with the other European colonial powers points up some of the reasons. The British Government was able on some occasions to mask its changes of policy by a change of individuals, blaming those it replaced for the failures of its own policy, and allowing their successors to experiment at their peril. This may have made it easier for them to win support or avoid criticism at home. In fact Labour seemed to think that the real task was to diminish Conservative criticism. In this they did not entirely succeed. But their parliamentary majority was so strong that it may be questioned why they tried so hard and why they were so ready to sacrifice local officers to do so. The contrast with France and the Netherlands is in any case striking. The domestic support their governments enjoyed was so limited and so insecure that they could display little flexibility. Moreover, when officials were replaced, they were replaced for their failure, but successors were rarely encouraged to experiment. The British found this inflexibility difficult to understand, and resented it particularly as it stood in the way of some of the region-wide implications of the adjustments they were themselves making. They failed to allow for the influence of local French and Dutch settlers; there being few British equivalents to consider. In Africa they were themselves to discover what settler pressures meant.

There were other and not unconnected reasons for the contrast. The Netherlands, occupied in the war, was seeking to guarantee its economic and political future: as after the Napoleonic wars, it could not envisage that future without renewing political and constitutional ties with its major overseas possession; and no politician who argued for loosening these ties could hope to sustain the kind of coalition that the Dutch parliamentary system involved. France, of course, was a state of greater substance. But there questions of prestige stood in the way of a change of attitude, and could be used in domestic politics in a similar way. Adjustment was made difficult in another sense. The question of 'collaboration' was not, of course, an issue in Britain, though it was, in respect of the INA, in India. It was for the Dutch at home, and that coloured the attitude towards those who could fairly be described as collaborators in Indonesia. Was it possible to deal with them? There was, however, a more profound way in which the British found it easier to adjust their post-war policies than the other colonial powers. Britain's policies were in any case transitional: the aim of its new imperialism—as, it liked with some good reason to think, of its old—was to prepare countries for a kind of world in which stable nation-states could securely coexist and provide secure conditions for trade and commerce. In essence the British still saw themselves as a great commercial, financial, and industrial nation. Its future would depend on successful activities in those fields and not on imperial rule. With minimum objectives of this sort adjustments were the more feasible. It took time for the Dutch and the French to realize that they too could survive in such a world. Some would say that in the event they managed it better than the British. There was another vein of wishful thinking among the British. They were no longer the great commercial, financial, and industrial nation they had been. The notion that they were made it easier in general to adjust their policy. There were certainly times when their economic difficulties were at odds with liberal colonial policies. By and large, however, the latter prevailed.

The aim of the British had been to build up an élite to which power could in due course be transferred in confidence that it would rule fairly and democratically and provide proper opportunities for trade and investment. The adjustment did not really alter this policy. It altered the direction of the search for such an élite; it altered its speed: cut corners and compromises ensued. As a result, it may have increased the problems that élite was to face. But it may also be argued that it reduced them, since holding up the transfer may only have exaggerated division, bitterness, expectation, and disappointment. And it is easy to be wise after the event. Did Britain cut too many corners, make too many compromises? Did it abandon or scuttle? The criteria for a flexible policy are uncertain. What we know happened as a result is not easily forgotten when we are assessing the deliberations of policy-makers at the time.

Harold Macmillan's speech to Parliament in Cape Town in February 1960 suggested in a famous phrase that the 'wind of change' was blowing through the African continent. The phrase was borrowed; and not apt, if, as has been suggested, the response was merely to drift.[7] In fact the policy the Prime Minister was advocating was not new, though its tempo had changed. The 'growth of national consciousness is a political fact. We must all accept it as a fact.' Policies must be based on it:

what Governments and Parliaments in the United Kingdom *have* done since the last war in according independence to India, Pakistan, Ceylon, Malaya and Ghana, and what they *will* do to Nigeria and other countries now nearing independence—all this . . . we do in the belief that it is the only way to establish the future of the Commonwealth and of the free world on sound foundations.

The British Prime Minister also argued that these 'great experiments in self-government' were aimed to make the 'uncommitted peoples of Asia and Africa' swing to the West rather than the East and come down 'in favour of freedom and order and justice'.[8]

Communism and the United States

One element in the shift in British policy deserves more attention in this context. Clearly some segments of the élite were not acceptable. It may indeed be that the British were overhasty in their anxiety to avoid the Communists, for long their antagonists in the colonial world, and to turn to safer politicians, though, if that was a fault of theirs, it was one the United States would redouble. To some extent the British were stepping in with new adjustments for fear that otherwise they would be able to make no adjustments at all, and, in particular, that the position of the moderates would be eroded. That did not seem, as perhaps it should have done, to undermine the confidence of the British in their policy, nor their belief that the élites whom they now accommodated could undertake the tasks set before them. Perhaps it was characteristic that they put so much emphasis on foreign intervention. It was international Communism, they persuaded themselves, that kept alive the local Communists. They may as a result have downplayed local sources of support for the Communists; they may have exaggerated their division from other elements of the élite, or the possibility or desirability of so dividing them; and they may have felt less disposed to deal with problems that helped the Communists elicit support. In so doing they risked rather than enhanced the long-term prospects of stability.

There were, of course, reasons to stress the international element in Communism. First, it was an international movement, and it had helped to support anti-British movements in Asia in the inter-war period. It offered an alternative view of the future to the one to which the British looked forward, a different framework in which states might operate, and a different international connection for the local élite. It did not merely challenge the British locally. It offered an escape from a system the development of which the British and their allies sought to determine and timetable, and an alternative external source of potential support. Second, it was at the same time a Russian-led movement. The Russians were the traditional antagonists of British empire and influence in Asia. There were good reasons to apprehend that Russian-backed Communism would take advantage of the postwar phase of vacuum in the old imperial world and capture the allegiance of its élites. 'It is a mistake to assume that nationalism in Asia is necessarily due to the evil machinations of Communists,' the envoy in Bangkok declared, 'though the latter will, of course, always exploit for their own ends the not unnatural desire of Asiatics to rid themselves of colonial rule....'9 The Russian moves in Europe only added to the apprehension. Those led the Russians to pursue policies that in the first instance helped European colonialism. Hopeful of success in France itself, for example, the Communists were unwilling to take up the cause of the Viet-minh. But in the longer term the threat was more visible. Churchill pointed it out in 1946. But it was made obvious to others in 1947–8, and perhaps crises in Europe exaggerated apprehensions in Asia.

It is possible to suggest that the British may have emphasized the international menace of Communism for another reason. The British wanted to involve the United States in the fate of the old imperial world. Pre-war they had seen the need for American backing against the advance of European Fascism and against the Japanese threat. But they had also been aware that, given American isolationism, they must not appear to push the United States into commitments. That might be counter-productive. Something of the same problem appeared post-war. The Americans had their own view of the future of the old imperial world. It comprised a mix of Wilsonian idealism with a realistic appreciation of economic opportunity. It had led them, even in the wartime years, to distrust the British, to criticize their role in the anti-Japanese war, and to suggest that their real concern was to regain their colonies. At the end of the war, it led them to disrupt what they saw as British plans for Thailand, and to cut off lend-lease help. It could be argued that the British were tempted to play up the threat of international Communism in order at once to involve the Americans in the area and to enlist them in the pursuit of what they considered more rational policies. Naturally they ran the risk that the Americans, more powerful in any case, would determine the line to be taken, and that as a result the emphases in South-East Asian policy, in respect of nationalism and Communism, of regionalism and the stance of the other Western powers, would be altered.

The British view of the future of the old imperial world was not in fact so very different from the American. The aim was to create stable states with which trade could be carried on in a regional framework which enhanced security and attenuated the conflict of East and West. At times mutual distrust obscured this congruence. Thailand is a case in point: the British were seeking a more democratic form of government, but they were seen as imperialists who wished to deny true independence. There were also differences of approach and timing, and different judgments about the way to reach the agreed objective, upon which distrust could feed. Though American policy in the Philippines involved, even more transparently than British policy elsewhere, the transfer of power to an élite, they were yet able to see it as part of a fixed timetable which other colonial powers might similarly follow. Though they were to secure, by quite stringent means, privileges in the Philippines for their trade and bases for their forces, they were critical of the kind of links by which the British wanted to sustain their influence and build stability. The gradualism and caution of others seemed more devious than their own.

Optimistically, the British hoped to play Greeks to the Americans' Romans. The British secured what Dean Acheson, the American Secretary of State, called 'a chance to talk the matter over with us before the thing crystallised . . . to go over it with us, pointing out their views and to be allowed to come in on the formulation at the start'.[10] In Cabinet discussion, it was suggested, perhaps too optimistically, 'that it should not be impracticable to maintain the political influence of the United Kingdom in South East Asia, while arranging for the United States to provide much of the capital investment that was required'.[11] The threat of the barbarians was an argument the British could use. But if they exaggerated the threat, it seems doubtful that very much of the exaggeration was in fact consciously or even subconsciously the result of a wish to persuade the Americans to accept their view of the proper policies for the old imperial world. Exaggeration, if such it was, derived more from the tendency of the British to perceive that area from an external point of view and to perceive its future in terms of the transfer of power to trustworthy élites who might work within and help to sustain the renewed framework, as co-operating groups had helped to sustain the old.

'Our interests and commitments in Asia . . . are greater and more varied than those of any other Western Power,' the Foreign Office declared in 1949. 'The question arises whether they are not in excess of our post-war strength. . . .' Commitments had been reduced in India and Burma. Now Britain's commitments 'should be for the purpose of maintaining internal security within our own territories, encouraging confidence in the adolescent nations of the region, and supporting local efforts to place defence establishments on a sound footing . . .'. The Foreign Office concluded that 'there is no other Power capable of undertaking the formidable task of trying to link South East Asia with the West and to create some kind of regional association which will be capable of effective resistance against communism and Russian expansion . . .'.[12] The Communist threat, intensified by the triumph of the CCP in 1948–9, gave a new emphasis to the promotion of regionalism. 'We should . . . do our utmost to encourage a spirit of co-operation and self-reliance in South East Asia with a view to the creation of a common front against Russian expansion in that area.'[13]

In any case the British had little success in their endeavour to involve the Americans in their policy. While the Americans abandoned Roosevelt's opposition to the return of France to Indo-China, they took few steps to support the regional approach that the British favoured, and that in fact might have made that return more acceptable. They came to realize that they needed to intervene in Indonesia, and there, despite their commitment to the Dutch in Europe, they came down in the end on the Wilsonian side. But their involvement in the area as a whole was limited and incoherent until the triumph of the CCP in China and the beginning of the Korean war. Then their policy changed. But it still did not fall into the British pattern. It put even more emphasis on the international sources of the threat of Communism and stressed its monolithic nature. It sought to draw a line of containment round the Communist states.

Southeast Asia is a vital segment in the line of containment of Communism stretching from Japan southward and around to the Indian Peninsula. The security of the three major non-Communist base areas in this quarter of the world—Japan, India, and Australia—depends in a large measure on the denial of Southeast Asia to the Communists.[14] The United States rushed to support any regime that seemed to be on the right side of the line, whether or not it was democratic. 'We must support against aggressive pressure from the outside even states which we regard unfavourably,' Dean Rusk declared in October 1949. 'We must preserve them merely as states. . . . Our first concern is not with the internal structure of states but with their safety from aggression.'[15] Even the French were now undeservedly to receive substantial support for their ill-conceived ventures in Vietnam. '[Can] we afford to be purists and perfectionists?' the American ambassador in Paris had asked.[16] On the defeat of the French, the United States set up the South-East Asia Treaty Organization (SEATO).

A decade earlier it may have seemed that an Asia of sovereign countries—held together only by membership of the United Nations and by the international monetary arrangements created at Bretton Woods, each following the principle of the 'open door' in its foreign relations— would be enough to satisfy American political and economic interests. But the effect of the Communist victory in China, immediately followed by the Korean War, convinced the United States that it needed positive allies and must create a system of collective security for the nations of the 'free world' in Asia. That in turn meant ensuring not only national independence from colonial rule but also the emergence in each country of a régime willing to identify itself with American strategy. Such a transition was easily achieved in South Korea, Taiwan and the Philippines. The situation was more complicated in other countries, and might even require covert American intervention. . . .[17]

Independent India

By this time, on the other hand, the British programme had advanced in ways that were consistent with its original aims, though nothing had gone quite as expected. Burma had left the Commonwealth, but India had remained within it at the price, however, of adjustments that effectively still further reduced that organization's overall coherence. The British approach to South-East Asia had always been influenced by Indian considerations. Now these considerations had changed their shape but they were still there. At the Foreign Office in May 1949 an official reasserted the British belief in both good government and local leadership.

R. A. Hibbert had doubted current analysis of the appeal of Communism, which depended in large part on physical force and organization rather than ideology. It was important that states should be 'well and liberally governed'. India, he thought, could set the example in Asia, as the United Kingdom had in Europe. 'India, by her example and influence, can do more than any other power to establish a healthy political system in South East Asia; and if such a system is established, the ideological attraction of communism will perhaps be found to be much weaker than we suppose.' The problem in South-East Asia was 'not primarily economic nor primarily ideological but primarily political...'. Communism was to be countered by 'the painful and piecemeal process of establishing political stability in individual countries, and Asian (necessarily Indian) initiative in Asia'.[18]

If India was to play a leading role in the area—and such was the design of the Indians—then the British hoped to shape it. But they recognized that their own policy would also have to allow for the character India wanted to give its role. That seemed not impossible in itself. For the British it could appear a development of their own policy. But it was hardly consistent with the new American approach. The difference was most apparent over Indo-China. Increasingly it seemed that Britain, in seeking to gather support from others, would be driven into policies that conflicted. Support would be bought at the expense of effectiveness. The impossible contradictions of an imperial position would reappear in the post-imperial world.

'If security against the spread of Communism is the objective,' B. R. Pearn wrote in 1956, 'surely this can best be attained by supporting India in her present domestic policy and by encouraging her interest in South-East Asia. India has the necessary strength, and India is striving to work out an Asian alternative to Communism.'[19] 'Indian policy in practice tends to be more realistic and satisfactory than the neutralism they preach....' Rallying South-East Asia round SEATO and Thailand was less desirable.

We do not of course want to weaken or disparage SEATO, but it is no use blinking the fact that except for the countries which had their own special reasons for joining SEATO the inhabitants of South-East Asia would rather trust the Communists not to attack than take military precautions against this in open association with the 'colonialists'.[20]

There was, of course, another danger, that India would be seen by South-East Asian countries as itself too much of a big brother, and the support it gave to independence movements might be seen as patronage. Prime Minister Nehru ran some such risk at the Bandung conference in 1955, where some British officials thought he played 'a surprisingly undistinguished part'.[21] India's geographical propinquity did not necessarily make its influence more welcome. It could not help being interested, like its British predecessor, in the security of the Bay of Bengal. The British transferred the Andaman and Nicobar islands to the new dominion, where they initially formed the only D-class state and later a union territory. In a decolonizing South-East Asia, the Andamans were the scene of colonization, particularly of settlers from East Bengal. They were also a melting-pot, a community, as K. R. Ganesh put it, 'which has its own cultural forms, which have been evolved in the islands itself. It has completely eliminated caste from its social system. . . . These people have developed a cosmopolitan outlook. . . .'[22] Indians were proud of the association of the Andamans with the imprisonment of those who had sought to overthrow British rule. They also became a significant naval base, in what the British had seen and now the Indians saw as an Indian sea.

The Emergence of Independent States in South-East Asia

In Malaya it was possible to believe that the British were pursuing an exceptional kind of policy. With the outbreak of the Emergency—and characteristically they emphasized its association with the machinations of international Communism more than with the frustrations of the Malayan Chinese community from which the Communists were largely drawn—the colonial power could rediscover the old 'purpose' of sustaining the Malay character of Tanah Melayu. Some have concluded that divide-and-rule had by this time at least become British policy. Indeed it might now be more actively pursued than pre-war, since it was now more necessary to engage in political manipulation, and it was also even more necessary to retain control over dollar-earning Malaya. Such ideas had been present earlier and were present again. But they had not been the prime motivation in British policy earlier, nor, though dollars were needed, were they now. The Malay community, more confidently led, saw no long-term future in continued British patronage. But the British also deliberately sought to bring about community reconciliation, and to put Malaya on the path of constitutional development. It would now depend, even more than Gent and others had hoped, on collaboration at the élite level. But that was consistent with the overall thrust in British colonial policy pre-war as well as post-war.

In their perception of the post-imperial world, the British saw the need for a viable international framework, supported by the United States, but also by their own retention of *points d'appui*. It was also necessary that the new states within that framework should abide by its rules and be themselves viable. The transfer of power to acceptable élite elements was designed to secure these objectives. But it was not clear that such states would in fact be viable. The British believed that states adopting constitutional and democratic systems would be more likely to sustain an acceptable code of international behaviour, and that perception was enforced by what they saw as the European lessons of the 1930s. They perhaps made too little of the problems standing in the way of setting up and developing such systems, given the limited experience of them, the problems of integration the states faced, particularly in the light of the existence and aspirations of minorities the old colonial frontiers had contained, and the high expectations of both élite and masses.

Their main criterion of viability was not necessarily consistent with the possession of a constitutional structure. That was a question of size. It was one of the arguments used against independence for Singapore. As Patrick Dean at the Foreign Office put it,

self-government and independence for Singapore seem to me doubtful propositions. The island is almost the same size as the Isle of Wight with about 1,300,000 inhabitants, 900,000 of whom are Chinese. It cannot exist effectively as an entity on its own, and it has no indigenous resources and virtually no industries.[23]

David Marshall, Chief Minister of Singapore, tried to counter this view. Singapore, he argued,

has both a larger population and a larger revenue than six of the States Members of the United Nations, namely, Costa Rica, Iceland, Jordan, Libya, Nicaragua and Panama. Its educational standards are probably higher than those of most States Members outside Europe and North America. The standard of living, though low on European standards, is high on Asian standards. . . .[24]

Small states, the British believed, could not survive in the harsh post-war world, having the resources neither to sustain economic development nor to defend their independence. Their tendency, therefore, was to push decolonizing territories into unions and federations. But that was often inconsistent, not only with their past, but also with any hope of developing workable constitutional systems. It was also likely to provoke rather than resolve minority problems, or to create new ones in place of old. Furthermore, it might upset other states and thus damage regional stability. In the post-war world frontiers were difficult to change. In a world dominated by one power, it had been possible to adjust them. In a world dominated by more than one, it was much less feasible. Furthermore, the new élites laid claim to the colonial inheritance and sought to build new states within the old frontiers. They were not the less attached to them because they generally corresponded to no long-standing sense of nationhood. Perhaps the reverse was true. Creating new states, even out of fragments of British territory, was thus a sensitive issue. It could appear as an imperialist anachronism.

The constitutional development of Malaya underlined the problem. The Peninsula was gaining independence. What future did the British envisage for the territories in Borneo, too small, it was assumed, to stand on their own? What future did they envisage for Singapore, also, they thought, too small to stand on its own, and in addition reckoned still as one of the strategic *points d'appui* the holding of which was necessary to support the emerging international framework as it had been a linchpin of the old? Incorporating Singapore with Malaya, though long envisaged as its ultimate fate, and seen by the rising People's Action Party (PAP) as its economic salvation, risked undoing the inter-ethnic agreement upon which Malayan stability rested. The Borneo territories, already distinguished one from another, were increasingly going their separate ways. Could they be brought together before it was too late?

In the early 1960s, an attempt was made to answer these questions by the creation of Malaysia, connecting Singapore and the Borneo territories with now independent Malaya. Associating these territories was not entirely a new idea, and indeed the pre-war Governor of the Straits Settlements had not only been High Commissioner but also Agent for North Borneo and Sarawak. But a restructuring difficult to carry through in the imperial world was many times more difficult in the post-imperial. Not only had the aspirations of those within the territories developed and their interests become more distinct. Their neighbours were no longer other colonial powers, but independent states, Indonesia and the Philippines, with different views of South-East Asia and its future. Perhaps surprisingly in view of their regional interests, the British took too little account of these changes. It was, however, difficult to do so: no machinery was available in the world of nation-states to attempt the kind of consultation that the European powers had earlier engaged in, for example, at the Berlin conference of 1884–5. A limited role for the United Nations and the Maphilindo consultation were inadequate substitutes. Malaysia was born, truncated by the absence of Brunei, amid international controversy and Indonesian confrontation. Though the contest with Indonesia committed British forces far more than anticipated or hoped, and ultimately prompted a further withdrawal from South-East Asia, in some sense it helped to hold the new state together, giving the Alliance a triumph in the 1964 elections. But Singapore left the Federation the following year.

Despite the prognostications of others and perhaps initial doubts on the part of its own leaders, Singapore survived and prospered. In the world of the 1960s and 1970s size was no longer seen as a criterion for independence. Rather, it was accepted, if not stated, that independence could be held in varying degrees, and that it could be theoretically absolute though in practice qualified. That was the only possible logic in a world of equal nations: they must recognize that they are not equal in power. That was not, of course, a new factor in the international life of states, but it was one that had itself attained a new dimension. Singapore was larger than some others, and more populous than many. But the survival of Singapore, and the subsequent emergence of Brunei as a fully independent state, indicated other factors that were at work. First, they were connected with the economic advance that most of South-East Asia shared. Second, even though it was in part still directed at a Communist threat, there was a growing sense of regional purpose among them. In some sense, it might even be said, Britain's hopes were being realized, though at a time when its chances of taking advantage of economic opportunities were entirely eclipsed by Japan's, and it had come to believe that its own future was more closely, though still not exclusively, tied to Europe.

No one document encapsulates British policy for South-East Asia in the post-war period. But much may be deduced from a range of policy papers and from political actions. There was, as a consistent element in British policy in this period, a desire for stable regimes under which trade and commerce could be carried on. The aim was consistent indeed with British policy over a much larger period, and it can be argued that, at least from the industrial revolution onwards, this was the primary aim of British policy, one particularly suited to a power of pre-eminent commercial and industrial capacity. The desire was to establish a framework of international order, within which national regimes would guarantee internal stability. Through that longer period, the aim had been sought by a number of means, by non- or limited intervention and by imperialist intervention, more or less in sequence. Now the aim remained, even though Britain's pre-eminence in industrial revolution had long since passed. The means to secure stability must, however, change. Account must be taken of the emergence of superpowers, of changes in Europe, of the relative decline of British power, of the emergence of new nations, and of the aspirations of nationalist élites. The answer was, however, both old and new.

In a sense, the objective was to revert to a situation where limited or non-intervention could again prevail. Then, in Palmerstonian days, it had been hoped that existing regimes could be brought to change without being revolutionized or displaced. The élitist view still dominated. Now it was desirable to transfer power to élites who would be collaborative. At the same time, however, they had to be democratic. That was not merely because Britain had just fought a war against Fascism, and had been a dependent ally of the largest of the democratic states. It was also believed, in particular because of the experience of the 1930s, that democratic states would help to provide for international stability. There was, as in the old system, but now even more, a mutuality between the framework and what it contained. It was stronger if its component parts were stronger, though it helped to strengthen them.

In the face of these policies, there were many obstacles. In part that was because they contained internal contradictions. The élite to which power was transferred might not be able to rule in a democratic manner; it might not even wish to do so. Nor was it clear that democratic states were necessarily more sophisticated in their approach to foreign policy than one-party states. If there were such conceptual difficulties, there were also practical ones. The policy was in part a recognition that Britain could no longer enforce its views to the extent that it had been able so to do in the past. But that meant that there were other policies to contend with. The Americans' view of the world was not so different, but they had different timetables and different tactics, and mutual jealousies also obscured the congruence of aims. It was hard, too, to fit the returning colonial powers into the picture, particularly when the Americans came to take a differing view of them, and when India made an input into British policy. Finally the impact of Communism distorted the views of the British and the Americans and divided the élites. No longer so powerful as in the past, Britain needed all the more to win the support of others. The risk was that it would be reduced to pursuing policies that contained internal contradictions or were restricted by the limited degree of consensus elicited.

Nevertheless a pattern can be discerned in British policy. It was a pattern that in some degree replicated Britain's wish to order the world. In a way its regional approach was thus a successor to its imperial approach. Again, it put its emphasis on framework rather than content, on élite rather than structure. In this respect it was somewhat unrealistic. The deficiency in Britain's own power only made it more so. Yet when all is said and done, it represented a vision of the future which, if ambitious, was rivalled only by others yet more deficient.

The Union of Burma

The development of British policy in Burma illustrated some of the contradictions within British policy for South-East Asia as a whole. The policy put forward in the White Paper of 17 May 1945 envisaged the development of a democratic Burma within the Commonwealth, and the subsequent House of Commons debate only emphasized that it had to be democratic. Yet in Burma itself, encouraged both by the events of the occupation and by the approach adopted by Mountbatten, power was falling into the hands of the AFPFL. While it aimed at setting up an independent republic, Mountbatten believed that it might accept the alternative of dominion status if it was readily accepted as the true political leadership in Burma and he more than once recalled the precedent of Smuts and Botha. Dorman-Smith, the returning Governor, could not endorse this line. It was not only not in accordance with his inclinations; it was not in accordance with his instructions. The Secretary of State in the Labour Government reinforced the view that the Governor could not accept the dominance of one party in his Executive Council. That more or less destroyed the chances of a collaborative approach, and Dorman-Smith's endeavours to negotiate with the AFPFL so that they might share power, but not absorb it, were vain.

His task was made no easier by the erosion of the armed force at his disposal. Perhaps Churchill would have considered using it to destroy the AFPFL. Perhaps, more likely, he would have wanted to negotiate the transition from a position of strength. In any case Dorman-Smith could do neither. Mountbatten took the opportunity to point out that, while British troops were being demobilized, Indian troops could not be used without grave risk. The loyalty of the Indian army might be undermined, and with it the hopes that Britain could retain a stable and intact India in the Commonwealth. Already Indian politicians queried the use of Indians in Indonesia and Indo-China: they could hardly be used to put down a freedom movement in Burma.

The Congress is making much capital out of alleged use of Indian troops, as mercenaries, for the suppression of so-called nationalist movements in NEI and FIC—even more capital than the party is making over our treatment of the INA—and our use of Indian troops for that purpose in Burma would give Congress material for agitation which might be even more damaging in its potential effect on the loyalty of the Indian Army. . . .[25]

The recall of Dorman-Smith was the occasion for a change of approach, though the Government tended to blame him for the inadequacy of its earlier policy, and leave his successor with the burden of developing a new one. The AFPFL took their opportunity to contribute by organizing the strikes of September and October, demonstrating that they could paralyse the government. Sir Hubert Rance, the new Governor, advocated concessions that would give them substantial power, believing that a Burma they ruled might still remain in the Commonwealth. But there was another argument for concession. The AFPFL was beginning to come apart. Earlier that might have been welcomed. But it was coming apart in a way that was now and might always have been both welcome and unwelcome. The Communist elements were breaking away. That might make the AFPFL in general more acceptable. But it also meant that it would have to have the reality of power, so that it might deny the Communists the opportunity to say that it had sold out to the imperialists, and so that it might itself cope with the Communists. The policy of working with the AFPFL was confirmed by talks in London, and the interests of the minority peoples were not allowed to divert the British from the determination on a deal with the Burmans. The Frontier Areas Commission of Enquiry was no more than a FACE-saver. It could be argued, as L. B. Walsh-Atkins of the Burma Office put it, that the British,

at the cost of looking a little foolish, have preserved our reputation in the eyes of the outside world and avoided the overt denunciation of promises we were unable or unwilling to meet, by the expedient of securing the free consent of the Frontier Areas to a course to which we had, in effect, arranged that there should be no alternative.[26]

Despite the hope that a late-found readiness to deal with the AFPFL might encourage them after all to drop their insistence on an independent republic, the AFPFL stuck to that objective. In part that was because the Commonwealth could not yet accommodate a republic and the example of Eire, adduced by the Burmans, was thought irrelevant by the British. Mountbatten's hopes as Viceroy of retaining the Indian successor-states as dominions made any concession to Burma impossible at that juncture. As A. F. Morley at the Burma Office put it, 'even if new forms are not unthinkable in all cases, Burma is not sufficiently important to warrant them'.[27] In part it was because the AFPFL could not risk abandoning their policy for fear of encouraging Communist accusations of a sell-out. The British preferred the greater prospect of stability under the AFPFL to the prospect of greater instability that might arise if they further exposed the AFPFL to attack by not agreeing to their demand for an independent republic outside the Commonwealth.

The chance of a deal was still further diminished with the assassination of the AFPFL leader, Aung San, in July 1947. His successor, Nu, was in no position, if he had been so inclined, to set out on a bold political adventure. He had to cleave ever more closely to the objective of setting up an independent sovereign republic in Burma. The British recognized this. 'The acceptance of Dominion status seems unfortunately now less likely than ever to be practical politics.'[28] What was not sufficiently recognized— or, if recognized, not sufficiently taken account of—was that a solution acceptable to the Burmans and the British was not acceptable to the non-Burman peoples. Always likely to be insecure in a majority-dominated Burma, they saw the end of the Commonwealth tie as a further undermining of their security, a final removal of the imperial arbiter. Their reaction meant that, whether or not Burmans followed their leaders, independent Burma was far from stable. Minorities were indeed to combine with Communist opponents of the regime.

Indonesia and Indo-China

While their own policy for Burma was less than fully successful, the British nevertheless considered the concepts behind it a model for other colonial powers in South-East Asia. Unless they pursued a similar pattern, some of the benefits British policy was expected to confer would not be secured. Their search was for stability, and that was to be based on an accommodation between ruler and ruled, West and East. That would be all the stronger if it had a regional thrust: it would be hard to attain in its absence. But if the policy was over-optimistic in Burma, it was even more over-optimistic in regard to Indonesia and Indo-China. 'If only the French will be reasonable and come forward with an imaginative offer, the war in French Indochina can be over,' Mountbatten told Tom Driberg late in 1945: it was 'heart-breaking to have to leave the political control to other nations when we are really in military control'.[29] Indeed the British found themselves almost willy-nilly pursuing policies at odds with their general objective, particularly in Indo-China. And the Americans were to follow in their wake.

In the case of Burma, the ability of the British to pursue their policies had been limited by their own weakness, by the organization of the Burmans, and by concern about India. There were yet other factors in the case of Indonesia and Indo-China. Neither of the colonial powers concerned was able or willing to take the broad view the British had been able to take. They were determined to regain a position, from which they might afterwards make concessions. Committed to releasing prisoners of war and securing the surrender of the Japanese and also to the maintenance of law and order, the British, without a clear policy on the nationalists, found themselves increasingly committed to restoring these colonial authorities. Concern for their support in Europe only made that commitment stronger.

The Dutch were later to realize that there were world-wide opportunities for their survival. But at the end of a destructive war they believed that the Indies, an earlier source of wealth, were their way to national revival as after the Napoleonic war. Their own democratic system, moreover, tended to confirm such an attitude. A multi-party system made for rigidity rather than flexibility. The openings for a statesmanlike approach were neglected and cruder methods came to dominate. Their policy in the Indies in the nineteenth century had been to mix diplomacy and force: isolating the Indonesians from the outside world, generally cajoling but if need be compelling them to come to terms with the colonial power. There was an idealistic side to their post-war federal approach, and it corresponded in some sense to the cultural and political diversity of the Indonesian peoples. But their idealism, and the federal approach, were compromised by the recurrence to a policy that in many respects resembled that of the nineteenth century in its attempt to isolate the Indonesians and set up élites that would collaborate on terms set by the Dutch.

While in some respects pressed to help the Dutch, the British sought to press compromise upon them. They had not realized the strength of Indonesian nationalism, while the interregnum that resulted from both the sudden Japanese surrender and the delay in accepting it enhanced the standing of the Republican Government Sukarno and Hatta had proclaimed. The British found themselves dealing with it and so, the Dutch thought, further strengthening it. There was little alternative. The British did not have the forces to overwhelm the Republic, even if that had been thought desirable. They had to secure the prisoners of war and the interned civilians without if possible provoking attacks upon them. The Dutch were frustrated by their lack of force. They tended not only to blame the British, but to think and act in extremes. Back in Europe, they pressed the British for stronger support, while in the East Britain's hopes of a conciliatory regional approach to South-East Asian nationalism seemed to diminish. Its answer was, of course, to try to use what influence it had to bring the parties to an understanding. With this in mind the British intensified their commitment to the Dutch, but they did not get what they wanted in return. The Hoge Veluwe talks failed. Perhaps no Dutch Government could undertake a policy of compromise—and with 'collaborationists'—just before the first post-war general election.

The British, still not evacuating, made a further attempt. The outcome was the Linggadjati agreement. But, while the Governments of the Republic found it difficult to contain those opposed to compromise, so did the Dutch. The first police action tended to confirm the view of those who believed that Dutch compromises had only been designed to temporize while they built up their strength with a view to trying to put down opposition by force. They did not, in any case, succeed. Not only did they not have sufficient force available; the Indonesians mobilized world opinion against them. In particular the Americans were brought to challenge the Dutch. The attempt to isolate the Indonesians was a total failure. The Dutch merely prevented themselves from internationalizing their cause. But in the post-war world, of course, nationalists were not alone, as they had been in the pre-war world. There was international support for them, and not merely from the Communists, but in particular from India, and also from Australia. Even the British no longer gave the Dutch the kind of guarantee they had in the cosier days of the 'exclusive Lords of the East'. Dutch policy was out-of-date and doomed to fail. The Foreign Office resented the police action. 'The Dutch will in the long run (and probably within the next few years) lose far more by this action than by trying to be patient and limiting their demands to what an Indonesian coalition would accept.' Britain would be 'in the embarrassing position of trying to follow an uneasy compromise between our own position *vis-à-vis* South-East Asia and our desire not to split Western Europe'.[30]

For the Americans, as for the British, there was a tension between European and Asian policies. The British in their heyday had restored the Indies because they wanted a strong Dutch kingdom in Europe. The Americans wanted one, too. But now they felt it necessary to pursue a Wilsonian policy in regard to Indonesia, and their determination to endorse the nationalist cause was reinforced by a growing perception that it was a better guarantee against Communism than upholding the colonial power. This lesson was driven home, in the context of a growing cold war, by the failure of the Madiun uprising of 1948. The Republic of Indonesia saved itself by this example 'Timing is of prime importance in the Indonesian situation', a State Department report declared in March 1949. 'The longer the delay in accomplishing a transfer of authority from the Dutch to representative Indonesians, the weaker becomes the position of both the non-communist native leaders and the Dutch and the stronger becomes the influence of all extremist elements including the communists. . . .'³¹ US policy on French Indo-China was quite different.

This followed on from a British policy that had also been rather different. Roosevelt had not wanted the French to return. But that opposition he had virtually abandoned before his death, and his successors dropped it altogether. The sudden end of the war, however, did not make the restoration of French authority easy. But the Communist-dominated Viet-minh were weaker in Saigon than the nationalists in Jakarta, while the British military were less disposed to work with them. The British were soon aiding the restoration of French authority in southern Vietnam far more than they aided the Dutch. Nor did they exact a price by pressing negotiations with the Viet-minh. The Viet-minh were, moreover, facing the Chinese in the north. That was their stronghold. But they had to relinquish the cities in the south, and in 1946 the French were to feel strong enough once more to move from south to north, as they had done in their initial nineteenth-century occupation. 'The fact that General Gracey permitted a French *coup d'état* in Saigon undoubtedly influenced subsequent developments in favour of the French. In NEI the Dutch could argue that the boot was very much on the other foot.'³²

Pressed at home, no French Government could work for compromise with the Viet-minh. Nor could the British effectively press for it, given their need for French collaboration in Europe. The fact that the Viet-minh were Communist, as well as nationalist, made any suggestion of compromise with them in any case difficult to urge. The alternative was to work with more moderate nationalists. But the policy of the French—who had ruled till March 1945—had always tended to discourage them and they were not now easy to find. If the élites in South-East Asia were often without mass backing, that was particularly true of moderate nationalists in Vietnam. The French had given and now gave them no scope. The attempt in 1947 to develop a new Bao Dai regime was half-hearted. It offered no concrete prospects to non-Communist nationalists and was unlikely to induce them to risk participation.

It was, however, at this time that US policy began to concern itself more directly with South-East Asia. In Indonesia it seemed best to meet the onset of the Communist threat by endorsing the nationalist cause. In Vietnam, by contrast, the United States began to aid the French, while urging them to give their puppet regimes greater reality. A policy statement of 1948 declared that 'we have an immediate interest in maintaining in power a friendly French government to assist in the furtherance of our aims in Europe. This immediate and vital interest has in consequence taken precedence over active steps towards the realisation of our objectives in Indochina.'[33] The French still failed. But the Americans were then tempted to offer support to the Ngo Dinh Diem regime in the south, giving the Viet-minh the task but also the glory of achieving reunification.

In the interim the Geneva accords of 1954 had sought to bring peace to Indo-China. British diplomacy was prominent. It was influenced by the concerns expressed by India. But in a sense it was also pursuing the aims long set for British policy in South-East Asia. The West should come to terms with nationalism and provide for the security of South-East Asia as a whole. That policy did not, however, square with the SEATO pact which the British felt obliged to join, though it offered them no promise of support in Malaya.

Post-war Thailand

Thailand joined the pact. Their concern about the advance of Communism in Indo-China helped to align the Thais with the United States, though the military nature of their regime also encouraged them to take that option. Earlier in the immediate post-war period, the Thais, then led by civilians, had looked to the United States for a rather different reason. They were concerned over British policy and looked to the Americans to limit its effects.

Over this policy there was some misconception, and there has been since. It was alleged by some Americans that it involved some sort of control over Thailand.[34] The idea derived in part from Churchill's concern over the Kra Isthmus and his wish to eliminate any repetition of the threat to Malaya that its position had posed at the outset of the Pacific war. In fact any such approach had long been dropped. But there was still something of a punitive air about British policy towards Thailand, which had, too, declared war on the Western powers. There seemed no reason why Thailand should benefit from the rice shortage that South-East Asia faced at the end of the war. The notion emerged that Thailand should make rice deliveries, if not as reparations, then as a contribution to the efforts of the Allies.

The idea was an unfortunate one. It was hard for the British to abandon it, since they needed the rice in Malaya, and they felt unable to ignore the fact that for much of the war the Thais had been belligerents. But the policy did not work. The Thai Government was both unable and unwilling to put it into operation and secured support from the Americans, who had never accepted the declaration of war in any case. The British were put into the humiliating position of dropping their demand so as to secure the rice they and the people they aspired to rule really needed. But they turned only reluctantly to this course. Meanwhile not only had the Americans improved their influence: the civilian politicians who had made the peace treaty with the British had been weakened.

The main objective of the British in Thailand, as elsewhere in South-East Asia, was to establish viable governments, with a democratic and constitutional base, that would guarantee internal stability and international security. 'It is my considered opinion', Lord Killearn wrote in May 1946, 'that in this concept of a bastion of good order and stability in South East Asia, an orderly, prosperous Siam inspired by sentiments of fullest friendship and of a sincerely cooperative spirit with us, both in political and economic field, is an asset of the greatest value. . . .' The Foreign Office agreed. Siam 'forms part of an area which will continue to be a bastion of vital, strategic and economic importance to the British Commonwealth'.[35] But other objectives conflicted with the main one. It was hard to behave punitively towards a government whose co-operation you sought, and hard to exact rice deliveries from an administration you wished to bolster. Once again British policy had too many aims, and some conflicted with others. That reduced its chance of achieving any objective, particularly as the policy was unwelcome to the Americans. Their policy was not dissimilar. But they could not resist the opportunity to undermine British influence and establish their own which British policy and Thai reaction to it offered.

The civilian regime, in difficulty in any case, was discredited by its attempts to fulfil British demands, without being endorsed by the British for its efforts. The wartime strong man was able to make a comeback even before the shift in US policy had taken place. But that shift only led the Americans to endorse him more fully. In May 1949 William S. Lacy was arguing in the State Department that, since 'diplomacy is the science of the possible, we should move quickly to strengthen Marshal Phibun's government'. The argument he advanced was that, 'for all his unsavory past and all his faults of character', he was 'anti-Communist, appears prepared to accommodate himself to the policies of the United States and the United Kingdom, and is eager and as able as anyone to bring the Army and Navy together again'.[36] The State Department moved towards this position, whatever Wilsonian concepts might have suggested. The Thai military for their part could hardly resist the opportunity the US alliance offered. Once they had abandoned neutrality for the advantages of the Japanese alliance. Now they attached themselves closely to the Americans. In neither case did they deploy the caution the monarchy had displayed when, accepting British predominance, it had yet sought to moderate it by keeping open relations with other powers.

There had been another aspect to collaboration with Japan. It had offered the opportunity to realize pan-Thai objectives by regaining lands and peoples over which the monarchy had established claims which it had had to abandon in the colonial period. These gains were, of course, lost at the end of the war. But Pridi and the civilians sought to enhance Thai influence in South-East Asia in other ways, in particular by associating Thailand with the end of colonial authority in Indo-China. The nature of the struggle that developed in Vietnam made that a difficult line to pursue, even had Phibun wished to pursue it. Even keeping Cambodia and Laos free of the Vietnamese proved impossible. But the Thais deferred rather than abandoned their aspiration to play a leadership role in Indo-China.

The comminatory attitude of the British towards Thailand at the end of the war had been based not only on their concern for their prestige but also on their interests in Malaya. While they did not attempt to upset pre-war frontiers and incorporate Patani into the new Malayan Union, they were anxious to guarantee Malaya's future security. Moreover, they did not wish to return amid conditions of scarcity and starvation: hence their pressure for rice deliveries. Their desire to guarantee cheap food was connected not only with the wish to avoid starvation: they also wanted to keep wages down in Malaya and promote the restoration of its economy, which would be even more important to Britain as a dollar-earner than it had been before the war.

Malaya and Malaysia

The British did not merely want to hang on in Malaya for economic reasons: they had ambitious political plans for the country. These again might be facilitated by the avoidance of scarcity and the restoration of prosperity. They involved a bold attempt to tackle the question of constitutional and political development in a communally divided Malaya. The war offered additional arguments for giving the immigrant communities the opportunity of political participation. The Union proposal that developed, however, did not fit the conditions that actually prevailed when the British returned, and the attempts to implement it provoked an unexpectedly substantial opposition from the Malays. Faced with this, the British promptly agreed to adjust their policy and the Union was replaced by the Federation during 1947–8.

For some, like Victor Purcell, formerly of the Malayan Civil Service, that was a sell-out, and historians, like Michael Stenson, have argued that the British, anxious to stay, allied with the weaker side in order to make their continued presence essential.[37] Perhaps the connection between these changes should not be seen quite in that way. What is more certain is that the British wanted stability in Malaya. The extent of Malay opposition suggested that it might be undermined by insisting on the Union plan: the Malays might even be encouraged to look for help from Indonesian nationalists. The immigrant communities, on the other hand, had treated the Union proposals with apathy rather than enthusiasm. Stability would help to guarantee prosperity, which would suit not only Britain's interest, but also help to promote the revised political scheme as it had been hoped it would have promoted the earlier one. The growing identification of the Chinese with a left-wing leadership seemed only to justify the new approach.

In fact the British again miscalculated, and their policy provoked not growing stability but what they called the 'Emergency'. For this, not without some justification, they could blame international Communism, and that both their habit and their interest inclined them to do. But the Emergency had other origins also, including the frustration of the political hopes of the immigrant communities and the dramatic foreshortening of their fortunes that the Federation seemed to symbolize.

This turn of events does not justify the view that Britain's policy was of divide-and-rule. They would have preferred to avoid the costly Emergency. Moreover, they reacted to it, not only by military and counter-insurgency campaigns, but also by political measures designed to win the 'hearts and minds' of the people.[38] That phrase did not mean that they had abandoned their emphasis on the élite. What they now sought was to bring out a moderate Chinese leadership and to encourage the Malay leadership to work with it. The Emergency pushed them down this line. But this was consistent with their long-term aim. If they could not produce stability in Malaya by Union or by Federation alone, they needed to promote community liaison and this they characteristically did by bringing community leaders together.

In fact the leaders found their collaboration was best based on winning further concessions from the British, obtaining power that they could share out and win the support of the communities with. The British went along with this approach: it was useful for the leadership to have to win its way; it would in fact help it to consolidate its support. At the same time the British must not put up too much resistance, since they wanted the leadership to remain moderate. They were thus encouraged to run rather quickly through their repertoire of devolution, dyarchy or the 'member system' making a brief appearance on the schedule, before the agreement on complete independence was reached in 1955.

Singapore had been kept aside from these developments. Its importance in British strategy was one argument for so doing; the fact that its inclusion in Malaya would tilt the demographic balance against the Malays was another. The association of Singapore and Malaya was seen, therefore, as something for the future rather than for the present, though the developments that meanwhile took place might well make that association more difficult to achieve and sustain, not less. While Malaya won its independence, Singapore won an increasing measure of autonomy. It was limited by Britain's continued interest in it as a base. It was also limited by the perception, on the part of Singaporean as well as British leaders, that the island could not survive on its own. The aim of the People's Action Party (PAP), victorious in the 1959 elections, was independence through merger with Malaya.

The concept of associating the Borneo territories with the Malayan was not a new one, but now it received a new impulse. For the British it offered the chance of diminishing their responsibility for the Borneo territories. It also seemed likely to provide for stability in South-East Asia through the kind of federal formula that they had elsewhere adopted as a partial replacement for the imperial order. At the same time, it would offer the Singapore leadership a form of the independence through merger it had been seeking, while the Malay leadership on the Peninsula would see the accession of Singapore as less of a threat if it was part of a larger federation. These were some of the objectives that lay behind the announcement of the Malaysia plan in 1961.

It ran into considerable opposition in Borneo and among its neighbours. The British had long had hopes of associating the Borneo territories with each other but the process had not gone far, and, as time passed, the territories became even more separate in interest and tradition. The approach of independence in Malaya had led the British again to raise the issue, but without any effective outcome. Sir Roland Turnbull, Governor of North Borneo, pointed out that, 'while the geographical proximity of the territories made the rest of the world regard them as naturally akin, in truth they were surprisingly different. With time the differences would become greater, and if there was to be a federation it should be soon. . . .'[39] Since the 1930s the oil from Belait had made Brunei rich, and therefore cautious over relations with its neighbours. The impact of development and of Chinese immigration since 1946 on those neighbours, on the other hand, meant that federation might increase internal tension and even risk domestic stability. In March 1959 *The Times* reported that the plans for 'a loose federation' had 'made no headway and are virtually dead for some years to come. The Brunei Malays, who jealously guard their oil wealth and fear Chinese influence in the other countries, do not want it; and the indigenous people of the other two countries, nervous also lest changes give more power to the Chinese, have given it no active support. . . .'[40]

Incorporation of the Borneo territories in a Malaysian federation was a different matter. It would avoid their assimilation to each other; but their individual development might be compromised by association with more populous, more powerful, and more politically sophisticated entities like Peninsular Malaya and Singapore. Sarawak and Sabah were encouraged to accept the concept through the offer of various constitutional guarantees. But Brunei did not join.

By this time it was possessed of great wealth, thanks to oil, though little territory, thanks to history. Incorporation in Malaysia offered little advantage, save, perhaps, that of greater security in a possibly hostile world. This in fact Britain was still prepared to offer, partly because Brunei could pay for it. But both the Brunei leadership and the British were also apprehensive that to force Brunei into the Federation might produce instability rather than stability. The 1962 revolt underlined the threat. That revolt was designed to challenge the autocracy of the sultanate. But it was also designed to challenge Malaysia in the name of North Kalimantan. The Partai Rakyat sought to associate Sarawak, Sabah, and Brunei under Brunei leadership. Such a reconstitution of the old sultanate had only a limited appeal in Sarawak and virtually none in Sabah. But, though suppressed by the British, the revolt no doubt made it quite unlikely that the already doubtful sultanate would enter Malaysia. It would not only lose control of its wealth; it would explicitly accept a federation the Partai Rakyat rejected and thus, perhaps, encourage a further political challenge.

Like some of their political experiments elsewhere the Federation thus undermined the main objective the British sought to realize, the promotion of stability in a decolonizing region. It did so in other ways, too. These were related in substantial part to the changed status it envisaged for Borneo, but related to other issues also. Setting up Malaysia, though in some sense a concept long in the minds of the British, could also be seen as a major restructuring of the political map of South-East Asia that affected other states in the area. Over this issue the British were insensitive. Taking too little account of the concerns of Indonesia and the Philippines, they perhaps made the birth of Malaysia more difficult than it need have been.

It is not, of course, certain that a different policy would have served them better. In the case of Indonesia, they faced a rather unpredictable regime, and though it later resolved to crush Malaysia, it initially had not opposed it. Perhaps, however, the British rather surprisingly paid too little attention to Indonesia's permanent interests as a state, and too much to the impact of domestic political manifestations. Any state in a world of states is bound to be concerned at changes on its frontier, and a state of the size and substance of Indonesia is bound to have pretensions to regional influence which have to be recognized if stability is to be preserved in a world where states, equal in theory, are unequal in fact. The British took too little account of this. Their relations with Indonesia had not been positive in the 1950s and they perhaps overemphasized the Communist influence in the expansionist nature of the Republic. What Sukarno's aims were is unclear even now. But it seems less likely that he sought to annex North Kalimantan than that he wanted to see there a safely weak state of which Indonesia might be patron. The fiery expression of Sukarno's policies no doubt made them more difficult to fathom, and opinions still differ as to his relationship with the Communists. But it is hard to escape the conclusion that the British had become more dismissive of Indonesian nationalism in the 1950s than they had been in later 1940s, and less inclined as a result to make a realistic appraisal even of the 'legitimate' interests of the Republic; still less of its 'revolutionary' language and of its avowed opposition to neo-colonialism. That the British might associate with Communism.

Their attitude towards the Philippines was also more contemptuous than it need have been or than it was profitable to be. In that case, however, the dismissive attitude dated from the 1940s. To some extent it was a legacy of the mutual antagonism of the British and the Americans. The Philippines, the first South-East Asian colonial state to gain independence, secured, partly for that reason, a rather poor bargain, as some Filipinos believed. Nehru agreed. His message of congratulation on Philippine independence showed his reservations.

We hope that this really signifies independence for this word has become rather hackneyed and outworn and has been made to mean many things. Some countries that are called independent are far from free and are under the economic or military domination of some great power. Some so-called independent countries carry on with what might be termed 'puppet régimes' and are in a way client countries of some great power. We hope that is not so with the Philippines.[41]

The British had their doubts, too, partly because they resented the urging they received to follow the American example and because they believed that it was necessary to prepare nations for independence. Critical of the Americans, they were therefore also critical of the Philippine Republic. Characteristically they did attempt to make a treaty intended as 'a prompt gesture of goodwill towards a new state',[42] but it proved impossible to negotiate. Their critical attitude seemed to have endured into the early 1960s.

Filipino nationalists had displayed an interest in the fate of Sabah back in the 1920s. Independence was gained in 1946, and at the same time North Borneo formally became a colony. That made the realization of any Filipino claim, derived from the claim of the Sultan of Sulu, more difficult, but the Filipinos decided not to add to their difficulties in establishing their new state by openly raising the issue at that point. However, the inclusion of Sabah in a nation-state was another, more once-for-all, matter. The Philippines might still have hoped to influence the future of a colonial territory as it emerged from its colonial status. It could have no influence on the territory incorporated into another sovereign state. Long aware of the claim, the British perhaps tried to brush it aside more than they should have done, and gave too little attention to the changed context in which it was now renewed. Perhaps, too, they gave too little attention to other aspects of the relationship. The Philippines, for example, had been left with a very insecure frontier to the south, particularly given the growing antagonism of the Moro peoples to rule from the north. Rejecting the Philippine claim the British alluded to the interest in the stability of South-East Asia which they believed, given the Communist threat, the Philippines should share. A public dispute about North Borneo might have 'undesirable repercussions', impair friendly relations, 'even lead to territorial claims being put forward by other South-East Asian countries. . . . Such developments would impair the stability of South-East Asia and the capacity of the peoples concerned for resolute united resistance to Communist encroachment and subversion. . . .'[43] But, though perhaps an indication of the interest of the British, this was hardly a sufficient recognition of the concerns of the Filipinos.

Maphilindo was, for the Philippines, an opportunity to express, not only their interest in the fate of Sabah, but their concern for a relationship with the Malay world as a whole, which their earlier nationalism had also expressed. For Indonesia, it gave expression to a claim to regional leadership. For both it was also a means of exerting pressure on the British and on the Malayan leadership. This latter function doomed it. The Malaysia proposal went ahead. It seemed in a sense all the more justified. Confrontation certainly added to the support it received on the Peninsula and in Borneo and from the United States. But its establishment also required a substantial military and naval commitment from the British which they no doubt had hoped to avoid. It helped to ensure that it was, however, a parting gesture, though the British retained their defence agreement with Malaysia.

Singapore left Malaysia in 1965. By then its strategic significance for the British had been further reduced, and the security of South-East Asia was maintained above all by the American presence in the South China Sea. Singapore now turned out to be a viable state. But that was in part because the PAP had used the colonial government to help it destroy the Communist opposition, and in part because it was an economic success in a South-East Asia the security of which now depended on the Americans and their relationship with the Russians, the Chinese, and the

Japanese. Within that framework, however, the South-East Asian states sought to co-operate in a regional approach, both in the political and the economic fields. That in some respect was bound to reduce the independence they each enjoyed, but it might also enhance their independence of outside powers in general. The outcome cannot have been unwelcome to the British. Though they had at one time been the most powerful of the states that had influenced South-East Asia, they had never fully exerted their power there. When their power declined, they sought, perhaps not entirely surprisingly, to use it more constructively, and they set targets that were far too optimistic. But their aim was a world of nation-states, in which security and stability would be enhanced by constitutional democracy, in which nationalism would not exclude internationalism, in which East and West might meet, and in which a regional approach might fill the power vacuum left by the end of colonialism and limit the impact of great power rivalries. It was also to be a world in which trade might be freely carried on and in which Britain might compete with others. The notion was not unlike the view of the world developed in the days of its primacy. But Britain was no longer so able to compete. Perhaps its hope to do so was the most unrealistic aspect of its policy. Some blamed the continued overcommitment of the British; some their lack of enterprise. Neither accusation is entirely fair. No other power seemed at the end of the war to be ready to take on the burden of stabilizing a new world of nation-states. Yet it had to be done, even at the cost of investment at home in a war-weakened Britain.

Concluding Remarks

Early in 1957 Prime Minister Macmillan had called for a 'profit-and-loss' account of the remaining colonial territories. The Colonial Office report concluded with these words:

Any premature withdrawal of authority by the United Kingdom would seem bound to add to the areas of stress and discontent in the world. There are territories over which jurisdiction might be surrendered without prejudice to the essentials of strategy or foreign relations, and at some modest savings to the Exchequer. But would we stand to gain by thus rewarding loyalty to the Crown which is an enduring characteristic of so many Colonial peoples? The United Kingdom has been too long connected with its Colonial possessions to sever ties abruptly without creating a bewilderment which would be discreditable and dangerous.[44]

The Colonial Office's words were not merely those of an interested party. They underlined the sense of responsibility that officials conceived lay behind the long history of the connection of Britain and its colonial peoples. The suggestion that rapid change would be dangerous went further. It implied a belief that, even in the late 1950s, Britain had still a major responsibility for preserving a stable and peaceful world. Bending too easily before the winds of change would be to abandon a wider responsibility. The Colonial Office view indicates that colonial policy was only an aspect of world policy. The British had long perceived that the world-to-be was one of independent states. In some cases they could develop themselves, if well led, following the right precepts, and given the right advice. In others a stronger and longer measure of intervention proved to be required. But the aim of colonization was the same. The Colonial Office feared that the work would even now be but partly or poorly done.

Ronald Robinson confessed that he and his fellow historian Jack Gallagher were, in writing of the imperialism of free trade, guilty of anachronism. 'They had projected the fall of empire in their own time, the triumph of nationalist subjects over waning rulers backwards into the interpretation of earlier empires which could hardly have been established and upheld without strong central power. . . .'[45] This book faces a similar peril. Its argument has been that the British developed a vision of world politics and stuck to it through a century and a half. There is a risk, as the author has recognized, that he will be accused of putting forward a 'Whig interpretation'; of taking too little account, for example, of what Bayly, in criticism of Harlow, terms 'a constructive authoritarian and ideological British imperialism' that 'came of age in the years between 1783 and 1820';[46] and of too readily accepting the myth that, as Macmillan put it, the independence of India was 'not a sudden whim or act of despair by an exhausted people', but 'the culmination of a set purpose of nearly four generations'.[47] Certainly he recognizes that there were periods in which and places at which such a vision seemed to have diminished or vanished. But he contends that even the 'imperialism' of the later nineteenth century is better understood in this particular context, while the hesitations of the inter-war period indicated a recognition that though the vision still beckoned, it was as impossible to move towards it as to abandon it. British activity in South-East Asia perhaps suggests that neither Harlow nor Bayly are wholly right, nor wholly wrong. 'Give no anxious thought for the morrow', enjoined the Bible in completion of the phrase Robert Meade had invoked. There was indeed confidence about the morrow. What is striking about the British view is its ambition. At the height of Britain's primacy, there was a remarkable degree of realism, even of caution. In the crisis of the Second World War, by contrast, Britain adopted objectives which it had not the resources to realize. Adaptation followed. But the British still preferred to adjust their timetable, rather than abandon it altogether. They aspired still to regulate the emergence of the modern world.

Decolonization, it is suggested, also makes better sense in this context. Superpowers had emerged, but the colonial and underdeveloped countries were still seen as needing guidance from the British. Perhaps they overcommitted themselves once more, but they had some remarkable successes. Their basic precepts after all helped them to adjust their views and to accept a world of independent states. They exacted from the countries concerned a smaller political price than the United States or the Soviet Union. It was a contribution to a stable post-war world. Victor Purcell wrote in his memoirs:

Wise statemanship on the imperialist side seems to consist in giving way to nationalism in such a way that there is as smooth a transition as possible from one regime to the other, so that the machinery of government was not wrecked in the 'hand-over'. In this way relations between the ex-colony and the ex-colonial power could have the best chance of being harmonious on a basis of equality.[48]

The policy was inherited from the days of economic primacy. The British retained it in days of straitened circumstances. They put their future, like that of the Britain of the Great Exhibition, on the basis of an economic relationship with other countries. Was that policy still valid? Britain's post-war economic performance did not suggest that it was a guarantee of success. Too much effort and too many resources had been diverted from domestic reconstruction, it was argued, and put instead into endeavours appropriate to a major world power. But it is hard to dismiss the latter-day endeavours to contribute to a world of nation-states as mistaken or unconstructive.

Their impact on South-East Asia is difficult to measure, given their limited power, the activities of the peoples of the region themselves, and the involvement of the superpowers and other states. The boundaries of the post-colonial states were one clear legacy of the imperial period, inherited by the new élites, and kept in being, too, by the international rivalry of the cold war phase. Within those states, governments pursued stability and prosperity with varying degrees of success and varying levels of adherence to democratic ideals. There has been considerable evidence, however, that the new states of South-East Asia, benefiting from renewed economic expansionism in the Pacific, could prosper in a world of states, and that they could conduct foreign and defence policies suited to their interests. There is also some evidence of the validity of Britain's latter-day regional approach, as a means both of regulating relations among the states of South-East Asia and of moderating the impact of outside powers.

1. D. J. Morgan, *The Official History of Colonial Development: Guidance towards Self-government in British Colonies, 1941–1971*, London: Macmillan, 1980, Vol. 5, pp. 11–12.

2. Minute, 7 February 1947, F.O. 371/63547[F1969/1969/61], Public Record Office, London.

3. Scrivener to Dening, 14 April 1948, and Minute by Christofas, 27 April, F.O. 371/69689[F5922/286/61], Public Record Office, London.

4. MacDonald to Dening, 3 February 1949, and Reply, 24 February, F.O. 371/76031[F3010/1072/61], Public Record Office, London.

5. R. D. Pearce, *The Turning Point in Africa: British Colonial Policy 1938–48*, London: Cass, 1982, p. 159.

6. F.E.(O)(46) 52, 16 April 1946, CAB 134/280, Public Record Office, London.

7. Elie Kedourie, 'A New International Disorder', in H. Bull and Adam Watson (eds.), *The Expansion of International Society*, Oxford: Oxford University Press, 1984, p. 352.

8. J. D. B. Miller, *Survey of Commonwealth Affairs: Problems of Expansion and Contraction 1953–69*, Oxford: Oxford University Press, 1974, p. 112.

9. Thompson to SEA Department, 12 January 1948, 2/2G/48, F.O. 371/69686[F1216/286/61], Public Record Office, London.

10. Quoted in D. C. Watt, *Succeeding John Bull*, Cambridge: Cambridge University Press, 1984, p. 103.

11. CM(49) 62nd, 27 October 1949, Item 8, CAB 128/16, Public Record Office, London.

12. PUSC 32, 28 July 1949, F.O. 371/76030[F17397/1055/61], Public Record Office, London.

13. Brief, 23 March 1949, F.O. 371/76023[F4487/1023/61], Public Record Office, London.

14. Memorandum by Louis Johnson, 14 April 1950, *Foreign Relations of the United States 1950*, Washington, 1976, Vol. VI, p. 781.

15. Quoted in Andrew J. Rotter, *The Path to Vietnam*, Ithaca: Cornell University Press, 1987, p. 113.

16. Ibid., p. 168.

17. R. B. Smith, *An International History of the Vietnam War*, London: Macmillan, 1983, Vol. I, pp. 39–40.

18. Minute, 9 May 1949, F.O. 371/76033[F6563/1073/61], Public Record Office, London.

19. Minute by B. R. Pearn, 10 August 1956, F.O. 371/123428[DF10340/10], Public Record Office, London.

20. Minute by M. S. Weir, 25 September 1956, F.O. 371/123212[D1052/10], Public Record Office, London.

21. Note by Chancery, Office of Commissioner-General, 7 May 1955, F.O. 371/116984 [D2231/345], Public Record Office, London.

22. N. Iqbal Singh, *The Andaman Story*, New Delhi: Vikas, 1978, pp. 303–4.

23. Minute, 9 March 1956, F.O. 371/123212[D1052/4], Public Record Office, London.

24. Memorandum, Singapore Constitutional Conference, May 1956, Cmd. 9777, App. 4. The talks are covered in Chan Heng Chee, *A Sensation of Independence: A Political Biography of David Marshall*, Singapore: Oxford University Press, 1984, Chap. 7.

25. Memorandum by Mayne, 29 November 1945, M/5/91, India Office Library, London.

26. Minute, 15 February 1947, M/4/2811, India Office Library, London.

27. Minute, 20 May 1947, M/4/2677, India Office Library, London.

28. Minute by Ledwidge, 25 July 1947, M/4/2714, India Office Library, London.

29. P. Ziegler, *Mountbatten*, London: Collins, 1985, p. 332.

30. Quoted in S. H. Drummond, 'Britain's Involvement with Indonesia 1945–63', Ph.D. thesis, University of Southampton, 1979, p. 164.

31. Quoted in G. R. Hess, *The United States' Emergence as a Southeast Asian Power, 1940–1950*, New York: Columbia University Press, 1987, p. 306.

32. Quoted in R. Buckley, 'Responsibility without Power: Britain and Indonesia, August 1945–February 1946', in I. Nish (ed.), *The Indonesian Experience: The Role of Japan and Britain*, London: London School of Economics, 1979, pp. 48–9.

33. Quoted in Hess, *The United States' Emergence*, p. 322.

34. Cf. L. A. Niksch, 'United States Foreign Policy in Thailand's World War II Peace Settlements with Great Britain and France', Ph.D. thesis, Georgetown University, 1976, pp. 65–6.

35. Telegram from Killearn, 2 May 1946, 386, and minute by Wilson-Young, 9 May, F.O. 371/54360[F6702/4/40], Public Record Office, London.

36. Rotter, *The Path to Vietnam*, p. 77.

37. V. Purcell, *Malaya: Communist or Free?*, London: Gollancz, 1954; Michael R. Stenson, *Industrial Conflict in Malaya*, London: Oxford University Press, 1970.

38. R. Stubbs, *Hearts and Minds in Guerrilla Warfare: The Malayan Emergency 1948–1960*, Singapore: Oxford University Press, 1989, p. 155.

39. *The Times*, 11 February 1958.

40. *The Times*, 5 March 1959.

41. Quoted in Hess, *The United States' Emergence*, p. 246.

42. Minute, 21 August 1947, F.O. 371/63872[F11460/605/83]. See N. Tarling, '"A Prompt Gesture of Goodwill": Anglo-Philippine Relations after the Second World War', *Pilipinas*, 5 (1985): 27–51.

43. Note of British Ambassador, 24 May 1962, published in *Philippine Claim to North Borneo*, Manila, 1964, Vol. I, p. 151.

44. Quoted in Morgan, *The Official History of Colonial Development*, Vol. 5, p. 102.

45. In F. Madden and D. K. Fieldhouse (eds.), *Oxford and the Idea of Commonwealth*, London: Croon Helm, 1982, p. 47.

46. C. A. Bayly, *Imperial Meridian*, London: Longman, 1989, p. 250.

47. H. Macmillan, *Pointing the Way, 1959–61*, London: Macmillan, 1972, p. 117.

48. V. Purcell, *The Memoirs of a Malayan Official*, London: Cassell, 1965, p. 302.

Bibliography

Sources for quotations in the text are given in the endnotes, together with bibliographical details. This bibliography comprises only publications related to various topics discussed in the text, and, for convenience, it is organized accordingly.

Abbreviations

HMSO	His/Her Majesty's Stationery Office
JAS	*Journal of Asian Studies*
JMBRAS	*Journal of the Malayan/Malaysian Branch of the Royal Asiatic Society*, Kuala Lumpur
JSEAH	*Journal of Southeast Asian History*, Singapore
JSEAS	*Journal of Southeast Asian Studies*, Singapore
JSS	*Journal of the Siam Society*
MAS	*Modern Asian Studies*, Cambridge
SMJ	*Sarawak Museum Journal*, Kuching
SOAS	School of Oriental and African Studies

Late Eighteenth and Nineteenth Centuries

Britain and the Dutch in Malaya and Indonesia

Bassett, D. K., 'British Trade and Policy in Indonesia, 1760–1772', *Bijdragen tot de Taal–, Land–, en Volkenkunde*, 120 (1964).

Bastin, J., 'Raffles and British Policy in the Indian Archipelago, 1811–1816', *JMBRAS*, 27, 1 (1954).

Marks, H. J., *The First Contest for Singapore, 1819–1824*, The Hague: Nijhoff, 1959.

Miller, W. G., 'Robert Farquhar in the Malay World', *JMBRAS*, 51, 2 (1978).

Reid, A. J. S., *The Contest for North Sumatra*, Kuala Lumpur: Oxford University Press, 1969.

Tarling, N., *Anglo-Dutch Rivalry in the Malay World, 1780–1824*, St Lucia and Cambridge: Cambridge University Press, 1962.

Wake, C., 'Raffles and the Rajas', *JMBRAS*, 48, 1 (1975).

Wurtzburg, C. E., *Raffles of the Eastern Isles*, London: Hodder and Stoughton, 1954.

Britain and the Malay States

Bastin, J. and Roolvink, R. (eds.), *Malayan and Indonesian Studies*, Oxford: Clarendon Press, 1964.

Bastin, J. and Winks, R. W. (comps.), *Malaysia: Selected Historical Readings*, Kuala Lumpur: Oxford University Press, 1966.

Bonney, R., *Kedah, 1771–1821*, Kuala Lumpur: Oxford University Press, 1971.

Cowan, C. D., *Nineteenth-century Malaya: The Origins of British Political Control*, London: Oxford University Press, 1961.

de Silva, J., 'British Relations with Pahang, 1884–1895', *JMBRAS*, 25, 1 (1962).

Khoo Kay Kim, *The Western Malay States, 1850–1873*, Kuala Lumpur: Oxford University Press, 1972.

Kiernan, V. G., 'Britain, Siam and Malaya: 1875–1885', *Journal of Modern History*, 28, 1 (1956).

Klein, Ira, 'British Expansion in Malaya, 1897–1902', *JSEAH*, 9, 1 (1968).

Loh Fook Seng, Philip, *The Malay States 1877–1895: Political Change and Social Policy*, Kuala Lumpur: Oxford University Press, 1969.

Mills, L. A., *British Malaya: 1824–67*, ed. C. M. Turnbull, *JMBRAS*, 33, 3 (1960).

Rubin, A. P., *The International Personality of the Malay Peninsula*, Kuala Lumpur: Penerbit Universiti Malaya, 1974.

____, *Piracy, Paramountcy and Protectorates*, Kuala Lumpur: Penerbit Universiti Malaya, 1974.

Sinclair, K., 'The British Advance in Johore, 1885–1914', *JMBRAS*, 40, 1 (1967).

Suwannathat-Pian, K., *Thai–Malay Relations*, Singapore: Oxford University Press, 1988.

Tarling, N., *British Policy in the Malay Peninsula and Archipelago, 1824–1871*, Kuala Lumpur: Oxford University Press, 1969.

Thamsook Numnonda, 'Negotiations Regarding the Cession of the Siamese Malay States, 1907–9', *JSS*, 55 (1967).

Thio, E., 'Britain's Search for Security in North Malaya, 1886–1897', *JSEAH*, 10, 2 (1969).

____, 'British Policy towards Johore: From Advice to Control', *JMBRAS*, 40, 1 (1967).

____, *British Policy in the Malay Peninsula, 1880–1910*, Kuala Lumpur: University of Malaya Press, 1969.

____, 'The Extension of British Control to Pahang', *JMBRAS*, 30, 1 (1957).

Tregonning, K. G., *The British in Malaya: The First Forty Years, 1786–1826*, Tucson: University of Arizona Press, 1965.

____ (ed.), *Papers on Malayan History*, Singapore: University of Malaya Press, 1962.

Trocki, C. A., *Prince of Pirates*, Singapore: Singapore University Press, 1979.

Turnbull, C. M., *The Straits Settlements 1826–67*, London: Athlone Press, 1972.

Wong Lin Ken, 'The Trade of Singapore, 1819–69', *JMBRAS*, 33, 4 (1960).

British Intervention in Malaya

Allen, J. de V., 'The Colonial Office and the Malay States, 1867–73', *JMBRAS*, 36, 1 (1963).

Bastin, J. S., 'Britain as an Imperial Power in South-East Asia in the Nineteenth Century', in J. S. Bromley and E. H. Kossman (eds.), *Britain and the Netherlands in Europe and Asia*, London: Macmillan, 1968, pp. 174–90.

Burns, P. L. (ed.), *The Journal of J. W. W. Birch 1874–5*, Kuala Lumpur: Oxford University Press, 1976.

Burns, P. L. and Cowan, C. D. (eds.), *Sir Frank Swettenham's Malayan Journals 1874–6*, Kuala Lumpur: Oxford University Press, 1975.

Chandran, J., 'Private Enterprise and British Policy in the Malay Peninsula: The Case of the Malay Railway and Works Construction Company, 1893–5', *JMBRAS*, 37, 2 (1964).

Chew, E., 'The Reasons for British Intervention in Malaya', *JSEAH*, 6, 1 (1965).

Gullick, J. M., *Indigenous Political Systems of Western Malaya*, London: Athlone Press, 1958.

Khoo Kay Kim, 'The Origin of British Administration in Malaya', *JMBRAS*, 39, 1 (1966).

McIntyre, W. D., 'British Intervention in Malaya', *JSEAH*, 2, 3 (1961).

_____, *The Imperial Frontier in the Tropics, 1865–75*, London: Macmillan, 1967.

Parkinson, C. N., *British Intervention in Malaya, 1867–1877*, Singapore: University of Malaya Press, 1960.

SarDesai, D. R., *Trade and Empire in Malaya and Singapore 1869–1874*, Athens: Ohio University Centre for International Studies, 1970.

Sinclair, K., 'Hobson and Lenin in Johore', *MAS*, 1, 4 (1967).

Tarling, N., 'Borneo and British Intervention in Malaya', *JSEAS*, 5, 2 (1974).

Britain, Borneo, and Sulu

Black, I. D., 'The Ending of Brunei Rule in Sabah', *JMBRAS*, 41, 2 (1968).

Brown, D. E., *Brunei: The Structure and History of a Bornean Malay Sultanate*, Brunei: Muzium Brunei, 1970.

Fry, Howard T., *Alexander Dalrymple (1737–1808) and the Expansion of British Trade*, London: Cass, 1970.

Galbraith, J. G., 'The Chartering of the British North Borneo Company', *Journal of British Studies*, 4, 1 (1965).

Harlow, V. T., *The Founding of the Second British Empire*, Vol. I, London: Longmans, 1952, 1964.

Ingleson, J. E., 'Britain's Annexation of Labuan in 1846', *University Studies in History*, 5, 4 (Perth: University of Western Australia, 1970): 33–71.

Irwin, G., *Nineteenth-century Borneo: A Study in Diplomatic Rivalry*, Verhandelingen van het Koninklijk Instituut voor Taal- land-, en Volkenkunde, Vol. XV, The Hague: Nijhoff, 1955.

Jacob, G. L., *The Raja of Sarawak*, London: Macmillan, 1876.

McArthur, M. S. H., *Report on Brunei in 1904*, ed. A. V. M. Horton, Athens: Ohio University Centre for International Studies, 1987.

Reber, A. L., 'The Sulu World in the Eighteenth and Early Nineteenth Centuries: A Historiographical Problem in British Writings on Malay Piracy', MA thesis, Cornell University, 1966.

Runciman, S., *The White Rajahs: A History of Sarawak from 1841 to 1946*, Cambridge: Cambridge University Press, 1960.

Rutter, O., *The Pirate Wind*, London: Hutchinson, 1930.

St John, Spenser B., *The Life of Sir James Brooke*, London: Blackwood, 1879.

Sandin, B., *The Sea Dayaks of Borneo*, London: Macmillan, 1967.

Saunders, G., 'James Brooke's Visit to Brunei in 1844: A Reappraisal', *SMJ*, XVII, 34–5 (1969).

Tarling, N., *Britain, the Brookes and Brunei*, Kuala Lumpur: Oxford University Press, 1971.

———, *The Burthen, the Risk, and the Glory*, Kuala Lumpur: Oxford University Press, 1982.

———, *Piracy and Politics in the Malay World*, Melbourne: Cheshire, and Singapore: Donald Moore, 1963.

———, 'Sir James Brooke and Brunei', *SMJ*, XI, 21–2 (1963).

Templer, J. C. (ed.), *The Private Letters of Sir James Brooke*, London: Bentley, 1853.

Tregonning, K. G. P., 'Steps in the Acquisition of North Borneo', *Historical Studies*, V, 19 (1952).

Wright, L. R., 'The Anglo-Spanish-German Treaty of 1885: A Step in the Development of British Hegemony in North Borneo', *Australian Journal of Politics and History*, 18, 1 (1972).

———, *The Origins of British Borneo*, Hong Kong: Hong Kong University Press, 1970.

Warren, J. F., *The Sulu Zone, 1768–1898*, Singapore: Singapore University Press, 1981.

Britain and Burma

Adas, M., 'Imperialist Rhetoric and Modern Historiography: The Case of Lower Burma before and after Conquest', *JSEAS*, 3, 2 (1972).

Muhammad Shamsheer Ali, 'The Beginnings of British Rule in Upper Burma: A Study of British Policy and Burmese Reaction 1885–1890', Ph.D. thesis, London University, 1976.

Aung-Thwin, Michael, 'The British "Pacification" of Burma: Order with Meaning', *JSEAS*, 16, 2 (1985).

Bennett, Paul J., *Conference under the Tamarind Tree: Three Essays in Burmese History*, New Haven: Southeast Asian Studies, Yale University, 1971.

Chew, E., 'The Fall of the Burmese Kingdom in 1885: Review and Reconsideration', *JSEAS*, 10, 2 (1979).

——, 'The Withdrawal of the Last British Residency from Upper Burma in 1879', *JSEAH*, 10, 2 (1969).

Cooler, Richard M., *British Romantic Views of the First Anglo-Burmese War 1824–1826*, De Kalb: Northern Illinois University Press, 1977.

Crosthwaite, Sir C., *The Pacification of Burma*, London: 1912; reprinted, Cass, 1968.

Desai, W. S., *History of the British Residency in Burma 1826–1840*, Rangoon: University of Rangoon Press, 1939.

Hall, D. G. E., *Europe and Burma*, London: Oxford University Press, 1945.

——, *Henry Burney: A Political Biography*, London: Oxford University Press, 1974.

Keeton, C. L., *King Thebaw and the Ecological Rape of Burma*, Delhi: Manohar, 1974.

Kitzan, L., 'Lord Amherst and Pegu: The Annexation Issue, 1824–1826', *JSEAS*, 8, 2 (1977).

Mukherjee, Aparna, *British Colonial Policy in Burma: An Aspect of Colonialism in South East Asia, 1840–1885*, New Delhi: Abhinau, 1988.

Pearn, B. R., *A History of Rangoon*, Rangoon: American Baptist Mission Press, 1939.

——, *Military Operations in Burma, 1890–1912. Letters from Lt. J. K. Watson*, Ithaca: Cornell University, 1967.

Pollak, O. B., *Empires in Collision: Anglo-Burmese Relations in the Mid-nineteenth Century*, Westport: Greenwood, 1979.

Ramachandra, G. P., 'The Canning Mission to Burma of 1809–10', *JSEAS*, 10, 1 (1979).

——, 'The Outbreak of the First Anglo-Burman War', *JMBRAS*, 51, 2 (1978).

Sarkisyanz, E., *Peacocks, Pagodas and Professor Hall*, Athens: Ohio University Centre for International Studies, 1972.

Singhal, D. P., *The Annexation of Upper Burma*, Singapore: Donald Moore, 1960.

Stewart, A. T. Q., *The Pagoda War: Lord Dufferin and the Fall of the Kingdom of Ava, 1885–6*, London: Faber, 1972.

Symes, M., *An Account of an Embassy to the Kingdom of Ava in the Year 1795*, London, 1800; reprinted, Gregg, 1969.

———, *Journal of His Second Embassy to the Court of Ava in 1802*, ed. D. G. E. Hall, London: Allen and Unwin, 1955.

Tinker, H., Review of D. P. Singhal's *The Annexation of Upper Burma*, *JSEAH*, 1, 2 (1960).

Woodman, D., *The Making of Burma*, London: Cresset, 1962.

Britain, Siam, and Vietnam

The Burney Papers, Bangkok, 1910–14.

The Crawfurd Papers, Bangkok, London: Farnborough, Gregg, 1915, reprinted 1971.

Crawfurd, J., *Journal of an Embassy to the Courts of Siam and Cochin-China*, London, 1830; reprinted, Oxford University Press, 1967.

Dhiravegin, Likhit, *Siam and Colonialism (1855–1909): An Analysis of Diplomatic Relations*, Bangkok: Thai Watana Panich, B.E. 2518 [1974].

Lamb, Alastair, *The Mandarin Road to Old Hué*, London: Chatto and Windus, 1970.

Tarling, N., *Imperial Britain in South-East Asia*, Kuala Lumpur: Oxford University Press, 1975.

Vella, W. F., *Siam under Rama III 1824–1851*, Locust Valley: J. J. Augustin, 1957.

The Twentieth Century

The FMS and Inter-war Malaya

Ahmat, Sharom, *Kedah, Tradition and Change in a Malay State: A Study of the Economic and Political Development of Kedah, 1878–1923*, Kuala Lumpur: MBRAS, 1984.

Allen, J. de V., 'The Elephant and the Mousedeer—A New Version', *JMBRAS*, 41, 1 (1968).

———, 'Johore, 1901–1914', *JMBRAS*, 45, 2 (1972).

Butcher, J. G., *The British in Malaya 1880–1941*, Kuala Lumpur: Oxford University Press, 1969.

Chai Hon-chan, *The Development of British Malaya 1896–1909*, Kuala Lumpur: Oxford University Press, 1964.

Chan Su-ming, 'Kelantan and Trengganu, 1909–1939', *JMBRAS*, 38, 1 (1965).

Chew, E., 'Swettenham and British Residential Rule in Western Malaya', *JSEAS*, 5, 2 (1974).

Emerson, R., *Malaysia: A Study in Direct and Indirect Rule*, New York: Macmillan, 1937; reprinted, 1964.

Heussler, R., *British Rule in Malaya: The Malayan Civil Service and Its Predecessors, 1867–1942*, Westport: Greenwood, 1981.

Khasnor, Johan, *The Emergence of the Modern Malay Administrative Elite*, Singapore: Oxford University Press, 1984.

Jackson, R. N., *Immigrant Labour and the Development of Malaya, 1786–1920*, Kuala Lumpur: Government Printing Office, 1961.

———, *Pickering: Protector of Chinese*, Kuala Lumpur: Oxford University Press, 1965.

Jones, Alun, 'Internal Security in British Malaya, 1895–1942', Ph.D. thesis, Yale University, 1970.

Mills, L. A., *British Rule in Eastern Asia*, London: Oxford University Press, 1942.

Milner, A. C., 'The Federation Decision: 1895', *JMBRAS*, 43, 1 (1970).

Purcell, V., *The Memoirs of a Malayan Official*, London: Cassell, 1965.

Sadka, E., *The Protected Malay States, 1874–1895*, Kuala Lumpur: University of Malaya Press, 1968.

Sheppard, M., *Taman Budiman: Memoirs of an Unorthodox Civil Servant*, Kuala Lumpur: Heinemann, 1979.

Sidhu, Jagjit Singh, *Administration in the Federated Malay States, 1896–1920*, Kuala Lumpur: Oxford University Press, 1980.

Thio, E., 'Some Aspects of the Federation of the Malay States, 1896–1910', *JMBRAS*, 40, 2 (1967).

Thompson, V., *Post-mortem on Malaya*, New York: Macmillan, 1943.

Winstedt, R. O., *Start from Alif: Count from One*, Kuala Lumpur: Oxford University Press, 1969.

Yeo Kim Wah, *The Politics of Decentralization: Colonial Controversy in Malaya 1920–1929*, Kuala Lumpur: Oxford University Press, 1982.

Yong, C. F. and R. B. McKenna, *The Kuomintang Movement in British Malaya 1912–1949*, Singapore: Singapore University Press, 1990.

British Borneo before the Second World War

Baring-Gould, S. and Bampfylde, C. A., *A History of Sarawak under Its Two White Rajahs, 1839–1908*, London: Sotheran, 1909; reprinted Singapore: Oxford University Press, 1989.

Black, I., *A Gambling Style of Government: The Establishment of Chartered Company Rule in Sabah, 1878–1915*, Kuala Lumpur: Oxford University Press, 1983.

Chew, Daniel, *Chinese Pioneers on the Sarawak Frontier 1841–1941*, Singapore: Oxford University Press, 1990.

Crisswell, C. N., 'The Mat Salleh Revolt Reconsidered', *SMJ*, XIX, 38–9 (1971).

———, *Rajah Charles Brooke: Monarch of All He Surveyed*, Kuala Lumpur: Oxford University Press, 1978.

———, 'W. C. Cowie and the British North Borneo Company', *SMJ*, XXIV, 45 (1976).

Digby, K. H., *Lawyer in the Wilderness*, Ithaca: Cornell University, 1980.

Doering, Otto C., 'Government in Sarawak under Charles Brooke', *JMBRAS*, 39, 2 (1986).

____, 'The Institutionalisation of Personal Rule in Sarawak', M.Sc. (Econ.) thesis, London School of Economics, 1965.

Horton, A. V. M., 'British Administration in Brunei 1906–1959', *MAS*, 20, 2 (1986).

Lockard, C. A., 'The Early Development of Kuching', *JMBRAS*, 49, 2 (1976).

____, 'The Southeast Asian Town in Historical Perspective', Ph.D. thesis, University of Wisconsin, 1973.

Pringle, R. M., 'The Brookes of Sarawak: Reformers In spite of Themselves', *SMJ*, XIX, 38–9 (1971).

____, *Rajahs and Rebels*, London: Macmillan, 1970.

Reinhardt, J. M., 'Administrative Policy and Practice in Sarawak: Continuity and Change under the Brookes', *JAS*, 29, 4 (1970).

Rutter, O., *British North Borneo*, London: Constable, 1922.

Saunders, G., 'James Brooke and Asian Government', *Brunei Museum Journal*, 3, 1 (1973).

Tarling, N., 'Britain and Sarawak in the Twentieth Century: Raja Charles, Raja Vyner and the Colonial Office', *JMBRAS*, 43, 2 (1970).

____, 'Sir Cecil Clementi and the Federation of British Borneo', *JMBRAS*, 44, 2 (1971).

Tregonning, K. G. P., *A History of Modern Sabah*, Singapore: University of Malaya Press, 1965.

____, 'The Mat Salleh Revolt', *JMBRAS*, 29, 1 (1956).

Ward, A. B., *Rajah's Servant*, Ithaca: Cornell University, 1966.

Wagner, Ulla, *Colonialism and Iban Warfare*, Stockholm: Department of Anthropology, University of Stockholm, 1972.

Warren, James F., *The North Borneo Chartered Company's Administration of the Bajau 1878–1909*, Athens: Ohio University, 1971.

British Burma before the Second World War

Cady, J. F., *A History of Modern Burma*, Ithaca: Cornell University Press, 1958.

Christian, J. L., *Modern Burma*, London: University of California Press, 1943.

Donnison, F. S. V., *Public Administration in Burma*, London: Royal Institute of International Affairs, 1953.

Furnivall, J. S., *Colonial Policy and Practice*, Cambridge: Cambridge University Press, 1948.

Moscotti, A. D., *British Policy and the Nationalist Movement in Burma, 1917–1937*, Honolulu: University of Hawaii Press, 1974.

Taylor, Robert H., 'The Relationship between Burmese Social Classes and British–Indian Policy on the Behavior of the Burmese Political Élite, 1937–1942', Ph.D. thesis, Cornell University, 1974.

____, *The State in Burma*, London: Hurst, 1987.

Britain and Other Powers before the Second World War

Tarling, N., 'King Prajadhipok and the Apple Cart', *JSS*, 64, 2 (1976).

――, 'Quezon and the British Commonwealth', *Australian Journal of Politics and History*, 23, 2 (1977).

――, ' "A Vital British Interest": Britain, Japan, and the Security of Netherlands India in the Inter-war Period', *JSEAS*, 9, 2 (1978).

Singapore and Imperial Defence

Haggie, P., *Britannia at Bay—The Defence of the British Empire against Japan 1931–1941*, Oxford: Clarendon Press, 1981.

Hamill, I., *The Strategic Illusion: The Singapore Strategy and the Defence of Australia and New Zealand, 1919–1942*, Singapore: Singapore University Press, 1981.

Kirby, S. W., *Singapore: The Chain of Disaster*, London: Cassell, 1971.

McIntyre, W. D., *The Rise and Fall of the Singapore Naval Base, 1919–1942*, London: Macmillan, 1980.

――, 'The Strategic Significance of Singapore, 1917–1942', *JSEAH*, 10, 1 (1969).

Miller, Eugene H., *Strategy at Singapore*, New York: Macmillan, 1942.

Montgomery, B., *Shenton of Singapore*, London: Cooper and Secker and Warburg, 1954.

Neidpath, J. L., *The Singapore Naval Base and the Defence of Britain's Eastern Empire 1919–1941*, Oxford: Clarendon Press, 1981.

Smyth, Sir J., *Percival and the Tragedy of Singapore*, London: Macdonald, 1971.

Tarling, N., 'The Singapore Mutiny', *JMBRAS*, 55, 2 (1982).

Wartime Planning

Donnison, F. S. V., *British Military Administration in the Far East, 1943–46*, London: HMSO, 1956.

Goldsworthy, D., *Colonial Issues in British Politics 1945–1961*, Oxford: Clarendon Press, 1971.

Lee, J. M. and Petter, M., *The Colonial Office, War and Development Policy*, London: Maurice Temple Smith, 1982.

Louis, W. R., *Imperialism at Bay: The United States and the Decolonization of the British Empire, 1941–1945*, Oxford: Clarendon Press, 1977.

Porter, A. N. and Stockwell, A. J., *British Imperial Policy and Decolonization 1938–64*, London: Macmillan, 1987, Vol. I, pp. 1938–52.

Thorne, C., *Allies of a Kind: The United States, Britain, and the War against Japan, 1941–1945*, London: Hamish Hamilton, 1978.

Britain and Other Powers after the Second World War

Crosby, J., *Siam: The Crossroads*, London: Hollis and Carter, 1945.

Dennis, P., *Troubled Days of Peace: Mountbatten and South East Asia*

Command, 1945–46, Manchester: Manchester University Press, 1987.

Drummond, S. H., 'Britain's Involvement in Indonesia 1945–63', Ph.D. thesis, University of Southampton, 1979.

George, M., *Australia and the Indonesian Revolution*, Melbourne: Melbourne University Press, 1980.

Oey Hong Lee, *War and Diplomacy in Indonesia, 1945–50*, Townsville: James Cook University of North Queensland, 1981.

Squire, C. W., 'Britain and the Transfer of Power in Indonesia 1945–46', Ph.D. thesis, SOAS, 1979.

Tarling, N., 'Atonement before Absolution: British Policy towards Thailand during World War II', *JSS*, 66, 1 (1978).

_____, ' "An Attempt to Fly in the Face of the Ordinary Laws of Supply and Demand": The British and Siamese Rice, 1945–7', *JSS*, 75 (1987): 140–86.

_____, ' "A Prompt Gesture of Goodwill": Anglo-Philippine Relations after the Second World War', *Pilipinas*, 5 (1985).

_____, 'Rice and Reconciliation: The Anglo-Thai Peace Negotiations of 1945', *JSS*, 66, 2 (1978).

_____, ' "Some Rather Nebulous Capacity": Lord Killearn's Appointment in Southeast Asia', *MAS*, 20, 3 (1986).

Valentine, D. B., 'The British Facilitation of the French Re-entry into Vietnam', Ph.D. thesis, University of California, 1974.

Singapore and Malaya Post-war

Allen, J. de V., *The Malayan Union*, New Haven: Yale University, 1967.

Chan Heng Chee, *A Sensation of Independence: A Political Biography of David Marshall*, Singapore: Oxford University Press, 1984.

Heussler, R., *Completing a Stewardship: The Malayan Civil Service 1942–1957*, Westport and London: Greenwood, 1983.

Lau, Albert, *The Malayan Union Controversy 1942–1948*, Singapore: Oxford University Press, 1991.

Nemenzo, F., 'Revolution and Counter-revolution: A Study of British Policy as a Factor in the Growth and Disintegration of National Liberation Movements in Burma and Malaya', Ph.D. thesis, University of Manchester, 1964.

Purcell, V., *Malaya: Communist or Free?* London: Gollancz, 1954.

Rudner, M., 'The Organisation of the BMA in Malaya, 1946–8', *JSEAH*, IX, 1 (March 1968): 95–106.

_____, 'The Political Structure of the Malayan Union', *JMBRAS*, 43, 1 (1970).

Silcock, T. H and Aziz, V. A., 'Nationalism in Malaya', in W. H. Holland (ed.), *Asian Nationalism and the West*, New York: Macmillan, 1953.

Simandjuntak, B., *Malayan Federalism 1945–1963*, Kuala Lumpur: Oxford University Press, 1969.

Stenson, M. R., *Class, Race and Colonialism in West Malaysia: The Indian Case*, St Lucia: University of Queensland Press, 1980.

——, *Industrial Conflict in Malaya*, London: Oxford University Press, 1970.

——, 'The Malayan Union and the Historians', *JSEAH*, 10, 2 (1969).

Stockwell, A. J., *British Policy and Malay Politics during the Malayan Union Experiment 1942–1948*, Kuala Lumpur: MBRAS, 1979.

——, 'Colonial Planning during World War II: The Case of Malaya', *Journal of Imperial and Commonwealth History*, 2, 3 (1974).

Stubbs, R., *Hearts and Minds in Guerrilla Warfare: The Malayan Emergency, 1948–1960*, Singapore: Oxford University Press, 1989.

Turnbull, C. M., 'British Planning for Post-war Malaya', *JSEAS*, 5, 2 (1974).

——, 'The Post-war Decade in Malaya: The Settling Dust of Political Controversy', *JSEAS*, 60, 1 (1987).

Yeo Kim Wah, 'The Anti-federation Movement in Malaya, 1946–48', *JSEAS*, 4, 1 (1973).

The Borneo Colonies

Baker, M. H., *North Borneo: The First Ten Years, 1946–1956*, Singapore: Malaya Publishing House, 1962.

Brooke, A., *The Facts about Sarawak*, London and Wisbech, privately printed, 1946.

Liang Kim Bang and Lee, Edwin, *Sarawak, 1941–1957*, Singapore: Department of History, University of Singapore, 1964.

——, *Sarawak in the Early Sixties 1961–1963*, Singapore: Department of History, University of Singapore, 1964.

Reece, R. H. W., *The Name of Brooke: The End of White Raja Rule in Sarawak*, Kuala Lumpur: Oxford University Press, 1982.

Sanib Said, *Malay Politics in Sarawak, 1946–1966*, Singapore: Oxford University Press, 1985.

Tregonning, K. G. P., *A History of Modern Sabah*, Singapore: University of Malaya Press, 1965.

'Rice and Reconciliation: The Anglo-Thai Peace Negotiations of 1945', *JSS*, 66, 2 (1978).

The Independence of Burma

Ba Maw, *Breakthrough in Burma*, New Haven: Yale University Press, 1968.

Collis, M., *Last and First in Burma*, London: Faber, 1956.

Silverstein, J., *The Political Legacy of Aung San*, Ithaca: Cornell University Press, 1972.

Tarling, N., *The Fourth Anglo-Burman War: Britain and the Independence of Burma*, Gaya, India: Centre for South East Asian Studies, 1987.

Taylor, R. H., *Marxism and Resistance in Burma, 1942–1945*, Athens: Ohio University Press, 1984.

Tinker, H. (ed.), *Burma: The Struggle for Independence, 1944–1948*, London: HMSO, 1983.

Chao Tzang Yawnghwe, *The Shan of Burma: Memoirs of a Shan Exile*, Singapore: Institute of Southeast Asian Studies, 1987.

South-East Asia in General

Andaya, L. Y. and Andaya, B. W., *A History of Malaysia*, New York: St. Martin's Press, 1982.

Cady, J. F., *Southeast Asia: Its Historical Development*, New York: McGraw-Hill, 1964.

Gullick, J. M., *Malaysia*, London: Benn, 1969.

Hall, D. G. E., *A History of Southeast Asia*, London: Macmillan, 1968.

Steinberg, D. J. et al., *In Search of Southeast Asia: A Modern History*, Revised edition, Sydney: Allen and Unwin, 1987.

Turnbull, C. M., *A History of Singapore 1819–1975*, Kuala Lumpur: Oxford University Press, 1977.

Wang Gungwu (ed.), *Malaysia: A Survey*, Melbourne: Cheshire, 1964.

The British Empire and Commonwealth

Adams, R. N., *Paradoxical Harvest: Energy and Explanation in British History, 1870–1914*, Cambridge: Cambridge University Press, 1982.

Baumgart, W., *Imperialism: The Idea and Reality of British and French Colonial Expansion, 1880–1914*, New York: Oxford University Press, 1982.

Bennett, G. (ed.), *The Concept of Empire: Burke to Attlee 1774–1947*, London: Black, 1962.

Darwin, J., *Britain and Decolonisation: The Retreat from Empire in the Postwar World*, Basingstoke: Macmillan, 1988.

——, 'Imperialism in Decline? Tendencies in British Imperial Policy between the Wars', *The Historical Journal*, 23, 3 (1980).

Eldridge, C. C., *Victorian Imperialism*, London: Hodder and Stoughton, 1978.

Gallagher, J., *The Decline, Revival and Fall of the British Empire*, Cambridge: Cambridge University Press, 1983.

——, 'Nationalisms and the Crisis of Empire, 1919–1922', *MAS*, 15, 3 (1981).

Gupta, P. S., *Imperialism and the British Labour Movement, 1914–64*, London: Macmillan, 1975.

Holland, R. F., *European Decolonization 1918–1981: An Introductory Survey*, Basingstoke: Macmillan, 1985.

Hyam, R., *Britain's Imperial Century, 1815–1914*, London, Batsford, 1976.

Johnston, W. R., *Great Britain, Great Empire*, St Lucia: University of Queensland Press, 1981.

Judd, D. and Slinn, P., *The Evolution of the Modern Commonwealth, 1902–80*, London: Macmillan, 1982.

Kahler, Miles, *Decolonisation in Britain and France*, Princeton: Princeton University Press, 1984.

Low, D. A., *Lion Rampant*, London: Cass, 1973.

Mansergh, N., *The Commonwealth Experience*, Revised edition, Toronto: University of Toronto Press, 1983.

——, *Survey of British Commonwealth Affairs*, London: Oxford University Press, 1952–8.

Mommsen, W. J., *Theories of Imperialism*, New York: Random House, 1980.

Moore, R. J., *Making the New Commonwealth*, Oxford: Clarendon Press, 1987.

Morgan, D. J., *The Official History of Colonial Development: Vol. 5. Guidance towards Self-government in British Colonies, 1941–1971*, London: Macmillan, 1980.

Pearce, R. D., *The Turning Point in Africa: British Colonial Policy 1938–48*, London: Cass, 1982.

Porter, B., *Britain, Europe and the World, 1850–1982*, London: Allen and Unwin, 1983.

——, *The Lion's Share*, Second edition, London: Longman, 1984.

Semmel, B., *Imperialism and Social Reform*, London: Allen and Unwin, 1960.

Thornton, A. P., *Imperialism in the Twentieth Century*, London: Macmillan, 1978.

Tomlinson, B. R., 'The Contraction of England: National Decline and the Loss of Empire', *Journal of Imperial and Commonwealth History*, 11, 1 (1982).

Wiener, M., *English Culture and the Decline of the Industrial Spirit, 1850–1980*, Cambridge: Cambridge University Press, 1981.

Index